NAPLES,

What most tourists never see

Also by Richard A. Lamb

"War in Italy" (John Murray UK, 1993)

"Mussolini and the British" (John Murray UK, 1997)

About the Author

Richard Lamb, born in 1911 in London, England, read Agricultural Economics and History at Merton College, Oxford prior to the second world war. He spoke fluent Italian and from 1943 to 1945 he played an important role in the Italian Army's operations on the Allied side. Following the War he stood as a candidate for the Liberal party. As a journalist, he edited "New Outlook", a Liberal magazine and "The City Press" as well as broadcasting on Radio 4's "PM" programme.

He wrote extensively about the Second World War and the post-war period in Britain. His "War in Italy" (John Murray UK 1993) was short listed for the Duff Cooper prize. He also wrote "Mussolini and the British" (John Murray UK 1997), and for War Monthly on the Risorgimento and Napoleon's armies in Italy.

He loved Naples and became well acquainted with the city during his war service. His last trip abroad was to Naples to write this book. He died in 1999 shortly after the completion of the manuscript.

NAPLES,
What most tourists never see

Library and Archives Canada Cataloguing in Publication

Lamb, Richard
Naples, what most tourist never see / Richard A. Lamb.

Includes index.
ISBN 0-9737545-0-8

1. Naples Region (Italy)--Guidebooks. I. Title.

DG842.L34 2005   914.5'73093'0222   C2005-901810-0

This edition published by Cybercom Publishing
Toronto, Canada

Cover, layout and text design: Tim Harrison

Printed and bound in the United States of America and London, England.

Care has been taken to trace the ownership of any copyright material in this text. The publisher will gladly accept any information that will enable them to rectify any references or credit in subsequent editions.

NAPLES,
What most tourists never see

Richard A. Lamb

CONTENTS

NAPLES, What most tourists never see

Acknowledgements

Cover Image

The publisher would like to thank Dr. Luca Lista c/o IFNF, Complesso Universitario di Monte Sant' Angelo, Napoli (Photographer) and Leonardo Merola, Director of INFA Section of Naples for permission to reproduce the cover images for this edition of "NAPLES What most tourists never see" from the IFNA Sezione di Napoli web site.

Editorial

Much appreciation is due to Mr. Nick Ross and his colleagues at Art History Abroad, 179c New Kings Road, London SW6 4SW for verifying the accuracy of the many places, names and historical facts contained within the manuscript.

On completion, he commented:

"Naples was once Norman, then French, Spanish and then Bourbon before becoming Italian. It was the largest port in the world in the eighteenth century when Nelson ruled the waves and it remains an essential port of call for anyone who wants to get under the skin of European history.

Richard Lamb dances with easy grace through this tortured history while even revealing the best place to order a shirt. He truly appreciated Naples and like the city, his text is full of life. This book is a masterpiece and should be on the shelves of all who love Italy."

Nick Ross

General Introduction

Until the First World War, the city of Naples itself was a very popular international tourist destination. Visitors used to stay in the centre of Naples and visit the 'surrounding area' by carriage or train from their Neapolitan hotels. Nowadays, Naples has become a type of 'surrounding area' for those staying in the modern tourist centres of Capri and Ischia, Sorrento, and the Amalfi coast.

Tourism to central Naples declined drastically in the 1930s and has never recovered. The disastrous cholera epidemic of 1973 and the shocking earthquake of 1980 sent the city into further decline, and today tourists tend to shy away from staying in Naples itself. After the 1980 earthquake, those wanting to see the churches and art treasures found them mostly closed for repairs. Thus the city was skipped and most tourists arriving by sea, train, or air took taxis to the boat and hydrofoil terminuses and set off for Amalfi, Capri, or another fashionable outside tourist destination. Their only relationship with the city itself would be a possible coach trip to the Museo Nazionale from their resort. The treasure house of art within the city is still largely neglected.

Now, strenuous efforts are being made to ensure the best of the old churches are open at reasonable hours; the Neapolitans like to say there is more art in their churches than in the whole of Florence and Venice! This is largely true. After the closure of so many churches because of the earthquake in 1980 a group of Neapolitan citizens led by Baroness Mirella Baracco, concerned at the desperate state of so many of the famous monuments, founded the Fondazione Napoli to focus world attention on what had happened to the city's art heritage. Considerable sums were raised to restore the most important monuments such as the marble arch at Castel Nuovo and the frescoes in the Genaro chapel in the cathedral. Under the auspices of 'Open Door Weekends', as many churches as possible were made open at certain weekends; they drew large crowds, almost entirely Italians with hordes of schoolchildren, but few international tourists.

More Neapolitan churches are open nowadays, but visitors are lamentably scarce and the lack of hotels of the secondary category, due to shortage of demand, is another factor in keeping tourists away. It is difficult to use a private car in Naples even in the depths of winter. Daily, hundreds of thousands of workers flock into the city by car and clutter up every street, often parking five abreast. However, I must say that Graham Hunter, my companion, was able to cleverly maneuver a car. He was prepared to drive and reverse down narrow lanes and to find his way around in an incredible manner. For this I am duly grateful. Still, unless you are an intrepid motorist and well used to hectic traffic, I advise you to park your car in a garage and go on foot or by taxi or make use of the excellent bus and train service. Remember always to buy your bus or tram ticket in advance at a tobacconist and stamp it when you enter or else you will be fined. If you hire a taxi, only use the licensed taxis and keep your eye on the meter. Most taxi drivers are honest, but you come up against the odd rogue and this can be extremely trying and costly.

The main tourist information office is in the Royal Palace in the Piazza del Plebiscito. There is also a kiosk in the Piazza Gesu (usually open) in the heart of the antique centre. Be warned however, there will be traffic jams and buses and taxis do get bogged down in the chaos. Naples is a town that lives by night, and traffic is still hectic at hours when other cities have gone to sleep.

The centre of Naples consists of three adjoining squares– Piazza del Municipio, Piazza Trieste e Trento and Piazza del Plebiscito. All result from Charles I establishing in this area the Angevin Court and his Royal Palace. The chief shopping street, the Via Toledo begins in the Piazza del Plebiscito. The Viceroy whose name it bears built it in the 16th century; it is 2 kms long, containing many excellent shops. The great Piazza del Plebiscito, the focus of the city, was until recently just a vast car park; miraculously, the cars have all been banished and today it is a pleasant spot from which to admire the Royal Palace and churches with a magnificent view of the bay.

The old city stretching north from the port of 'Naples on the Sea' is the promontory of S Lucia to its west. Further west there is the suburb of Chiaia, through which a splendid riviera and the Via Caracciolo sweep along the bay toward the small port of Mergellina. To the west above Mergellina rises the still attractive height of Posilippo - 'Naples on the hills'. Between Posilippo and the Certosa di Sanmartino and the Castel of S Elmo, which are landmarks visible from all over, the city there lies a vast modern built-up suburb called the Vomero.

Naples is a delight to explore. Whereas the main treasures of Rome, Florence, and Venice are familiar to everyone from coloured photographs and guidebooks, the magnificence of Naples is largely unknown to outsiders and many of its most important monuments are not even signposted. The fabulous 18th-century Palazzo Sessa where Nelson stayed, and home to the 18th-century British ambassador to Naples, Sir William Hamilton, is dilapidated and hidden in an alley off the shopping street Via Chiaia, with its crumbling walls covered with graffiti from spray guns. There is no plaque and one can hardly imagine that it was here that the irresistible Emma

Hamilton dazzled Horatio Nelson.

The large Piazza Garibaldi around the Central Station (*Stazione Centrale*) is an unsavoury spot. Touts, pimps, prostitutes of both sexes, pickpockets, and gangsters abound. There are plenty of hotels, some good but some little better than brothels. There are excellent restaurants; however, a few keep their doors locked for fear of a clash between rival Camorra gangs. Artists and musicians mix with the gangsters and produce a stimulating atmosphere in these restaurants. The Camorra are the Neapolitan equivalent of the Sicilian Mafia. They are more difficult to stamp out because they consist of many different families at war with each other, whereas in Sicily snuffing out one family exterminates the whole of the Mafia of that regime. Contrary to government accounts, the power of the Camorra gangs is as great as ever; blackmail and corruption in the public service flourish and the Neapolitans are cheated out of great sums. Nearly all of the businesses have to pay protection money and it is estimated this takes £60 million out of the Neapolitan economy. While the chief activity of the Camorra is the sale of heroin and hard drugs as would be expected, if you go to the Piazza Garibaldi you would be well advised not to wear a necklace or carry a handbag.

Piazza Garibaldi is near the antique centre. The best way to become acquainted with this fascinating quarter is to try and secure a room in one of the comfortable low star hotels, which exist in some of the quiet old palaces. Their rooms are comfortable and large and the owners are obliging. Such rooms are scarce so you must book well in advance and you may sometimes have to carry your keys as the desks are not manned all of the time. The tourist office produces an excellent monthly multilingual handbook, *Qui Napoli,* available free in their offices and in most of the hotels. This has much useful information with timetables, lists of events, and good maps. You will find there are accompanied walks with knowledgeable guides around the old city. Enquire about these walks in the Piazza del Gesu Nuovo.

Shopping

There are fascinating and elegant shops in Naples, especially in the Via Chiaia and Via delle Mille. There you will find some of the same names as in Bond Street or Rue du Faubourg, St Honoré in Paris, intermingled with equally distinguished Naples shops. The variety of clothes for both men and women is greater than in Paris or in Rome; obviously, a great number of

Neapolitans as well as the Camorra are very rich. One specialty is dresses for small girls – not all in the best of taste, but many exquisite ones at high prices–over £100 sterling. Men's clothes are attractive; I strongly recommend the shirt maker Buccafusca, 13 Via Chiaia. The elderly owner has charming old world manners and will supply shirts to measure in six days. I much liked his old fashioned shop with the shirts in mahogany drawers and cupboards. Martino in Piazza S Catarina is an excellent tailor with a good supply of interesting Italian hats for men. Children's clothes are especially featured in the Via Chiaia and the Via della Mille. There are plenty of good jewelers and coral sellers, but you will not find any bookshops. For these, go to Porta Alba off Piazza Dante where around twenty are congregated. Some buy and sell secondhand students' books. As I had just had a book published in Italian I was especially pleased to see a display in the biggest bookshop, Guida, and in another a copy of a full-page review in the *Corriere della Sera* posted on the wall. A great number of art books and guidebooks on Naples and its environs, both in English and Italian, can also be bought there.

Via Chiaia begins at the corner of Piazza Plebiscito. Here is the typical and most popular Neapolitan café - Gambrinus, established in 1860. Foreign tourists go there for excellent ice cream, coffee, and cakes. At the Piazza S Catarina at the far end of the Chiaia, you find the Café Calflisch. The owner was a Swiss who set up his café in 1820 and it has been continuously open ever since. During the British/American occupation of 1943–1945, sugar was almost non-existent but Calflisch bought it on the black market and continued to make their delicious cakes. The Neapolitan aristocracy flocked there, along with a few British and American officers who had already made friends with Neapolitans. I well remember the eerie feeling over fifty years ago of stepping out of the elegant Calflisch into my jeep to go back to a muddy tent on the Casino front, which was only 25 miles away, amid the noise of the guns. At Calflisch today you will find no tourists, only Italians, but the food and drink is of exceptionally high quality and reasonably priced. You can even buy a tasty snack lunch while you enjoy the surroundings. The Via Chiaia and Via del Mille are only a stone's throw from the seafront and very cheerful. I liked the contrast between the elegant shops and the narrow slummy streets of the Spanish quarter, which run into them.

In the Via del Mille the street divides with one way continuing with expensive shops and the other dropping down into a typical attractive Neapolitan quarter with only small inexpensive shops and houses.

Via Calibroso at the bottom of Via Chiaia is full of internationally well-known fashion shops. In the Via Morelli there are many interesting antique shops. In the antique centre opposite Pio Monte you will find an old-fashioned typesetter who has his original Heidelberg printing press. This is a wonderful piece of printing archaeology and the typesetter would be delighted to print off complimentary slips, at home cards or visiting cards for you while you wait. It is fascinating to see the skill of the workmen operating these old and well-maintained machines. The address is Severini, Via Tribunale 132.

At Port Alba near Piazza Dante there is a spate of bookshops, some secondhand, some new. If you want to find a guide to Naples of whatever period you can have a field day here. Prices are reasonable. The little streets of the antique centre are full of small workshops with one or two operators. They sell exquisite coral and cameos; cameos are the typical products of Naples made from special seashells. You see them everywhere and with a bit of bargaining they can be purchased very reasonably. Beautiful porcelain and ceramic figures made at the old Royal Factory of Capodimonte can be bought at some of the better shops, however they tend to be expensive. If you are interested in classical remains, there is a 150-year-old foundry, Fonderai Chiurazzi, Via Ponti Rossi 271, whose workers make and specialize in reproductions of the ancient bronzes in the National Museum. If you have enough money, they will even make you one, life-size.

Another great joy about Naples is the open street markets around Piazza Garibaldi and the centre. Daily catches of every type of fish - squid, octopus, mussels etc. are displayed on benches; the colour is amazing. The fruit stalls are also photogenic and some sell lemons from Sorrento that are so big you cannot cup them with both hands. Still, unless you have a flat, you need to go to a restaurant to sample these wonderful fish. It will give you an idea of the excellent food available in the restaurants; Neapolitans will not tolerate bad cooking and demand a very high standard.

Naples is the town of nativity cribs. Here it is an art form, which shows Neapolitans at their best, like their music and pizzas. The biggest, the size of a bus, is in S Martino and much beloved by Neapolitans. All the cribs have fine well-carved ceramic or wooden figures and the one at S Martino dates back 200 years. Each face is an authentic portrait. For modern Christmas cribs go to Via S Gregorio. It is full of shops and stalls exclusively selling both conventional and modern figures. You will find numerous Mother Teresas, trees, sheep, donkeys, goats, dogs, salami, angels and other items that appeal to the Neapolitans.

If you set up an annual crib in your home at Christmas you will find it impossible not to buy some fresh figures in the Via S Gregorio - especially the attractive cooked foodstuffs or the Turks, beggars, dwarfs, and those with other deformities that delight the Neapolitans. Lady Blessington wrote in 1839: "The more I see of the Neapolitans, the more I like them. I have not detected any of the individuals spoken of generally and I am inclined to think, so unjustly attributed to them by strangers."

Not everyone falls for the charm of Naples and the Neapolitans. Perhaps it is an acquired taste. At the end of the 19th century, John Ruskin described Naples as "the most loathsome nest of human caterpillars I was ever forced to stay in." To some, Naples comes as a shock because it is so unlike the rest of Italy. It is obviously of Byzantine origin not Roman, and displays a taste of Constantinople and the East. But the friendliness of the Neapolitans cannot be denied.

You will not find much English spoken but with a few words of Italian a conversation is possible. Italians love talking, and everywhere you are surrounded by animated conversations coupled with the liveliest gestures. Most visitors find the streets of the old quarters hold great attraction. They are full of passers-by who seem to have nothing else to do and whose volubility and gesticulation have to be seen, to be believed. The food shops and stalls, the music and antique shops, the jewelers and cameo sellers belong to a non-European world. Old men sell eggs from carts; widows sell contraband cigarettes; and there are masses of young boys (*scugnizzi*) but not girls, so that one wonders when the schools are open.

Be careful, however, of older groups of boys who will steal your bag or wallet with impunity, as they are so desperate to obtain cocaine. These are the petty thieves, as the main commerce in heroin is carried out by the Camorra who wear white ties and lounge suits.

On Saturdays and Sundays motorcars are not allowed to circulate in the main city until 2:00 p.m., and then Naples reverts to its former pace with dozens of cyclists, roller skaters, and horses on the seafront. From the rocks in the centre of town swimmers dive into deep water and bathe in an unfortunately rather dirty sea.

The generous warmth of the Neapolitans' reception charmed the Allied soldiers in 1943 and 1944; at that time this was coloured by the hope of receiving gifts of chocolates and cigarettes. Yet the same warmth is given to foreign travellers today. Mind you, poverty still abounds; many of the 1¼ million citizens can only just afford to live. No wonder crime flourishes. However, with the influence of Mayor Bassolino and his administration, a

14

lot of the criminal elements have been banished to the Torre del Greco and Castelamare, which are very dangerous places. Even so, the risk of being pick-pocketed or mugged still exists in Naples.

The city of Naples is a crowded pulsating city with its own charm and much fascinating history. The islands, Sorrento, and the Amalfi coast are for most visitors a welcome contrast, with gardens, orange, lemon, and olive groves everywhere and a feeling of peace. You do become more conscious of being in a tourist paradise than when in Naples itself. Bathing from beaches is only good on Ischia and Procida and very limited until you get as far south as Paestum. From Paestum to the south the coast is a bather's paradise, as yet hardly exploited by British tour companies. To enjoy Campania as far south as the Calabrian border one needs to travel by car although there is a railway line that unfortunately does not follow the coast. In this area there are nests of tourist hotels and bathing establishments catering to Italians.

The sea to the west of Naples is best left to the Italians although there is a small pleasant area with good hotels north of Volturno toward Formia. However, it is better to explore the wilder unspoiled and delightful coast, which extends from Paestum to Maratea, where you pass many out of the way places in which you can experience the Italian way of life of fifty years ago, which has almost vanished from the spots popular for package holidays. However, the islands of Capri and Procida (on Procida there are virtually no hotels) have retained their erstwhile charm. I would say the same of the island of Ischia were it not for its excessive "Germanization", which makes one feel it is no longer for the English-speaking tourists, with its signs in the shops and cafés written in German.

Naples and the Gulf are desperately hot in August with temperatures reaching an excessive 35°C although the drought, which scorches the vegetation, is usually relieved by occasional bursts of rain. August is the most forbidding month for the Gulf of Naples. The roads are crowded and the main sites like Pompeii are jammed with tourists. Too, the seaside hotels are full because the Italians find their towns are too hot, and fantastic numbers take seaside holidays to catch any sea breeze in July and August. Mid June (and often October) are the best seasons; then the trees of the countryside assume a wonderful variety of colours and in spring there wild flowers abound. The winter climate is good with nearly always a reasonable temperature. The Victorians looked on the Bay of Naples and the islands as winter resorts. Today this has changed but the pleasant climate is only marred by occasional cold and wet spells.

15

Whatever time of year you go, whether to Naples itself, to the islands or the coast, you can be sure of plenty of sun and a warm welcome from a carefree people, but avoid driving if possible, as the overcrowded coast to the west of Naples. Caserta and Capua can easily be reached by train or bus. To explore the whole region of Campania with such delightful medieval towns as Sessa, Aurunca, and Teano, etc., a bicycle is ideal.

Sorrento has the advantage that you can quickly go by train to explore the antique centre of Naples. From Sorrento and all the Amalfi coast resorts, bus excursions run to Pompeii, Herculaneum, the Naples museum, and even to Caserta and Casino. Again, a car is of little use on the Amalfi coast except in winter because the roads are so overcrowded.

Salerno has a few hotels and is ideal for exploring not only the treasures of Salerno itself, but also because Paestum and the Certosa di Padula can easily be reached by bus or car. To fully enjoy the fabulous empty beaches and gorgeous mountainous coastline from Paestum to Maratea one does need a car; however there is usually very little traffic. There are plenty of hotels, many in delightful settings, occupied almost exclusively by Italians; the railway is rather a delusion because it does not follow the coast. British package holiday companies have not yet discovered this area, although they probably will do so before long as it is the only completely unspoiled seaside area left in Europe. It is easily reached by plane from Britain and it retains the unique old-world charms of Italy.

1
History of the Kingdom of Naples

The Greeks settled on the island of Ischia in the 11th century BC; Cumae (Greek Kyma, Latin Cumae) was their original Greek settlement on the mainland of the Bay of Naples. The rich culture of the Greeks flowered at Cumae, and Cumaen colonists built the Greek town of Naples (Neapolis) in the late 6th century BC. The former Greek site is now the ancient centre (*centro antico*).

The Greeks revelled in the climate and the fertile soil with its magnificent fruit and vegetables, and the beauty of the bay. The area became prosperous, with a healthy import and export trade as well as farming and fishing.

Cumae successfully resisted the Etruscans whose power in the Bay of Naples was broken by the Syracusans in the Battle of Cumae in 474 BC. In 421 BC the Samnites seized Cumae and settled alongside the Greeks, building strongholds with huge blocks of stone, which can still be seen, especially at Pompeii.

The Samnites succeeded the Etruscans as a threat to the Greek colonists; they were ancient tribes from the Central Apennines, which bordered the fertile Campanian plain. They were farmers and pre-eminent warriors, and surprisingly, in view of their great military success, do not seem to have had a large city base or nerve centre; none has been identified.

The lack of evidence of the existence of a large Samnite centre may be because of the Italian failure to conduct fully equipped expensive archaeological excavations in Samnium. Today it is Italy's smallest province, with attractive towns and villages and oak and walnut forests not unlike Umbria.

Telesé (the ancient Telesia), near Lazio, has been excavated and has remarkable perfectly octagonal walls with gates at cardinal points. Pietrabbondante, the most promising site, has only been sporadically excavated. They were mainly a rural society but evidence shows the existence of various urban centres, which must have been towns of some importance. Benevento, originally known as Maleventum, was probably their main centre. Their culture resembled that of Romans, and they had the same gods. However, the excavations at Pietrabbondante revealed temples and altars in Greek style, as at Pompeii which was later an outlying Samnite town. Particularly interesting are the Samnite tomb paintings, which can be seen in the museums at Naples and Paestum, showing chariot races and gladiatorial combats and other scenes with a strong Greek influence.

When in 421 BC Cumae fell to the Samnites, many of her Greek inhabitants fled to nearby Naples, which was never taken by the Samnites and remained a Greek town though it received an influx of Samnites c400 BC. As well as Cumae, Capua, Pompeii, and Herculaneum became important Samnite towns after a successful Samnite invasion of that part of Campania. The Samnites liked the Greeks and, albeit reluctantly, absorbed much Greek culture. On the other hand, they always disliked the Romans and had constant border battles with them. The Romans and Samnites made a Treaty of Peace in 354 BC. Eleven years later the first Samnite war broke out which the Samnites won, but they lost the next two wars and also the Pyrrhic War from 281-275 BC when allied with Pyrrhus, who invaded Italy from Greece to save the Greeks in Magna Grecia from Roman domination. Pyrrhus won two striking victories over the Romans only to lose the war at Benevento in 275 BC; hence the term 'Pyrrhic victory.'

The Samnites were then forced to become Roman allies, and gradually they disappeared from history. However, their influence in Campania was very strong, and one is constantly reminded of this while visiting ancient sites like Pompeii, which had once been occupied by them.

After Pyrrhus left Italy and returned home, the Romans strengthened their power over the Greek cities and Italian tribes, treating them as nominally independent states while planting Roman colonies everywhere. Prosperity under the Romans was disturbed during the social war of 91-90 BC when the aggrieved magistrates of the central and southern Italian tribes led their retainers in a revolt against Rome, and also because debt and Roman law pushed large numbers of them into slavery. The revolt was snuffed out by the campaigns of Marius and Sulla and by an offer to extend Roman citizenship to all free Italians. The Samnites made a heroic last stand against Sulla in 83 BC, but under Sulla's dictatorship, the dominance of the aristocrats was strengthened and many opponents were murdered or dispossessed. There was a remarkable revolt in 73 BC by Spartacus, an escaped gladiator of Capua, who led a strange army of dispossessed peasants and runaway slaves, some 70,000 of them, backwards and forwards until the Roman legions finally defeated him in 71 BC.

The later civil wars - Pompey versus Caesar, and Augustus versus Antony - largely spared the south, although many of the plots were hatched in villas around Naples. A revolt in Campania by impoverished victims of the harsh Roman law of debt was crushed in 48 BC. Under Augustus, the Bay of Naples prospered greatly. The original Greek town of Naples was laid out in straight lines, which still form the attractive roads of the ancient centre. Little remains of the Greek town except in the extensive catacombs. (See Chapter....). Still, at S Paolo Maggiore in the heart of the old city, you can see two Greek Corinthian pillars within part of an architrave - all that remains of the Temple of Dionysius. Under S Lorenzo and the Duomo there are underground passages revealing traces of Greek building, but only by going to Paestum (....) can one form a clear idea of the Greek scene; there you will find the majestic Doric temples which give an idea of what Greek Naples must have been like. However you can see magnificent Italo-Greek vases in the Museo Nazionale in Naples.

Naples was brought under the aegis of Rome in 327 BC, and in 326 BC, in return for accepting Roman domination; the Greeks and Samnites became part of the Roman Empire. The Neapolitans, loyal to Rome, fought against Hannibal in the second Punic war, and Naples never fell, although Capua and the surrounding territory did.

As Naples drifted into the orbit of Rome whilst retaining Greek laws and Greek ways, Pozzuoli (ancient Puteoli) became the most important port in Southern Italy and one of the biggest in the Mediterranean. At Pozzouli stand the remains of the second largest Roman amphitheatre, and an impressive forum. In 90 BC Naples was given Roman citizenship; it may then have had 30,000 inhabitants, mostly of Greek origin.

The great eruption of Vesuvius in AD 79 must have caused havoc because the sizeable towns Pompeii, Herculaneum, and Stabiae ceased to exist, and much fertile land was covered in volcanic ash. This was a period of rapid expansion when northern Italy was thriving with centres like Milan, Padua, and Florence.[1] But despite earthquakes and the AD 79 eruption of Vesuvius, Naples continued to prosper under the Romans.

Even after the harbour of Ostia, Rome's port, was improved, Pozzuoli maintained its importance. In the Augustan age, Virgil and Horace came to the Bay of Naples. Virgil wrote the *Georgics* there, and his much advertised tomb might be authentic. The warm thermal water had much appeal to the Romans. St. Paul landed at Pozzuoli, and there is evidence that he found a small Christian community here. Extensive remains of early Christian churches in Naples can be seen in the catacombs of SS Gennaro e Gaudioso and under S Marla di Sanità, but it was not until the edict of Constantine in 313 AD that Christians were allowed to construct churches above ground. The chapel of S Restituta is the oldest surviving Christian church (now within the Duomo).

Pozzuoli, while still the leading port of Italy, was the terminus for the grain coming from Sicily, North Africa, and Egypt. The whole of

---

[1] Venice emerged later.

Campania was booming, largely from the manufacture of ceramics and luxury goods as well as agricultural produce, and its metropolis, Capua, was renowned for scent and the beauty of its women. Gradually Greek culture gave way to Roman, and Naples became bilingual. Baiae and the coast to the west of Naples became fashionable resorts for the Roman nobility, and magnificent villas and baths were built - the remains of which are dramatic. In 476 AD, the Goths overran Italy, and after capturing Rome they took Naples. Then the rule of Imperial Rome in the west finally came to an end. The Ostrogoth Odoacer humiliatingly deposed the last Emperor, Romulus Augustus. Odoacer considered that Romulus Augustus was not important enough for a public execution and banished him with a pension to the villa of Lucullus at Misenum. He actually died in the Castel del'Ovo. The occupation of Naples by the Goths can be considered a fifty years' breathing space. Their first king, King Theodoric and his successor but one, King Totila, were tolerant, and Naples and Campania were reasonably well governed.

However, the eastern Roman Empire attempted to recover southern Italy, and the Byzantine General, Belisarius, captured Naples by passing his troops through an aqueduct in 536 AD. The ensuing Gothic war caused extensive damage to the south of Italy, and the Goths recaptured Naples. The Goths had abandoned paganism in 340 AD and for twenty years Justinian, the Greek Roman Emperor, wasted his forces in trying to drive them out of Italy where they were acting as reasonable rulers. Eventually, after hard fighting, another Byzantine general, Narses, defeated the Goths in 554 AD but Italy, including Campania and Naples, had been devastated by long years of fighting. Naples remained subject to the Byzantine emperors of Constantinople for nearly six centuries, being ruled by provincial governors. The Church, which had been left in peace by the Goths, became stronger and was an important element in the Byzantine rule of Naples. However the long drawn out battles between Goths and Byzantines had done grave damage to Naples and surrounding towns and weakened the Byzantine army.[2] Only five years later, the Lombards, a Germanic tribe who really deserved the title of barbarian[s], overran northern Italy and part of the south. After capturing a large tract of land in Campania, they established the Lombard duchy of Beneventum there in 571. At first the Lombards persecuted the Church and heaped fresh ruin upon that caused by the Greek Gothic war. The Lombards never took Naples.

---

[2] The Greek and Roman temples in Naples were destroyed during the period.

However, in 653 the Lombard kingdom was converted to Catholicism. The Lombards did not reduce the inhabitants of their conquered lands into second-class citizens even while pagans. In 774, Charlemagne pronounced himself King of the Lombards, and the Lombards, who had controlled most of Italy, ceased to exist as a separate state. Still, the Lombard duchy at Benevento continued until 840 when it disintegrated, but the Lombards there were progressively absorbed by the indigenous culture; their language fell out of use as the Lombards took part in the intellectual life of the Italians. Yet Lombard art had a strong effect on monumental ornamentation in Campania.

The coastal area around Naples was successfully defended by Byzantine dukes against the Lombards. Meanwhile, Amalfi and a small mountainous surrounding area became an independent republic with a large fleet and considerable mercantile power. Establishing its independence from Naples in the 9th century, it became directly subject to Constantinople, giving them such considerable commercial and naval privileges that Amalfi almost rivalled Venice. The whole coast of Campania was subject to ferocious raids by Saracen pirates, who sometimes maintained a presence on land, and the coastline south of Naples is dotted with castles called 'Saracen'- put up for defence in that period, which can still be seen.

Normans first arrived in southern Italy in the 9th century as mercenary soldiers, or pilgrims to Monte Sant' Angelo in Apulia. They saw opportunities for booty and conquest, so that younger sons of the great Norman landowning feudal families with their followers moved south, acquiring large tracts of land in return for military service. They soon controlled most of Puglia and Calabria under Robert de Hauteville (1015-1085) - who came to Calabria in 1047 with a handful of knights and led the life of a robber chief by cattle lifting and other plunder. In 1059 at Melfi, he came to terms with Pope Nicholas II and was formally invested with his lands, styling himself Duke of Apulia and Calabria. With his younger brother, Roger, he conquered much of Campania and all of Sicily. In 1074 Pope Gregory VII excommunicated him, but found him too powerful. Robert, after an abortive expedition against Constantinople, marched on Rome and sacked it in 1084, carrying off the Pope to his Norman capital at Salerno. Gregory died there in 1085. (....) Robert's sacking of Rome was worse than anything the Goths and Vandals did there. His younger brother Roger I, King of Sicily, (1031-1101) was a finer character. He completed the conquest of Sicily from the Arabs, beginning in 1061, six years before the Norman Conquest of Britain, and at his death was one of the leading princes in Europe. His son Roger II (1097–1154), on the death of his cousin the Duke of Apulia in 1127, united the south of Italy with Sicily as a Norman Kingdom with Naples under him in 1139. The United Kingdom under Roger II became the cultural centre of the Mediterranean, with its glittering partly oriental capital of Palmero. The 12th century was a boom time for Naples and the south of Italy, and the Romanesque churches began to be built. William the Bad succeeded Roger II and William the Good (neither was particularly bad or good), and in 1194 the Hautevilles male line became extinct.

Then the unattractive and sinister Holy Roman Emperor Henry VI of Hohenstaufen (1165–97) brought an army from Germany and claimed the kingdom successfully in 1194 after capturing Richard I of England, but only lived for three years to enjoy it. He was married to Constance, the heiress to the Norman Kingdom of South Italy and Sicily. His son, the legendary Frederick II (1194–1250), *Stupor Mundi*, was both Holy Roman Emperor and King of Sicily. He preferred southern Italy and presided over a brilliant court, brought in liberal reforms, and founded the University of Naples - the first in the south, although the medical school at Salerno, which Frederick II also endowed, was already famous. Frederick II had a good relationship with England, having married Isabella, sister of Henry III. He was an enlightened ruler, whom Dante called the father of Italian poetry. When he died in 1250, the Guelfs[3] began to gain the upper hand. Frederick's son Conrad claimed the throne in 1252 but was killed. His illegitimate brother Manfred attempted to do the same, and was crowned King of Sicily in 1258, but he was killed in 1266 at Benevento by troops led by Charles of Anjou (1226–1285), who had been entreated by the Papacy to oust the House of Hohenstaufen.

Manfred's younger brother Conradin then tried to reclaim the throne in 1268. He was only 15, and at a battle between Rome and Naples at Tagliacozzo, his army was badly defeated by the Guelfs and he was made prisoner. He was brought before Charles of Anjou at Naples, who had him beheaded in the Piazza del Mercato, and in the nearby Church of the Carmine his coffin and his body can still be found (....). Charles of Anjou, brother of King Louis IX was the first in the line of Angevin kings who ruled Naples for nearly 200 years. Robert the Wise, who ruled from 1309 to

---

[3] The Guelfs were the chief rivals of the Hohenstaufens among German princely families. Their name was given to the Italian party, which championed national unity under the Pope, against the Ghibellines who urged submission of all Italy to the Holy Roman Emperor.

1343, was a patron of the arts; he encouraged poets, writers and artists to come to Naples. Giotto came to Naples to paint in 1328, and fragments of his work can still be seen. Petrarch came twice, and Boccaccio came from Tuscany; he spent his time at court collecting material for his tales of *The Decameron*, which he wrote in the 1350s. Under the Angevins, the splendid Gothic churches were built. Robert the Wise left only a granddaughter, Giovanna I, and under her rather feeble rule the barons increased their power. The Black Death (1347) cost her kingdom almost one-third of its population, and a civil war began between different Angevin factions. This civil war continued for a century and thoroughly weakened the Angevin dynasty, and opening the way for the Spanish Aragonese, who already ruled Sicily. Alfonso V of Aragon (Alfonso I of Sicily) succeeded his father in 1416 as King of Aragon and Sicily. In 1420 the childless Joanna II appealed to him for help against her Angevin cousin Louis III of Anjou. Alfonso was adopted as her heir but soon lost her favour. Nine years later he renewed his designs on Naples, but she disinherited him in favour of René of Anjou. Alfonso threw out the Angevins from Naples in 1442. A student of the classics, he knew how Belisarius had taken Naples in the Greek Gothic war by sending men through an aqueduct, and repeated the feat. Naples was then again united with Sicily. Alfonso, unlike his Norman and Hohenstaufen predecessors, made Naples his capital, and attracted artists and scholars to his court. After his state entry, he never returned to Spain.

The Aragon dynasty was less enlightened than the Angevins. However, Alfonso celebrated his victory by building a beautiful white marble arch at the entrance to the Castel Nuovo. This should not be missed (......). He was a harsh ruler, and his bastard son and successor Ferrante I was worse. He exploited women, killed feudal barons who revolted, and even mummified his enemies. The mild Alfonso II, Ferrante's son, was a better character, and enticed good architects to come to Naples.

In 1494 Charles VIII, King of France, who had a good claim to Naples by descent from the Angevins, tried to invade Naples. The last Aragonese King, the ineffectual Alfonso II, fled. However the Spaniards were then at the height of their powers under Ferdinand and Isabella and they sent El Gran Capitano, Gonsalvo di Cordova with a strong army, and after some fighting, Naples and its kingdom were put under Spanish rule. King Alfonso was not restored and the Kingdom was ruled directly under the Spanish Crown from 1503. A long line of viceroys from Spain then governed Naples. The most important of these was Don Pedro de Toledo. He greatly enlarged the city, made the Via Toledo, which runs in a long ribbon from north to south, and built Castel Sant' Elmo, also to keep the Neapolitans in order.

Spanish rule lasted for over two centuries, and baroque art, of which there is so much to admire in Naples, flourished. However, as Spain lapsed into decadence the government grew more oppressive. In 1647 there was a popular uprising against the Spaniards incited by the French and the citizens were free for nine days. The Viceroy summarily put the leader of the revolt, Masaniello, to death. He became a legend, and spasmodic revolt continued for over a year, but he was ruthlessly put down by the Spaniards, having receiving insufficient aid from the French.

In 1707, during the War of the Spanish Succession, Naples came under the rule of Archduke Charles of Austria. The Treaty of Utrecht confirmed this. Uninspired Austrian viceroys ruled the city for 27 years, but the city had a monarch of its own again under the Spanish Bourbon Charles III in 1734. The Spanish Bourbons remained in power until 1860, except for the years when Naples was under Napoleon. Charles III was responsible for many lavish buildings in Naples. He built the San Carlo Opera House, the Caserta Palace, and Capodimonte with its famous porcelain factory. He also played a leading part in organizing the excavations at Herculaneum and Pompeii. His mother was Elizabeth Farnese, and thanks to her inheritance, the wonderful Farnese collection now rests in the Capodimonte and National Archeological Museum. But the Bourbons killed Neapolitan baroque and introduced classicism, although some baroque work went on until 1770.

At the age of 43, Charles was called back to rule Spain in 1759, and his third son Ferdinand was crowned King of Naples at the age of seven. The eldest son Philip was insane, and the second son Charles was destined to become King of Spain. Ferdinand was known as King Nasone or 'King Nosey' because of his big nose. Poorly educated, he spent his time shooting pheasants, partridges, quail, deer, and wild boar, and fishing. An army of gamekeepers bred pheasants for him, and a splendid collection of his sporting guns can be seen at Capodimonte. Nevertheless, he was fond of the Neapolitan people and was much liked. His wife, Maria Carolina, sister of Marie Antoinette, was an astute and more intelligent politician..

In 1799 Napoleon's armies, under General Championnet, took Naples; the King fled to Sicily, but thanks to Nelson and the British in 1802, after the Peace of Amiens, he returned. He then inflicted savage reprisals on all those who had sided with the French. In 1806 Napoleon's armies returned. First, Napoleon made his brother Joseph King of Naples, succeeded by Joachim Murat, his brother-in-law. The French ruled sensibly

25

and made many liberal reforms. However, much resentment was caused by the manner in which the French sent young Neapolitan soldiers to fight in Russia. With some regret of the population, Murat left in 1815 after he had foolishly attempted to chase the Austrians out of North Italy and lost the Battle of Tolentino against superior forces. Stupidly, he tried to start a revolt at Pizzo in Calabria in 1816, and was executed on the orders of the Bourbon King.

Under the rule of the Bourbons, British tourists flocked to Naples, and the British Ambassador Sir William Hamilton, who lived there for 35 years, formed a wonderful collection of classical antiquities, whilst his young wife Emma used to pose for impressive drawing room performances. When Stendhal visited Naples in 1817, he found it so difficult to find a hotel room that he remarked, 'There must have been two or three thousand English in the city'.

On his return from Sicily in 1815, after the flight of the Murats, Ferdinand I was popular with the lower classes but was resented by the more educated because he was too reactionary. He died in 1825 after a reign of sixty-five years, and was succeeded by his dull son Francis, who died in 1830. Then Ferdinand II came to the throne; he was a colourful character with coarse geniality like his grandfather, although likewise stupid and reactionary. He became popular especially with the riffraff of Naples. He was known as King Bomba because he had ordered the bombardment of Messina when the Sicilians demanded a constitution in 1848.

Still, the reign of the Bourbons should perhaps in some way be looked on as a golden age for Naples. The Bourbons built the first railways in Italy, spent vast sums on the excavations at Pompeii and elsewhere, and provided a lavish museum for their finds. Yet it was a backward state, described by Gladstone as 'a negation of God erected into a system of government'.

On his death in 1859, Ferdinand II was succeeded by his son Francis. Francis was weak and ineffectual: against all the odds, Garibaldi and his thousands, aided by Mazzini's propaganda agents, conquered Sicily, and in 1860 he entered Naples by train to become dictator. Francis II escaped to Gaeta and fought back, but unsuccessfully largely due to the fact that King Victor Emmanuel II brought his Piedmontese army into Neapolitan territory to help Garibaldi. When Francis II abdicated, Naples became part of a united Italy, but the Savoy kings never regarded it as a royal capital, and the Bourbons were badly missed. For more than sixty years after 1860, British travellers still saw Naples as an essential part of their Grand Tour; but in the

1930s, with the rise of fascism, the Abyssinian war, and Mussolini's increasing involvement with Hitler, British tourism dwindled. Naples was badly affected by intrusion in the Second World War – first by the Americans, then by the Germans. As Naples was the principal port for supplying the Axis armies in Libya and Tunis, it was a legitimate target. However after the Axis surrendered in Tunisia in April 1943, the port was no longer used for military purposes, yet the Americans continued to bomb without justification. With its being the main port of entry for the Allied armies after October 1943, the Germans launched many air raids. As Naples was never a strong fascist city, Neapolitans spontaneously rose against the Germans and fascists on 29 September 1943 as the Allies broke out of the Salerno bridgehead, and without any help from Allied troops, drove the Germans out of the city in four days after a series of heroic actions and many casualties. Today the Neapolitans are immensely proud of their glorious four days of 1943.

In the years immediately after 1945, life in Naples was at low ebb, with few monuments being repaired after the bombing and few attractions open to the public. Few tourists came to Naples itself, although the Amalfi and Sorrento coasts quickly became popular again. Then the disastrous cholera outbreak of 1973, followed by the earthquake of 1980 which damaged many attractions that remained closed for a long time, made Naples a no-go area for tourists. Nowadays, tourists are returning, but not in great numbers. There is an acute shortage of second category hotels. Instead, package tours go to Capri, Sorrento, and the Amalfi coast, but few tourists spend more than a day in Naples itself.

The time is ripe for a return of mass tourism to visit the art treasures of the city of Naples, and at last efforts are being made to achieve this end, with most of the main monuments being repaired after the 1980 earthquake. Perhaps this book will encourage the British to stay in Naples and enjoy its art as their forbears did.

2
Churches

Naples has 350 churches; this is more than in Florence or Venice. Most of the important historic ones lie in the antique centre between Piazza Dante and the Duomo (Spaccanapoli). This area is crossed from east to west by two ancient Greek–Roman streets - Via Tribunali and Via Biagio Librai, and covers the site of the old Greek Roman city of which you still see many traces. Fascinating crowded alleys criss-cross the zone, and it is difficult to suggest routes. Arm yourself with a plan with the churches clearly marked (and a stick if you fear up and down pavements) and take a bus or taxi to Piazza Dante, Piazza Gesu Nuovo, or the Duomo. Then continue on foot. Here you encounter the throbbing vibrant life in the centre of historic Naples - innumerable people of every age all talking animatedly and gesticulating to great effect with their hands; countless small shops mostly selling hand-made jewellery, and many bars with trays of coffee being continuously carried out to shops and offices. Here is one of the great attractions of South Italy, quite different from and more cheerful and picturesque than Rome, Florence, or Venice. Alas, too many motor scooters still push up and down the narrow streets, which cry out to become a large pedestrian precinct.

The number and richness of the closely packed ancient churches in the Centro Antico is impressive. It is extraordinary how close together they are. The Neapolitans like to say there is more art in their churches than in the museums of other Italian cities, and this is largely true. Neapolitans have always been celebrated for their piety, and today large devotional congregations flock to the churches to hear mass. In past centuries, rich Neapolitan nobles spent vast sums on building churches as well as endowing masses for the repose of their own souls, and as well, many rich fathers with unmarriageable daughters, or surplus sons, found it more economical to pay a dowry for them to enter a convent or monastery. Thus in size and wealth, and in Old Master paintings and sculpture, religious houses in Naples surpassed other Italian cities. The historic centre became clustered with churches, convents, and monasteries that have come down to us over the centuries almost intact.

Few tourists today visit the ancient centre, whereas in Victorian days the old churches were a must for visitors. Interestingly, the famous guidebooks of the Victorian travellers - Augustus Hare, Murray's handbook (1855), and the 1865 Baedeker - are still largely valid. You will find it a great joy walking in the footsteps of the British doing the Grand Tour in Naples.

My favourite church in Naples is S Giovanni a Carbonara in the street of the same name - a short distance to the east of the Duomo. You should give this church priority.[4] It is the best Gothic [example], and unspoiled. No other building brings one so close to the Angevin rulers of Naples. The church stands well above the street and is approached by an imposing double staircase designed by Sanfelice. Inside it is pure joy. Founded in 1343, the nave is filled by the large arched tomb (1428) of King Ladislao of Durazzo, who died young in 1414, having eaten and drunk too much and indulged in too many women. The tomb was erected by his sister Queen Joanna II, and is a masterpiece by Andrea Ciccione. It is a unique Gothic tomb of three storeys, rising to the whole height of the church. The lower storey consists of four big statues of the virtues that support the whole monument. Above an architrave are seated figures of King Ladislao and his sister. In the third storey, angels are gracefully drawing aside a curtain to display the coffin containing the King's body, while on the summit is an equestrian figure of Ladislao with a sword in his hand.

According to an 18th-century writer Pietro Giannone, Ladislao was planning to attack Florence and the Florentine envoy in Naples. Knowing that he was sleeping with the daughter of a doctor from Perugia gave the man a 'huge' bribe to anoint her private parts with poison, and by this means the King was struck down by an 'unknown and lingering disease' from which he died, as presumably did his lover.

He was renowned for his sexual powers and the number and quality of his concubines. According to the same chronicles, his sister Joanna II was not 'inferior' to her brother in her tastes for multiple sex, as no sooner had she been left a widow by the Duke of Anjou than she provided herself with plenty of lovers; and their father King Charles III was said to have brought two monsters of lust and filthiness into the world.

Nevertheless, the atmosphere produced by the delicate and tasteful tomb of Ladislao makes one hope that his sister's and his sins have been pardoned. Before leaving, cast a glance on the dignified tomb of Gaetano Argento by Sanfelice (1730).

Behind the tomb is a beautiful octagonal chapel that contains the tomb of Sergianni Carracciolo del Sole, the favourite seneschal of Queen Joanna. Sadly, finally after a quarrel, she agreed to have him assassinated and he was buried in secret by four monks in the chapel he had built. His statue, with a dagger in his hand alluding to his murder, is characteristic and

---

[4] Since writing this I am pleased to read that Sacheverell Sitwell also writes that it is his number one.

the chapel shows the transition to Renaissance. There are damaged - but in places still perfect - frescoes of the life of the Virgin around the walls of the chapel in the Giotto style, dating back to the mid 15th century. They are by a pupil of Giotto, Leonardo di Biusuccio, with lifelike faces and animals and attractive landscapes showing the lives of the hermit monks, with colours still vivid. The 1440 floor of the chapel (recently restored) is a fine example of early pavement in majolica, with emblems of the Caracciolo family. To the left of the nave is another fascinating circular Caracciolo chapel, one of the best pieces of Renaissance architecture in Naples, with statues of knights in armour interspersed with saints by Neapolitan sculptors of the 16th century. In the Sacristy there is a small picture by Bassano, and fifteen by Vasari, commissioned in 1546, and interesting walnut cupboards of the same period designed by Vasari.

After the 1980 earthquake, S Giovanni was closed until 1997 but has now been well restored. On the piazza in front the Neapolitans held bloody gladiatorial conflicts, which even Petrarch viewed with horror during the reign of Joanna II. It is worth lingering in S Giovanni to imbibe the atmosphere of five centuries ago.

From S Giovanni plunge westward into the Via Tribunali, and before you arrive at Via Duomo you find my favourite early Spanish church in Naples – that of Pio Monte della Misericordia, the church of the charitable order of the same name. The chapel and the adjoining palace, which still houses the order, were built in 1601 during the Spanish vice regency. Originally the order bought a palace and church, but in 1658 considered the church inadequate so the order had it pulled down, and the excellent architect Picchiati was instructed to plan a magnificent chapel. We must be grateful to Picchiati because he built the finest example of 17th-century early Baroque with seven altars; it is the first octagonal church in Naples. It is not flamboyant, but dignified. There are six side altars with doorways, giving the impression they open into each other, but in fact they do not. Each has an Old Master picture. The marble floor is radiant.

The chapel is beautifully lit and the steep dome is particularly striking. Behind the altar is a Caravaggio, one of the most important religious pictures of the 17th century. (It is worth visiting Naples alone to see this and the Caravaggio of *The Flagellation* at Capodimonte). All seven works of mercy are in the Misericordia Caravaggio - help for the down and out and sick, clothing the naked, feeding the hungry, aid for prisoners, burying the dead, drink for the thirsty, and lodging for pilgrims. The picture is a delight and might be a scene from Neapolitan life, and it is fascinating

NAPLES, What most tourists never see

that the order carries on the same works of mercy today.

Caravaggio painted it between September 1606 and January 1607, having been specially invited to Naples. He was asked to include both the *Madonna of the Misericordia* and the *Seven Acts of Mercy* in a single vertical canvas. Traditionally, each act had previously been represented in separate pictures. He set the acts, described in Matthew's Gospel 25; 35–36, in a small piazza typical of the ancient centre of Naples. It has the same contrast of light and shade as in Caravaggio's *The Flagellation* at Capodimonte. In the light is the figure of a beautiful woman, Pero, breast-feeding her father Cimon through the bars of his prison ('I was hungry and you gave me food').

In the shade is a young bravo, Saint Martin, cutting his cloak to share it with a naked beggar who is in the foreground ('I was naked and you clothed me'). In the shadow behind is a youth with twisted legs ('I was sick and you visited me'). The group of loiterers is completed by a husky man, Samson, in the desert of Lechi (Judges 15; 19), pouring water into his mouth from the jawbone of an ass ('I was thirsty and you gave me drink'). In the background, a vested priest holds a torch to light up the hurried transport of a corpse, recalling the plagues that periodically decimated the population of Naples, (Burial of the dead, the seventh Act not mentioned in the Gospels). Above hover the Madonna and Child, with two angels giving divine acknowledgement to the acts of human charity and especially to the figures in the painting who probably portray members of the community.

The picture lit up above the dark altar gives the appearance of the church's being invaded by part of the crowd from the adjoining narrow streets, full of the animated Neapolitan squalor, which must have impressed Caravaggio when he first came from Rome to Naples. The scene in the picture is most apposite for the Misericordia who are dedicated to the daily performance of the works of charity depicted and who have been performing them for hundreds of years.

In one side chapel is a splendid picture by Giordano of the burial of Christ. It was commissioned in 1670 to replace a similar picture by Forli, which did not satisfy the Governors of the Guild. In the adjoining palace you can still see the banished Forli, and may agree how much better a picture Giordano's is. Another chapel has an interesting picture of the Guild ransoming Christian slaves from the ferocious Turks, who at that period made frequent raids on the Campanian coast. This is by Azzolino, and represents an important part of the charity's former work.

The adjoining 17th-century palace, still used solely for administering the Guild's charities, is fascinating, with a fine collection of furniture and pictures on the *piano nobile,* all in excellent condition. You find yourself in a magnificent 17th-century house with everything in place as it was then. It is a gem seldom visited by tourists, and its silence and dignity evoke the continuity of a patrician dwelling standing naturally amid the slums of old Naples. You must phone in advance (446973) to pay a visit; there is a lift from the courtyard, and the staff of the Guild is most courteous and helpful. Little has changed here since the 17th century, and the Governor's table is set out with the name cards of present-day Neapolitan nobility who currently manage the charity; the palace leaves a strong sense of the history of an aristocratic Guild carrying on the same tradition over the centuries. There are numerous attractive pictures by first-rate Neapolitan painters - many by Francesco de Mura, who was closely associated with this Guild; a good one by Stanzioni, and others by Vaccaro and Santafede. It is a rich picture gallery, all the more enjoyable for the pictures being in their original setting amongst furniture of the same date, and for the peace of the old palace.

Three hundred yards to the west, up Via Tribunali after crossing Via Duomo, you come to the present-day convent of Mother Teresa's nuns. They carry on, in a much humbler way, the same type of charity in Naples as the Guild of Pio Monte has been doing for so long. There are six nuns – two Italian, one Spanish, and three Indian. They occupy the premises of a dilapidated disused seminary, with a mouldering chapel and an old palace in slightly better repair. Here they lodge 50 men, and each day they have a soup kitchen for 200. The very young Spanish nun I spoke to was most welcoming; she told me they do NOT solicit alms, but welcome contributions. There is a notice, SUORE DELLA CARITA, on the battered front door, but to enter you must go to another door down the narrow lane immediately to the east. (Another Mother Teresa convent for women is at Capodimonte). As there are no men on the staff, they cannot accept drug cases. The complete dedication of these nuns is moving, and the need for their service demonstrates the poverty of Naples today, with 26% of the population out of work.

Stepping down a narrow lane into the Via S Biagio brings you, just before the Piazza S Domenico, to the small Gothic church of S Angelo a Nilo, built in 1384; but this has greatly changed and alas, now the interior is baroque. It belongs to the Franciscans of S Lorenzo, and has a sweet small cloister. No monks live there now. In it there are two important monuments; the first of the founder, Cardinal Brancaccio, who died in 1427, by Donatello and Michelozzo. The angels with cymbals on top are charming, as are the folds of the curtain coming down over the coffin. The central relief of the *Assumption* is definitely by Donatello. The second important monument is an exquisite statue of St. Michael, recently restored to its original whiteness after being covered in dirt for centuries. It was here that my grandson was highly amused to see the reticent sacristan casually filling the holy water stoop from a Coca Cola bottle.

Anthony Blunt ascribes the Brancaccio tomb to the new Renaissance style because of the small Corinthian pillars on the sarcophagus. The whole tomb was sent by ship in 1428 from Pisa, but the style was not imitated while Naples was under the Angevins who stuck to French Gothic for their few remaining years after 1428. Like others, Blunt thinks Donatello did only the relief of the *Assumption* himself.[5]

Turn right off the Via Biagio, a few yards past S Angelo a Nilo and down Via Grande Archivio, and you are at SS Severino e Sossio. The church and monastery (one of the richest, oldest and largest in the city) were founded in the 9th century, but in 1835 Ferdinand II decided to use this former Benedictine Monastery to house the enormous quantity of documents relating to the affairs of Naples that had accumulated since the Angevin period. (Access to these archives is freely granted to students and researchers from any nation.)

The renovation entailed remodeling the 9th-century monastery, which had been enlarged in 1494. There are four attractive cloisters, indicating how numerous were the Benedictines formerly here; it was even believed that a very old, enormous plane tree with a fig tree grafted onto it, which only died in 1955, had been planted by St Benedict himself. This cloister is still known as the Cloister of the Plane Tree.

Ask to see the twenty 15th-century frescoes known as *Lo Zingaro,* or the gypsy. They are very evocative of Benedict's life. Especially good is one of the young saint on his way to Rome with his father and nurse, and all are full of the quiet calm of the contemporary life of the saint. Look also at the pharmacy.

The splendid vaulted ceilings, frescoed by de Mura with the life of St Benedict, dominate the current monastery church rebuilt in 1490; they are a real masterpiece. De Mura also painted the canvases of saints and popes by the large windows, and a Supper in the House of Pharisees in the church after falling from a scaffold when he was in his 80s. The high altar by

---

[5] See Palazzo di Carofa (1466) 121 Vla Biagio dei Librai for a mixture of Gothic and Renaissance. (Page .....)

Cosimo Fanzago is typical and delightful, but the putti statues on it are from a later date. The lower church is older and has a Renaissance appearance. Note the remains of Gothic arches in the wall. In the seventh chapel on the left is the Crucifix, given before the battle of Lepanto by Pope Pius V to Don Juan of Austria; this will please the historically minded. At Lepanto, in the Gulf of Corinth in 1571, a united papal Spanish and Venetian fleet under Don Juan completely defeated the Turks, whose barbarisms had horrified Europe, and much reduced Muhammadan power. Without doubt there were Neapolitan ships in the fleet because of the Spanish involvement, and the fleet sailed from Messina in Sicily. S Severino is a magnificent church. You gasp at its size. When last I visited it in 1999, the altar and choir could not be seen following the earthquake damage of 1980, which has necessitated scaffolding. Many of the frescoes are in a sad state. The church is only open on Sunday morning, but is well worth seeing.

Close to San Severino is the lottery office (Ufficio Lotto e Lotterie) at 17 Via Del Grande Archivio. The lottery dates back to the 17th century, and for a few minutes in the streets and alleys of old Naples at noon every Saturday, the bustling life comes to a halt as a crowd waits impatiently for the result. For many Neapolitans this is the great event of the week.

Proceeding up Via St Gregorio in Armeno, you find dozens of shops selling cribs and figures for them. The shepherds around the manger are famous, and in the last century eminent sculptors contributed to this form of art. Neapolitans still love them.

The church of S Gregorio in Armeno on the left is striking. Built on the site of the Greek Roman forum, right in the centre of classical Naples, it was finished in 1579.

The inside is richly decorated with frescoes by Luca Giordano around 1679 to celebrate the 100th anniversary of its construction, and shows the arrival of Greek nuns in white habits as refugees in Naples. The high altar is magnificently composed of white marble; note the Giordano frescoes and the *Adoration of the Sacrament* by de Matteis. The dome, well lit by large windows, is most impressive; even more interesting are the two large organs on either side of the nave, with balconies and paintings added in cheerful typical mid-18th-century Neapolitan style in 1745, before the reaction against baroque set in and the return to classicism after the deaths of Sanfelice and Vaccaro.

Equally exhilarating is the adjoining convent. There are still 45 nuns who enjoy their splendid surroundings. Originally they belonged to the Greek rite, but in 1569 they were forced by the Council of Trent to change to the rule of S Basilio under the Roman rite and to wear black. They had been expelled from their original convent in Greece in the 16th century. On the top of the steps leading to the convent are two turntables where unwanted babies could be left to be raised as orphans by the nuns. The convent is three storeys high, with covered balconies, and is still full of life, with many open French windows leading from the nuns rooms to the balconies. The Italian nuns are very friendly but you need to speak Italian for a sustained conversation. They have in their care the blood of S Patrizia, the female patron saint of Naples which, like that of S Gennaro, is said to liquefy periodically. The cloister of S Gregorio is an oasis of peace in the middle of the crowded streets of Spaccanapoli.

In the centre of the large attractive cluster is a splendid 17th-century fountain by Matteo Bottiglieri showing Christ and the Good Samaritan. A device beneath a fresco of St. Benedict regulates the water flow. A stone inscription reads: '... No dishonest person may live near this monastery and no person of whatever station or condition may engage in any game or sport near this monastery on pain of paying a royal fine of 28 ounces of gold.' Perhaps a joke! From S. Gregorio it is only a few paces to the important church and monastery of S. Lorenzo Maggiore, where a few amiable Franciscans still live.

The present-day church of S Lorenzo is relatively modern, being remodeled by Sanfelice (1732). However, it occupies the site of a church built by Charles of Anjou in 1266. The tower dates to 1487. The greater part of this building was destroyed in the earthquake of 1732. Only the main door, the side door towards the cloister, and the chapels around the choir, with Angevin tombs, remain of the Gothic architecture. Petrarch recalls praying with the monks after being wakened by a fearful storm in November 1343, and here Bocaccio beheld the beautiful 'Fiametta' (Mary – illegitimate daughter of King Robert).

Petrarch wrote that a bishop, who was also an astrologer, had forecast an earthquake for 23 November 1343: he had gone to bed in apprehension, and had only just closed his eyes when suddenly there was the most terrible noise; not only were the shutters rattling horribly but the actual walls themselves, built of hewn stone, were rocking on their foundations. His night-light had gone out, but the whole community, groping in the darkness with one single lamp, was led by the saintly Prior David to the church to sing hymns. They all spent the night in the church, expecting they were about to die, and that 'everything was collapsing in ruins.' The scenes of devastation amongst the ships in Naples harbour the next day were so shattering that Petrarch recorded that he would only travel by land again 'throughout the rest of my life.'

The baroque interior decoration has been removed recently, so despite its 18th-century restoration, the large fine church is pure Gothic. The nine Gothic chapels, much damaged in 1732, are intact, and in the seventh chapel was a very interesting picture on a gold ground by Simone di Martini (1319). This depicts the Coronation of King Robert of Naples by his brother, St Louis of Anjou, adorned with many fleurs de lys; while in the chapel of the right transept is an important picture by the 15th- century Neapolitan artist Solario.

Over the high altar is a magnificent white marble screen by Giovanni da Nola (1536), with a bas-relief with fascinating views of old Naples, and behind the altar there are Angevin tombs. In the large chapel of S Antonio there are paintings by Mattia Preti (1660). The most important tomb is that of Catherine of Austria, while the remarkable Gothic frescoes (1320) in the Barrile chapel, behind the high altar, must not be missed. Giotto himself may have worked on this. The chapel of the family Carace was designed by Fanzago in 1643; it is splendid baroque, as is Fanzago's other chapel - that of S Antonio (1638). Do not miss looking at the inlaid floor by Fanzago in the chapel Carace.

In the attractive cloister there is a staircase leading to fascinating archeological remains, showing the old Greek Roman street, which joined Via Biagio with Via Tribunali. There is a Greek wall of 500 BC, a vast Roman building of 100–200 AD, together with a number of recognizable shops (dyers, vase makers, and a baker), and a public meeting place of 800 AD. Digging is continuing. These excavations are well worth visiting (closed Tuesdays).

Almost opposite San Lorenzo, on the other side of the Via dei Tribunali, lies S Paolo Maggiore, approached by an imposing flight of steps. It was built on the site of the ancient Temple of Castor and Pollux in 1590, and originally incorporated the beautiful portico of the ancient temple. Unfortunately, the Greek portico was destroyed in the earthquake of 1688, although interestingly, two Corinthian columns and part of the architrave can still be seen, together with fragments of inscriptions.

Inside the church there is a splendid ceiling by Solimena; fortunately, mirrors are provided so you can see its detail comfortably. There are also paintings by Corenzio and Stanzioni; a most interesting sacristy with frescoes by Solimena, and an attractive typical baroque chapel dedicated to the family Firrao. Alongside the church is an entrance to an underground area where you see interesting Greek, Roman, and early Christian remains – the area being in the heart of the Greek Roman city. The cloister with Roman columns is attractive.

On another visit to Spaccanapoli, start in Piazza Bellini, easily reached under the Port Alba arch from Piazza Dante, and look at the largest concentration of new and second hand bookshops in Europe. In the green and attractive Piazza Bellini there are several pleasant coffee shops, one of which is also a library, and under the arch of Port Alba there is an excellent pizzeria, which I can strongly recommend.

From any chair outside the Piazza Bellini cafés you get a good view of Palazzo Firrao, 99 Via Constantinapoli - a typical 17th-century Spanish home of the nobility - on the opposite side of Via Constantinapoli. Note the statues of the Spanish Royal Family and that the enticing balconies are 200 years older, as they come from the original building that was pulled down and rebuilt in the 17th century. The cafés adjoin the remains of the Greek walls (4th century BC) that used to surround the ancient city; they are well-exposed and evocative, while in the middle of the shady picturesque square sits a monument to the famous composer Vincenzo Bellini. The Monastery of S Antonio a Port Alba, up many steps, glowers down on the square; it incorporates the 15th-century Palazzo Conca. It is firmly closed and has a persistent air of neglect. On leaving the square to the south, you arrive at the west end of the always fascinating Via Tribunali. At No. 1 is the Church and Monastery of S Pietro Maiella (1313) - a fine early Gothic church, nearly always open, and welcoming. The original Gothic architecture was at one time heavily overlaid with baroque additions. From 1888 to 1927, meticulous restoration uncovered fine 14th century frescoes in two side chapels, and painted vaulted ceilings. There are splendid gilded wooden ceilings with paintings by Mattia Preti, which are some of the best examples of 17th-century Neapolitan painting.

Owing to the debaroqueization of S Pietro, you experience the glory of true Angevin Gothic. You must not miss the fresco of the Madonna in one of the side chapels. At one time the whole church was painted, and there are enough paintings left to give a good idea of how spectacular it was in its former Gothic splendour.

In the cloisters and monastery adjoining is the Naples Conservatorio di Musica, always bristling with talented young men and women. Concerts are frequently held in the evening; tickets are cheap, and the quality of the music as one would expect in Naples is fantastically high. My wife and I were lucky enough to hear a full-scale orchestra and several leading singers from the San Carlo theatre without booking in advance.

Below S. Pietro is Via Sebastiano, full of musical instrument shops. It is worth making a diversion down it to No. 12 Via Benedetto Croce, where the famous Neapolitan philosopher historian and anti-Fascist politician (1866–1952) of that name lived. It is called Palazzo Filomarina. This is one of the best preserved noble buildings of the old centre, and still keeps its air of splendour whereas so many similar palaces are falling down. Inside is an historical library with 40,000 volumes in which students of all nationalities are welcome. It is open to the public three days a week, but a polite request to visit is seldom refused. The Palazzo dates back to 1512, and has an arcaded loggia, which is rare in Naples; the palace was altered in the 17th century. Inside you will be impressed by Croce's own library on the first floor; look also at the 18th-century entrance by Sanfelice, enlarged by him to allow the big coaches of the period to enter the courtyard. Almost next door at 45 Via Benedetto Croce is a very imposing baroque doorway at the Palazzo Carafa della Spina.

Turn back to the ever-fascinating Via Tribunali and you will come, on the left, to the small but elegant Capella Pontano, built in 1492 and based on a design for a pagan temple. It was built by Giovanni Pontano, secretary to King Ferdinand of Aragon, and its harmonious design makes it one of the most attractive Renaissance chapels in Naples. There is a good funeral triptych by Caiazzo, and the original 15th century pavement of coloured tiles is in good condition. Giovanni Pontano himself wrote the numerous Latin epigrams.

Close by on the left you find the campanile (bell tower) of S Maria Maggiore della Pietra Santa. This dates back to the 6th century AD and it's the most important surviving Romanesque Paleochristian remains in Naples. On the base of the tower there are fragments of friezes from Roman tombs. In the Middle Ages the road, which was then lower, passed under the bell tower arch. S Maria Maggiore della Pietra Santa is named after a holy stone; Fanzago built the church, separate from the bell tower, over the ruins of an early Christian basilica, traces of which can be seen in the crypt, and is an attractive church.

A few yards to the east is the church of S Maria Anime del Purgatori ad Arco, founded in 1604 to collect alms for masses for the dead to be said. There are bronze and stone skulls, bones, and other funeral objects on small stone columns on the facade and also inside. This church has a single nave; Fanzago designed it. On the left of the entrance, stairs lead down to an underground cemetery still much used by Neapolitans to pray for the souls of dead relations in purgatory whose bodies lie buried there.

Under the arcades on the right are piles of fish and vegetables – a tremendously colourful scene. The lower storeys of all the houses are clearly Roman; opposite the excellent café on the right is a shop selling fine wines in a three-storey house that is entirely Roman.

Naples is an acquired taste. If in the Via Tribunali you cannot find the charm of this timeless city dating back 2500 years and of its inhabitants, it has passed you by. However, you cannot fail to be impressed by the manners and friendliness in the cafés and in the innumerable shops selling shells, cameos, corals, and other typical handiwork. Keep a tight hold on your purse, and enjoy the medieval streets and the crumbling palaces with their soaring staircases within, and the sharp contrasts of various periods in the architecture.

If you plunge into any of the medieval alleys on the right of the Via Tribunali, within a few yards you are at Piazza del Gesu Nuovo. In the middle of the square is a slightly grotesque baroque statue, Guglia dell' Immaculata. Opinions vary about its artistic merit. It is definitely striking, so form your own view. To the north of the square is the large well-known Church of Gesu Nuovo, built at the end of the 16th century on the site of a 14th-century palace, San Severino, of which the distinctive facade alone remains. The main doorway, however, is dated 1685.

For many peoples' taste, Gesu Nuovo is too brightly coloured. My daughter did not care for the inside. It is a triumph of rich decoration, multicoloured marble, glass candelabra, altars aflame with flowers and candles, and many brilliant and worthwhile paintings. It also has its own modern saint, a Neapolitan priest who died recently, and his cult brings great numbers of the faithful into the church with obvious strong devotion.

The high altar was redesigned by Astarita in the 1750s and shows the return to classicism; it is bold and attractive. Brilliant and exciting baroque is the chapel of S Ignatius in the left transept by Fanzago (1637), with columns and statues, including marble and pictures, all contributing to an exciting and harmonious whole. Anthony Blunt describes the Guglia in front of Gesu Nuovo as ebullient rococo with the Putti floating, in flight in sharp contrast with the outside facade of the church.

The best picture is behind the portal by Solomena in 1725 of the chase of Eliodoro from the temple. It is worthwhile coming to the Gesu Nuovo just to see this picture. Other highly coloured pictures, all in tip-top condition, are a *Conception* by Paolo de Matteis, and several fine works by Corenzio (1638). Stanzione and Giordano have also contributed, especially to the magnificent painted ceilings. My favourite glimpse of this church is at dusk from the piazza through the main door when the rich colours inside become startlingly spectacular compared with the gloom outside.

A few steps to the east bring you to the Franciscan church and monastery of S Chiara, begun in 1310. Unfortunately American bombs did terrible damage here in August of 1943 at a moment when the Italian emissaries were talking to General Eisenhower and trying to negotiate an armistice with the Allies, and the Germans were no longer using the Port of Naples or the city. Naples port had been the main point of departure for Axis troops proceeding to North Africa, but with the fall of Tunis in April 1943, this came to an end. In August 1943 Naples was not a legitimate target.

Fortunately S Chiara has been well reconstructed and restored, with almost all the mid- 17th-century baroque of the interior removed so that you see the church now in its Gothic glory. The impressive large campanile was built to celebrate the completion and consecration of the church in 1340. Only the first storey is original, with Gothic inscriptions on the fascia. The top fell down in 1456 and was not rebuilt until 1604. Traces of the original bell tower can however, be seen on the building. The original design was a tower to stress that the whole complex was a fortress.

You come into the church of S Chiara by a finely worked marble 14th-century doorway. Inside immediately, one is struck by the simplicity of the large single Gothic nave, although it has been compared to an aircraft hangar. The style of the nave and chapels is typical Neapolitan Gothic, influenced perhaps by Tuscan architects from Siena. The windows high up were destroyed by American bombs and now have modern stained glass. The floor of the nave is marble and was designed by Vaccaro.

Behind the main altar is the magnificent tomb of Robert of Anjou, seated on the throne with his Queen and relatives around. This is one of the great medieval monuments of Italy. The Bourbon kings are buried in a fine baroque chapel to the right. This chapel was designed by Fuga, and is one of the few 18th-century works in the church that survived the bombing of 1943. It was built for the idiot first son of Charles III, who died in 1777. In 1984 the Cardinal of Naples, in the presence of the Bourbon claimant (the Duke of Castro the heir of Francis II), placed the coffin of Francis II, the last Bourbon king, here after a Requiem Mass. Poor Francis ruled only from May 1859 to October 1860 after succeeding his father, King Bomba, and was quite unprepared to order and control his people rigidly like his father had done. Instead of playing the hero, he preferred to save his subjects from the ravages of war and did not resist Garibaldi's entry into the city in 1860.

His Bavarian wife, Maria Sophia, lived until 1925 and was glimpsed from afar by both Proust and Sacheverell Sitwell in the early days of Fascism. (The reinterment of Francis II was the subject of an interesting article in the *Spectator* on 25 January 1984.)

Pause awhile in this Bourbon Commemorative Chapel and reflect on the history of this strange dynasty that, from 1734 until 1860, ruled Naples always with affection and sympathy, but sometimes brutally and far too often without intelligence. While they were kings, Naples was a capital; their successors, the House of Savoy, treated Naples as a province or a colony. Harold Acton, in two books, brought the times of the Bourbons of Naples to life ('*The Bourbons of Naples*; *The Last Bourbons*'), and in them we see Naples, with an endless flow of famous visitors, as a famous royal capital which Shelley called 'the Metropolis of a ruined Paradise.' Remember at least that when faced with revolution in the streets of Naples in May 1848, King Bomba refused to allow his troops to shoot at the mob at the barricades, crying out 'Spare my misguided subjects. Take prisoners. Do not kill.'

The crowning glory of S Chiara is the lovely cloisters – another oasis of calm and a meeting place for Neapolitans; these cloisters cannot fail to charm the visitors. They are simple 14th century arches, and Vaccaro redesigned the garden in 1742. Seats punctuate 64 octagonal pillars at intervals on which Donato and Guiseppe Massa decorated all the surfaces with colourful majolica painted tiles. These are exquisitely done with scenes of fishing and rural life, evoking Campania in the early 18th century. No finer majolica exists.

Going back inside the main church, you find that the Nuns Choir behind the main altar contains remains from the bombing of the church; it was frescoed by Giotto and his assistants. Unfortunately, only fragments of the original frescoes remain - just enough to tantalize you and make you wring your hands that you did not see it in the days of Giotto. Majolica scenes in the Nuns Choir have been protected from the weather and have even more brilliant colours than those outside.

Next to the cloister is the Museo dell'Opera, which houses decorative ornaments and sculptures from S Chiara. In the section of the museum devoted to archaeology, you can see the ruins of a Roman bathhouse that extended outside the museum. There is so much to see at S Chiara that you will want to pay a second visit.

Proceeding down the Via Biagio, after the Piazza San Domenico, you come on the left to a fascinating large Roman statue, which was sculpted in honour of the Egyptian god of the Nile. It is said to represent the River Nile lying down and reclining against the sphinx, his feet supported by a crocodile's head, while little children playing around him are proofs of his fecundity. According to Gunn, this recumbent male figure recovered from the ancient theatre is evidence that a colony of Alexandrians lived in Naples during the time of Nero. It was unearthed in the 15th century, but the bearded head was not found until 200 years later. It is a good memorial to the Naples traditional links with Egypt and the Middle East, and fits well into the antique centre.

A short distance further down the Via Biagio, to the right, brings you to the stately palace of Monte di Pietà, built by Cavagni in 1600, and now the headquarters of the Bank of Naples. Unfortunately, the magnificent chapel is only open to the public on Saturdays. Bernini designed the chapel, and on its facade is a statue by him. Inside there are colourful frescoes by Corenzio, and it is rich with golden stucco. On the three altars of the single nave there are good pictures – the *Resurrection* by Imparato; the *Deposition* by Santafede, and the *Assumption* by Borghese. They are all in excellent condition. In the sacristy there is a monument by Santafede, and all the floors are splendid. The *Pietà* should not be missed if you can be there when it is open, as it contains wonderful examples of Neapolitan painting around 1600.

Continue down Via S Biagio, and facing you to the east and at the corner of the Via Duomo and Via S Biagio, is S Giorgio Maggiori. This is one of the oldest churches in Naples and was originally an early Christian basilica. It was completely rebuilt in the mid-1600s by Cosimo Fanzago. However, it is most interesting that there is a surviving part of the original church at the entrance, in a semi-circular apse with Corinthian columns. This apse makes one realize how important the Christians were in the early days. The third chapel has frescoes by Francesco Solimena. On leaving S Giorgio Maggiore, look up the Via S Biagio and you get a fine view to S Martino.

Continuing east down the Via S Biagio you come to the Misericordia (....). In the square in front is a *guglia* statue by Fanzago. This is worth looking at, as is the portico built on to the facade of Pio Monte della Misericordia to shelter the needy. A short distance to the east, at the end of the Via Tribunali, is the Castel Capuano and Porta Capuana. These were a palace and fortress built by the Normans in 1165 to defend the city. Castel Capuano remained a royal residence for the Angevins and for the Aragonese rulers even after Castel Nuovo (...) was constructed. In 1540, Don Pedro de

Toledo turned the castle into law courts, and this is its function in the same place today. On the first floor to which you will be admitted is a huge fresco in the Court of Appeal that leads to the splendid Renaissance chapel della Sommaria, decorated by a Spanish painter, Pietro Rovisle. A short distance away from the Courts stands the gateway of Porta Capuana. Although it is much older its current appearance is the result of late 15th century reconstruction by Guiliano da Maiano. Two towers, called Honour and Virtue, enclose the marble arch, repeating the pattern of the Arco di Trionfo in Castel Nuovo. The marble arch glistens in the sunshine, and it is worthwhile staying a few minutes to appreciate its detail.

On the north side of the square is the elegant Renaissance church of S Caterina a Formiello. Begun in 1519, but not finished until 1593, its design is attributed to a Florentine Balsimelli and it is one of the most Tuscan churches in Naples. The dome dominates the surrounding area, and the church was called Formiello because it was built next to Formali, the ancient city aqueduct. The interior, with its fine 17th century baroque decoration, is delightful and there are interesting tombs of the Spinelli family in the apse area. In one of the chapels are some of the macabre relics of the martyrs of Otranto, where in 1480 the Turks massacred 800 Christians because they refused to renounce their faith. Blunt thinks the most interesting part of the church is the black and white facade, which is typical Renaissance and has a good sculpture over the ornate doorway. Fragments of an early cloister can be seen in dwelling houses to the north of the church; it must have been very fine - a double cloister in two parts, separated by a loggia open on both sides. Look at the carved choir stalls made before 1566, and the coloured tiles in the floor of the nave before you leave. One important point about the architecture of this church is that it emphasizes how, in Naples in the middle of the 16th century, they were ignoring the revolution in architecture which was taking place in Rome, and as Blunt points out, as far as Neapolitan architects were concerned then Bramante and Michelangelo might never have lived, and it was only considerably later that Naples created its own variant of baroque.

From S Caterina a Formiello, turn south to the Porta Nolana, the Aragonese gateway off Corso Garibaldi, and look at the colourful fish market in the narrow Via Carmigano. Here wooden pails are filled with black and blue silver mussels (*cozze*) and red shellfish (*frutti di mare*), which contrast with the glowing yellows of the lemons and roses. Continue south to the Church of the S Annunziata, built by King Robert in 1304 and rebuilt by Vanvitelli in white marble after a fire between 1760 and 1782.

Note the large gravestone of Queen Joanna II (1435), who succeeded her brother Ladislao, and with whom the French house of Angevin came to an end. From the 1300s, the Annunziata was a charitable institute that took care of abandoned children. To the left of the church an impressive archway leads to the former foundling hospital, now used as a general hospital. Here you can see the turntable on which the unwanted babies were placed until 1875; at the other side a nun, who stamped them with a number, received them.

The church of S Annunziata is light, and in the classical style eschewing the ornamental 18th-century Neapolitan baroque. However, the sacristy was undamaged by the fire and has well-preserved frescoes by Corenzo and 16th-century inlaid cupboards. From S Annunziata, go south across busy streets and you come to the Piazza del Mercato where there is a large market on Mondays and Fridays. Here stands the fine church of S Maria del Carmine. Formerly, the sea used to lap this piazza. The Piazza del Mercato, for anyone with a sense of history, brings back vividly tragedies from the story of Naples. The piazza used to have always in readiness an execution block for the aristocracy, a gallows for common people, and a gibbet for the dregs of society. Here Charles I of Anjou beheaded Conradin Hohenstaufen, the grandson and rightful heir to Frederick Barbarossa, in 1268 when he was only 16 years old.

With a German army, Conradin in 1267 entered Italy to try and recover his father's kingdom of the Two Sicilies from Charles of Anjou. Repulsed by the Pope near Rome, he met the army of Charles, and after a defeat was captured in August 1268. Taken to Naples, he was kept in the Castel dell'Ovo and after a pretence trial was taken to the Piazza del Mercato and beheaded, together with his young and lifelong friend Frederick of Baden. The only time the people of Naples saw their legitimate King was as he was conveyed along the seafront from S Lucia to his death in the Piazza del Mercato. He was playing chess with Frederick of Baden when he was told he was to be beheaded. He could hardly believe the news. It was the end of the Normans in southern Italy.

In 1647 Masaniello, a fisherman from Amalfi, was beheaded in the Piazza del Mercato. He had led a revolt against the Spanish Viceroy because of high taxation, and armed 200 rebels with sticks, disguised them as Turks, and paraded them in front of the Royal Palace. The Viceroy parleyed with Masaniello and lifted a detested tax on fruit, which he had imposed a few months before. Masaniello then proclaimed the Parthenopean Republic. This did not please the Spaniards, who arrested him and put up the price of bread, which so enraged the Masaniello supporters that they stitched his head back on to his body and paraded it through the streets of Naples.

The Piazza del Mercato was also the scene of the execution on the orders of Ferdinand I of a good number of Neapolitan nobility who had openly collaborated with the French army during the short lived Championnet occupation of the Kingdom in 1799. Their punishments were brutal.

Once inside the church of S Maria del Carmine, you become very conscious of Conradin. On the left in the nave he is commemorated by a life size statue of a strikingly beautiful youth, modelled by Thorwaldsen for Maximilian II of Bavaria, Conradin's kinsman, in 1847. Two reliefs on the pedestal show Conradin parting from his mother and from his friend Frederick of Baden, who was three years older.

The body of the executed prince lies behind the high altar under a stone marked R.C.C. (Regis Corradini Corpus). It is alleged that the original church on this site was founded by Margaret of Bavaria, daughter-in-law of Frederick II, with the ransom money she had brought to Naples in anticipation of saving the life of her son. Masaniello is said to be buried in the church, but there is no evidence of where his body lies.

The church is now beautiful and typical baroque, and although founded in the 13th century, was not completed until 1631. There is an enormous crucifix, seldom exposed, which is said to have bowed its head to avoid a cannonball, which passed through the nave in 1439. Behind the altar, close to Conradin's body, is shown a 14th century painting, *Madonna Bruna* of the Madonna and Child. After mass, the faithful flock behind the altar to venerate this painting, usually ignoring Conradin. There are frescoes and paintings by Solimena in the wings of the transept. The 75 metre striking majolica topped bell tower by Fra Nuvolo dominates the square and is the tallest in Naples.

The choir and high altar are very ornate, with magnificent 17th-century inlaid marble; there is an especially fine carved and gilded ceiling, and the side chapels are equally impressive. The cloister (1603) is pre-baroque. The congregation here seems to be still mostly the less prosperous, and fishermen. Franciscan monks run the parish and are jolly and friendly, as are their flock.

Cross the Mercato to the north-west and you will find S'Eligio Maggiore, which closes off the square to the west. It is usually open in the mornings. It is a unique small Gothic church, being the first to be founded in Naples by the Angevins. The three nave Gothic interior is austere, but the church is a gem. The left hand nave leads to a vaulted area, decorated with 14th century frescoes of the Giotto school, and possibly the master painted here himself. This historic church was badly damaged in the same needless American air raid, which so nearly destroyed the sumptuous S Chiara. In the process of restoration after the war, all the later baroque decoration was removed, so nowadays you see it in the state the founders intended.

Sant' Eligio Maggiore has an especially beautiful pure French Gothic portal and a fascinating 15th century bell tower forming an arch over the street to the right (Arco dell'Orologio). This spot is an evocative reminder of the days of the Angevins, and we should be grateful that the church is restored so well after being nearly destroyed by the Americans.

Close by is the church of S. Giovanni a Mare, which is known to have existed since the 12th century, but I have found it firmly closed for many years. It contains Greek and Roman columns, as well as a crucifix said to be that of S Brigida. Between the two churches is a damaged Greek stone head on a wall, which the locals revere, calling it '*Donna Marianna*', considering her almost a goddess of Naples.

An enjoyable morning can be passed in the southern extremities of the ancient city, which would have been nearer to the sea in olden days, and is less densely packed than the area around the Via Tribunali.

Take a bus or taxi to the Palazzo Gravina in Via Monte Oliveto. It is a fine 16th century building in black stone, with a typical Renaissance facade; this was damaged by fire but has been well restored. From the courtyard you get a good impression of a great Neapolitan nobleman's house in the 16th century. It is now the seat of the Faculty of Architecture of the University. Note the heads above the first floor windows - so often a feature of Neapolitan architecture, and at the windows of the *Piano Nobile*.

To the north on the right, also in Via Monte Oliveto, is the Monastery and church of Monte Oliveto, known also as Sant' Anna dei Lombardi. (Lombard monks came here in 1805 after their church had been destroyed in the earthquake). There are four attractive cloisters. Immediately on entry, one comes to the tomb of Domenico Fontana, who completed the dome of St. Peter's in Rome for Pope Sixtus V before spending his final days in Naples, where we see much of his work. The sculpture on the tomb gives a good indication of his appearance. The church was built in 1411, and is one of the best worth visiting in Naples. Perhaps the most popular sculpture in Naples is down a corridor to the right before the high altar. This is the *Pietà* (1492) of Guido Mazzoni of Modena, consisting of eight life size figures that are especially realistic, gathered around the body of the dead Christ, and considered to be portraits of the court of King Ferrante, with Alfonso 11 of Aragon and Pontano, who built the Renaissance chapel of his name. According to Augustus Hare, the Christ is 'unworthy and obviously by another hand.'

The Piccolomini Chapel, built in 1475, has two very important and intriguing works by the sculptor Antonio Rosellino – the *Adoration of the Shepherds* and the tomb of Mary of Aragon. They are unique Renaissance features.

The Curiale, or Mastroquidace chapel, has an altar piece made in Florence in 1489 by Benedetto da Maiano. Both these chapels show strong Florentine influence. Blunt thinks Piccolomini employed the better Tuscan architects. Certainly the Piccolomini frescoes are impressive, although damaged.

Blunt much admired a third chapel - the Capella Tolosa, that was completed in 1511. The altar piece by Pinturicchio has now been removed to Capodimonte, as have the inlaid choir stalls, with views of Naples and Rome to the sacristy. The Capella Tolosa is completely frescoed by Guilano de Maiano (who designed the arch at Porta Capuana). Its fine architectural detail and the colourful illusionistic frescoes are striking. Note the barrel vault ceiling, containing coloured rosettes carved in stone. A fine painting by
Giorgio Vasari is in the Capella del'Assunta, and there are frescoes by him in the sacristy. Several writers disparage these works by Vasari.

Suddenly, at the back right of the church, you come across the sacristy; formerly the refectory of the monastery. It is beautiful, with wooden panels done in 1506-1510 by Giovanni da Verona, which are most imaginative.

The church is not well looked after, and is only open on Saturdays and Sundays. The tiled floors are unprotected. The families to whom the chapels are dedicated have died out and there is no one to maintain them. Before leaving, look at the della Robbias high up on the ceiling of the Tolosa chapel. Although the frescoes in the church are damaged, you can still see how beautiful they were. The relief above the high altar of the *Nativity,* with fine palm trees and a delicate circle of saints, is particularly striking. The monastery was used as the first Neapolitan Parliament in 1848, and is now a police headquarters.

On coming out of Sant' Anna di Lombardi, turn toward the sea and take the second turning to the left after Palazzo Gravina. Here you are in a pleasant quarter, with four piazzas, and it is almost a pedestrian precinct with two or three elegant and relaxing cafés where foreigners are scarce but welcomed.

You come immediately on the right to the dignified church of S Maria la Nova, dating back to 1279 when it was given to Franciscan friars by Charles of Anjou. Owing to earthquakes, it was rebuilt in 1599, and has a splendid Renaissance facade with an entrance up a double flight of steps. The high altar in coloured marble is by Fanzago and Corenzo, and others painted the interesting ceiling in gilded wood. The interior of S Maria la Nova is one of the most remarkable in the city, and you should use a mirror to look at the 46 spectacular paintings on the ceiling which show how well developed painting was in Naples even before the arrival of Cavaraggio. The altar and the pulpit are masterpieces of the art of inlaid marble. The majolica cupola from the 18th century is attractive.

The two cloisters of S Maria la Nova are as noteworthy as the church itself, especially for their frescoes. Simone Papa decorated the first with bright frescoes, and there are also elegantly sculpted 15th-century tombs, which survived the fire. The second cloister to the east was originally kept as a cloister for the monks, and has nice arches on each side and Ionic capitals. The east cloister has now been turned over to the local government offices, and both are quiet and pleasant places to wander in.

Stroll eastwards and you come to the Palazzo Penna, built in 1406 by Antonio Penna, secretary to King Ladislao. The facade has a handsome portal and interesting original doors: the stones have the insignia of the owner repeated in the rustication (*penne* = feathers), which are covered with feathers and also Angevin lilies. It is the only palace to survive in its original condition from the 15th century, and for this reason should be looked at carefully.

Adjoining the Palazzo Penna is the fine Palazzo Casamassima (which also has an entrance from Via Banchi Nuovi). This keeps intact its 17th century layout, with an impressive open staircase and a double loggia in front of the entrance. It was enlarged in the 18th century. If you can get in, look for a vaulted ceiling with a fine fresco.

A little further on lies the Capella Pappacoda in the pleasant Piazza of S Giovanni Maggiore, built in 1415, with a spectacular late Gothic portal and a small bell tower with interesting different coloured stones. It was begun in 1415 by Artusio Pappacoda, seneschal to King Ladislao, and restored in 1772 when the frescoes were covered and a new altar built by Solimena. Fortunately, the outside of this exquisite chapel, so typical of late Gothic architecture, was not contaminated by the baroque mania; the portal of the facade is especially notable for its flamboyant Gothic style with rich decorations in frames of garlands and flowers.

Facing the Capella Pappacoda is Palazzo Giusso, now the School of Oriental Studies for the university. It was founded as the Chinese College in 1725 when the missionary Matteo Ripa brought back from China, 15 young Chinese to convert and educate as priests and missionaries. The Pope encouraged this project, and the institution was extended to other oriental nations. Alas, today this fine palace has suffered ravages from its use as part of the university.

Continue to the east and you will find yourself in the old centre of Naples - now given over to the university students. The church of S Giovanni Maggiore has an entrance from the Piazza S Giovanni Maggiore, where the Cappella Pappacoda is situated. The original church was 6th century, constructed from the ruins of Hadrian's temple and dedicated to Hercules and the Emperor's favourite, Antoninus. As a result, there are still two Roman columns on either side of the high altar. On the wall of the left transept is a marble tablet commemorating the reconsecration of the church in the time of Pope Sylvester II 999-1003. Note the terracotta crib of the 18th century in the first chapel on the right, which is a good example of this art.

Now we are in a pleasant district of narrow streets and little squares, which have a medieval feel. In the Piazza Banchi Nuovi in the Middle Ages stood the houses of the bankers of Naples, who were nearly all Florentines; most of their houses remain, but in sadly battered condition.

Further to the east is the university, which starts almost from the Via Tribunali in the north behind Sant' Angelo a Nilo and runs south down to the Corso Umberto. At the south end, where we are, is a very large shady well-kept garden, ideal for a picnic with views over the bay. The university was established in 1224 by the Emperor Frederick, but is mainly modern, being built around 1990. Part of the ancient Jesuit Convent Gesù Vecchio to the north of the university is incorporated in it. There is a fine library with good access for foreign students. Under Angevin rule, the university was housed in S Domenico Maggiore, where Thomas Aquinas taught; later it was moved to the Palazzo degli Studi, now the famous Archeological Museum. After that it was housed in the convents of S Gregorio Armeno and S Lorenzo Maggiore, but with the suppression of the Jesuits, was moved to the Jesuit Convent behind the current university, from where it has expanded enormously.

The university also owns the nearby large monastery of SS

Marcellino e Festo, which dates from the 8th century. Alas, this is in very bad condition, and it is useless to try and get inside the church. The cloister is enormous and lush, with plants and fountains, and open to the side facing the sea. In the evening the sun streaks across the gardens, casting long thin shadows from the palms under the deep stone arcade of the cloister and reflecting off the pools of water in the small fountain. It is enchanting, and one of the most evocative places in Naples. Perhaps someday the monastery will be repaired and used by the university, when it would rival Oxford or Cambridge colleges.

The university has used the Gesù Vecchio since 1777; it is late 16th century and was the first Jesuit College in Naples. One remaining part of the original college is the Court of Statues, from where you can ascend to the first floor and see the upstairs rooms occupied by the college library, with 850,000 volumes. At 38 Via Paladino, to the west of S Marcellino, is the 16th century college church, worth seeing because of works by Solimena and Fanzago.

An equally pleasant morning can be spent at the northern edge of the antique city. Take a bus or taxi to the crowded Via Foria. Then turn left on foot northwards to the Largo dei Vergini (so-called because in Greek times there was a burial ground for the bodies of the Eunostedi who practised chastity), and come to the Palazzo del Spagnuolo. It dates from 1738, and has splendid balconies with striking foliage decoration, but its pride is the wonderful outside double staircase by Sanfelice, which had a great influence on the later staircases of Naples. It is one of the most charming and distinctive 18th-century staircases in Naples, and the whole palace is magnificent.

After the 1914–1918 war, this palace was the seat of the Fascist party and there is an interesting tablet, now very dirty, recording this with the signature in stone of Mussolini. From 1943-1998 the palace was neglected, but now ambitious restoration is being undertaken and before long it is to become the museum of the Neapolitan circus clown Toto (born 1898).

You are now in the centre of the Sanità quarter - a very poor area with a nasty reputation for drugs. Nearby in the same square, is the Church of the Padri della Missioni, which behind a dull facade is most interesting architecturally - being by the classic architect Vanvitelli. Over the main altar is a picture by de Mura - S Vincenzo in Gloria. Next door is the church of S Maria dei Vergini (17th century), also interesting architecturally.

Walk up the Via della Sanità and you find San Felice's own

spectacular palace (Palazzo San Felice). Here you see another double round staircase, resembling and rivalling San Felice's Spagnuolo design. Note especially the two fine symmetrical doorways and the statues above the fourth floor windows.

Do not be put off by the poverty and untidiness of this crowded part of Naples and push on to the excellent large baroque church of S Maria della Sanità – known to locals as the church of S Vincenzo because this saint's statue is in the church. It was designed by Fanzago and begun in 1612. There is a magnificent scenic double flight of steps leading to the high altar, with as good inlaid baroque marble decoration as you will find anywhere, and a charming if slightly heavy marble pulpit by Andrea Lazzari, a pupil of Fanzago. There are sweet little angels (putti) at the base of the staircase on both sides. In the church are colourful pictures by Giordano, Vaccaro, Vaccherino and others, all in excellent condition.

From the attractive crypt access can be gained to the catacombs of S Gaudisio where there are 5th and 6th-century frescoes and mosaics and strange wall tombs. Blunt thinks Nuvolo's plan for this church is closely based on Bramante's for St Peter's in Rome. Nuvolo also designed a monastery behind S. Maria della Sanità. This was largely swept away when the bridge carrying the road to Capodimonte was built in the 19th century. An octagonal sacristy still exists as does part of an oval cloister. The view from the cloister was much admired by 18th century writers.

Continue east from S. Maria della Sanità and you find a quieter part of the old city. Continue up the Via Foria until you come to the Via Michele Tenure, which takes you up a slight hill to the fascinating church and convent of S. Maria degli Angeli alle Croci.

The name arises because the ascent to the church was originally marked by wooden crosses (*croci*). It was entirely rebuilt for the Franciscans in 1638 by Cosimo Fanzago. The facade is simply decorated with white and grey marble, which is a remarkable contrast to the lavishness of most Neapolitan baroque. Blunt thinks Fanzago originally designed a further storey with a loggia. The pulpit designed by Fanzago is typical, and Blunt believes he carved the eagle on it himself and also the statue of St Francis on the façade. Fanzago designed the large, exceptionally attractive holy water stoup and the niches near the entrances, now made slightly ridiculous by modern statues on them.

Well worth visiting is the church of Maria Regina Coeli (1590). It is up the Via Gaudisio, which runs north from the Via Sopienza, a parallel street to Via Tribunali to its north, right in the heart of the ancient centre.

The church has an elegant façade, and was designed by Di Palma the Second, who later changed his name to Mormanno - and who was also the architect of SS Severino e Sossio. According to his usual design, it has a single nave and side chapels. It was completely redecorated in the 17th and 18th centuries so that one cannot form any idea of its original appearance. Inside today it is stupendous and in an especially good state of preservation. The magnificent ceiling paintings consist of three canvases by Stanzione of the Virgin Mary (1634), and even more spectacular between the two big windows are ceiling paintings by Luca Giordano of the life of St. Augustus. Giordano also painted canvases and frescoes on the walls of the second and fourth chapels on the left. Behind the high altar is a Madonna by Carraciolo.

Entry to the church is not easy. I had to go to an early mass there on Sunday to find it open, and it was very cold, with a far too long sermon. Try at the convent behind, and the obliging nuns, if they are not too busy, may let you in. There are still 60 nuns at S. Maria Regina Coeli, and it was nice to go to mass in a church where the congregation consisted mainly of a thriving community of nuns. The original Franciscan community, who wore white and grey, were suppressed by Murat and replaced by another Franciscan French order in black, who still prosper. They run a large secondary school. Their spacious convent is on the right, up a slight hill to the left of the church - and is also worth visiting as they have the largest garden in the ancient center - an oasis of peace. One fine looking French nun, who was ordained at 16, lived to be 100, dying in 1921 having witnessed much of the later turbulent history of Naples. Opposite the church is a very comfortable café where they display in Italian an interesting history of both the church and the convent. Do not fail to look into the courtyard of the neighbouring Palazzo Bonifacio, where on the wall is an outstandingly good Gothic carving of a warrior that evokes the days of the Angevins.

To the north east of S. Maria degli Angeli is another pleasant oasis of peace – Orto Botanico, or Botanical Garden. It is one of the two most important botanical gardens in Italy. Originally a layout for the gardens was made under the Spanish Viceroys in 1615, but the project only came to real fruition thanks to Joseph Bonaparte in 1807 - although Ferdinand I had issued a desire for it to be created in 1796 - which was not properly followed up. Today it is an attractive green island in the centre of a crowded noisy city where you can relax in peace and enjoy a picnic, oblivious to the nearby teeming traffic.

There are thousands of trees, shrubs, and flowers, including a mass of tropical and semi-tropical ones, which flourish in the mild Neapolitan climate. The collection of desert plants from all over the world and the tree ferns are outstanding. Look at the collection of orange and lemon trees. There is a splendid terrace, and the whole area is around 30 acres. It has a gorgeous neo-classical greenhouse.

Next door is the ambitious Palazzo del Poveri, with a facade over 1000 feet long. It was begun on the orders of Charles III in 1751 to the design of Ferdinand Puga as a haven for old people and a place to educate orphans without families to support them, and to rehabilitate tramps. Never finished, it was badly damaged in the 1960 earthquake; today it is decaying. Efforts at restoration and repair cannot compete with the pace of its deterioration, and it is best admired from the outside. The roof is green like a jungle, with magnolias flowering at one corner. Still, it is a beautiful relic.

At the end of the Via Foria to the east lies Porta S Gennaro, rebuilt in the 15th century, and in a niche, is a sadly decomposed painting by Mattia Preti - the only surviving remains of the pictures he painted on all the gates of Naples.

If you have done all this you will need refreshment, and I advise a bus or taxi back to the Piazza del Plebiscito as enticing cafés and restaurants do not abound around Porta S Gennaro.

I have left some of the most fascinating churches in the old centre to the end. The long Via Duomo, which begins to the south in Piazza Bovio - a square with four fine palaces and a magnificent fountain - has on both sides shops selling bridal clothes, and outfits for spouses and parents of the happy couples. Nowhere else in Europe are so many of these specialist shops congregated. For a family it must be well worthwhile, from the price point of view, making a visit to Naples to pick up the necessary clothes inexpensively.

The cathedral in the Via Duomo is tremendously impressive. The medieval façade was largely restored in 1877, following extensive damage by an earthquake. The first glimpse of the interior is exhilarating. The nave is supported by sixteen pillars in which are incorporated 100 columns, all with different capitals encased in marble from the Roman temples of Apollo and Neptune, which originally occupied the site. On the walls and ceiling above the arches in gorgeous colours, are painted 46 saints by Luca Giordano and Salvatore Rosa.

The current cathedral was begun by Charles of Anjou in 1272 and is dedicated to the city's patron, St Gennaro. La Capella del Tesoro or S Gennaro is hailed as the jewel of the Duomo, and mighty impressive it is. It is the third chapel on the right as you come in; protected by a beautiful 17th century bronze grill designed by Fanzago and executed in 1688. The chapel was built because of a vow made by the citizens to the saint during the terrible plague of 1527. His skull of the saint is preserved within a silver bust, kept behind the high altar; the bust is studded with a variety of precious stones, including exceptional emeralds and diamonds given by Joseph Bonaparte during his brief reign as King of Naples. The ampoules of the saint's famous blood are also kept behind the high altar, and its famous liquefaction is celebrated on the Saturday preceding the first Sunday of May, on 19 September and on 16 December. The Neapolitans believe that if the blood does not liquefy it portends catastrophe, and quote the cholera outbreaks of 1826 and 1973[6] as examples of what happened when there was not satisfactory liquefaction.

The liquefaction celebrations are very crowded and perhaps best left to Neapolitans. To the strains of a brass band the ampoules are taken out and carried in procession to S Chiara. The travel writer Ian Thomson reports that when he was present in May 1988, liquefaction did not occur properly and then Naples lost an important home soccer fixture. Norman Lewis records a successful but slow liquefaction in 1944 when the presence of US military top brass in seats near the altar was ill received, and when liquefaction was going too slowly, there were shouts of 'Out with the heretics.' However, once the descendants of the family of St Gennaro approached the altar, all was well. Lewis also records that the flow of lava from Vesuvius, which was knocking down houses - the March 1944 eruption of Vesuvius was halted when the statue of St. Gennaro was unveiled in front of it.

Murray's 1855 handbook prints a letter from Lord Perth from Rome in 1698, the last Stuart Chancellor and a Roman Catholic, stating that he had held the 'glasses' in his hand and 'no blood from a vein could appear more lively'- and it was one of the happiest forenoons of his life; thanks to St Gennaro he felt no pains in his knees despite kneeling on marble for 3½ hours. The chapel of St Gennaro contains magnificent frescoes by Lanfranco and the Bolognese Domenichino and a hairpiece by Ribera. It is all high Neapolitan baroque, with the most striking inland marble. Particularly attractive are the little balconies, and a visit is a unique experience. Domenichino came especially from Rome to paint in this chapel; the Neapolitan artists were jealous of him and persecuted him systematically. There is little doubt they were responsible for his death.

For many, the high spot of the cathedral is the chapel of S Restituta.

---

[6] In 1973 24,000 Neapolitans died of cholera.

This is the oldest church in Naples, built shortly after Christianity was legalized, and it was the cathedral of Naples until 1592. Alongside it was built the basilica of S Stefania in the 10th century, so there were two cathedrals, one catering to the Latin rite, the other to the Greek.

In S Restituta we are in the period of Ravenna, the impression of which is heightened by a fine mosaic of Our Lady which however dates back only until the early 14th century. The baptistery of S Restituta is 5th century and contains a large piscina from which the faithful undergoing baptism, could look up at the ceiling frescoes (still there) of the divine mysteries and perhaps contemporary with the tub.

In 1969, extensive excavations were carried out under S Restituta. They revealed traces of Roman and Greek roads. A staircase leads down, and a small fee is required. Below, you find a Roman column and rooms and vaults from the early years of the Roman Empire and the remains of an early Christian structure. Part of a Greek road shows ruts from chariot wheels, and in a Roman pavement one can read the name, 'Aureila Ytician', probably the name of the man who built it.

After passing the Greek road, one comes to a large excavated area with extensive fragments of mosaic pavements, probably part of the ancient basilica of S Stefania. There is also a small apse with a mosaic floor, again part of the S Stefania basilica. A visit is not recommended for anyone who suffers from claustrophobia.

The most luxurious public lavatories in Naples are at the Duomo, and adjoining the Bishop's palace; behind glass, are the pillars and mosaic floor of a large Roman temple.

Leaving the Duomo to the north leads one into the attractive Spanish-looking square, Largo Donna Regina. Here there are two churches, both named S Maria Donna Regina. The later church contains frescoes by Solimena but is rather messy baroque. Behind it is the earlier Angevin church, finished in 1307, containing the tomb of the founder Queen Maria of Hungary, wife of Charles II of Anjou. The church has been restored to its original Gothic form and the queen's tomb is particularly interesting, being splendid Gothic, with angels holding back curtains to show the body of the dead queen. It is a fine memorial of French rule in Naples. The choir, built like the dress circle of a theatre, is attractive and has splendid frescoes of the last judgment and passion by the Roman painter Cavallino, which are sometimes compared with Giotto's frescoes at Rome and Assisi.

The church of S Filippo Neri, opposite the Duomo, should not be missed. It is part of a convent for Oratorians, and is also known as the church of the Gerolamini after the church used by St Filippo Neri in Rome. G.A. Dosio began it in 1592 while St Filippo Neri was still alive and at the height of his influence from designs. The Neapolitan Oratorians have many connections with the British Oratorians at Birmingham and Brompton who followed Newman.

One hundred years ago this convent held fifty Oratorians. Today, there are only three. The former aristocratic and scholarly order has fallen on sad times in Naples, whereas in England the cult of Newman is having a limited revival. All the same, the convent is still full of vibrant activity as ecclesiastical and secular students flock to the magnificent library and occupy the living quarters.

The Oratorian I spoke to told me that postulants now studied at the Rome oratory, whose building was mostly confiscated by the State after Rome was occupied by the Piedmontese in 1670; Roman Oratorians, unlike the Neapolitan Oratorians, occupy only a tiny part of their former magnificent building. However, when I was in Rome some years ago, there was only one aspirant and he was British. A scandal arose in the 1950s when the Oratorians in Naples sold off chalices, candelabra, lamps, etc. to delighted local dealers, who got them very cheaply.

The church is magnificent, with twelve columns brought at great expense from the island of Giglio. It is loaded with frescoes and pictures by Giordano and other Neapolitan masters. The most noteworthy is the fresco over the entrance of the *Expulsion of the Moneychangers* from the Temple by Luca Giordano. There is a picture gallery in the convent well worth seeing, with good pictures by Giordano, Caracciolo and Vaccaro.

There is no lighting, so it is essential to visit on a fine day. The library is also of great interest, and there are two fine baroque cloisters. Amongst the manuscripts in the library is a celebrated Lucius Seneca (the Roman writer of the 14th century), with beautiful miniatures by Zingaro. It is not difficult to obtain permission to see the library, which is in a magnificent room.

Having done the Duomo, S Maria Donna Regina, and S Filippo Neri you will need refreshment, and the Caffé del Duomo a few doors to the south of the cathedral front is very polite and makes excellent coffee.

To the west of Via Duomo is the old City Centre, replete with the fascinating churches. In the Via San Biagio dei Librai you will find jewellers shops and old palaces. The palaces are mostly deserted by the nobility and are in multiple occupations. Fine staircases and fountains can be seen in their courtyards, and the odd aristocratic families still occupy part of the family palaces, sharing the residences with numerous other families - many poor - as described by Anna Maria Ortese in her well known book, *Il mare non togna Napoli,* (unfortunately one of her novels not translated into English).

A short distance up Via Biagio, (passing disfigured palaces), brings one to the Piazza S Domenico, with one very good café and one not so good, and an interesting baroque obelisk – the *guglia* of Pichiatti and Vaccaro, built by the Domenican order in fulfilment of vows made for the ending of the plague in 1656 with a statue of St Domenic on the top. It is much admired by Sacheverell Sitwell, but despised by Augustus Hare as 'foolish', although 'picturesque.'

The old main entrance to the large church of S Domenico is through the Domenican monastery behind it, but today you must use a double flight of steep steps leading down to the piazza. Charles II of Anjou founded it in 1289, and the earlier monastery is world famous because St Thomas Aquinas studied here as a youth and returned as a Professor of Theology in 1272, making it the premier theological college in Europe. His small cell has been converted into a chapel. It is moving for someone like myself, brought up on heavy doses of *Summa Theologica* at a Roman Catholic public school, to come so close to him. How much of the convent monastery is 13th century is hard to discover. You have to ask the monks for permission to visit, and the hard-working sacristan is not all that gracious. The church is pure Gothic, but spoiled by the restoration of 1850 with ugly stucco and gilding.

Originally S Domenico housed the famous *The Flagellation* by Caravaggio, which is now at Capodimonte, but a fine copy by Andrea Vaccaro remains. In the seventh chapel on the right is a very early crucifixion, that is said to have once spoken to Aquinas, 'You have written well of me. What reward would you like?' Aquinas is alleged to have replied 'Nothing! I only want you.'

There is much more of interest in the noble S Domenico. Amongst many good pictures there is a picture of the *Virgin and Child* in the chapel of St Stephen attributed to Giotto; two pictures of *S John Baptist* by Matteo Preti, and fine pictures by Giordano. Alas, frescoes by Corenzio in one chapel have almost disappeared, although Corenzio's picture of *S Thomas Aquinas with Pope Urban IV* remains.

The large sacristy is very impressive, with the ceiling painted by Solimena, but its chief claim to fame lies in its 45 historical tombs among which are 10 of the Aragon princes and princesses, all in large wooden chests covered with crimson velvet. The body of Alfonso has been removed to Spain. In Victorian times, the mummified corpse of Antonello Petrucci, still dressed in Spanish costume, used to be shown to curious visitors. He was Ferdinand I's secretary, who joined the 'Conspiracy of the Barons.' But you would have to find the sacristan in a very good mood before he would show it to you. The coffins are all on a gallery high in the air on a balustrade, which visitors are not allowed to mount.

Originally, the church was Gothic and this is still apparent, although the earthquake of 1456 and a fire in 1506 obliterated some of the 1298-1524 origins, as did the baroque alterations in the 17th and 18th centuries. Americans will be fascinated to find the tomb of the first Catholic Bishop of New York, originally Neapolitan, who died in Naples just after he was consecrated.

Be sure to look at the very remarkable Gothic frescoes from the time of Giotto's visit to Naples (1320s) in the second chapel on the right, looking towards the high altar (Cappella Brancaccio). They show the life of St Andrew, Mary Magdalene, and St John the Evangelist, and are by Pietro Cavallini.

Anthony Blunt claims to have visited 200 churches for his book, and saw 50 others from the outside. Out of the 350 churches in Naples, alas, it is difficult to get entry to some of the smaller ones except on Sundays, and like the old palaces, you really need a bit of Italian to seek out the curators and sacristans.

If you have only a short time in Naples, you must visit the Angevin Gothic churches of Donna Regina and S Giovanni e Carbonara, the early baroque of the Misericordia, the Oratory church of the Girolamini, the cathedral, Gesù Nuovo with its brilliant baroque decoration and the Gothic S Chiara with its flamboyant majolica cloister. All these churches are huddled close together near the Cathedral.

3
Capodimonte Museum and Palace

The Royal Palace of Capodimonte was the brainchild of Charles III, the first Bourbon king. He cleared several hundred acres at the top of the hill nearest to Naples, and began designs for a palace and a hunting forest; there were already delightful woods there, and another attraction was the stupendous view over the Bay of Naples. Charles was the son of Philip V of Spain and Elizabeth Farnese, last descendant of the powerful and rich Roman family who had an unparalleled collection of pictures, statues, and antiques at the Palazzo Farnese in Rome and also at the Farnese palaces in Palma and Piacenza.

Charles and Elizabeth, to the disgust of the Romans, originally brought the vast Farnese collection to the Palazzo Reale in the centre of Naples. Here it lay in a disgraceful state. The French President, Francis de Brise, wrote in 1740 that the collection lay around in complete disorder, with some of the most famous paintings still in their crates.

However, King Charles had decided that he would house the collection in his new palace at Capodimonte. Giovanni Medrano was chosen as architect, and he was assisted for a short time by the more expert Roman architect Antonio Canevari. They decided with the King, to build an enormous palace 170 metres long and 87 wide. On the *piano nobile* there were to be placed a monotonous series of rooms destined for official receptions, royal apartments and for the Farnese collection.

The foundation stone was solemnly laid in 1738, and it was decided that those rooms facing south and towards the sea were less prone to dampness and had the best light, so they were reserved for the Farnese paintings, while the back rooms facing the woods were destined for books and other antique objects. Ferdinando Sanfelice had already started work, laying out the park with tree-lined avenues and many marble statues. He did not get very far, and it was left to Frederico Fuga to finish the park project in 1766. The palace was not completely finished until 1835.

Work on the palace proceeded slowly, mainly because many other heavy expenses were being incurred at the Caserta and Portici Royal Palaces to which Charles gave preference. Still after twenty years in 1758, twelve of the twenty four rooms making up the *piano* nobile were ready, and the collection of pictures and antiques were mounted in them - but this arrangement was only completed after Charles III had gone back to Madrid to resume the throne of Spain.

In 1758, Winckelman visited the palace and was immensely impressed by the Farnese pictures. Fragonard, Angelica Kaufmann and Canova also came to study them, while in 1787 Goethe praised the highly valuable works. Alas, no catalogue or list of the original exhibition has survived. In 1759, Ferdinand I had come to the throne at a young age, and between 1761 and 1765 royal apartments were joined to the rooms housing the Farnese collection. Pictures were also purchased for the King, and in 1799 when the French plundered the museum, 1783 items were listed in the catalogue.

When Ferdinand fled from Naples to Palermo in 1799, he took with him only 14 pictures, but the whole Farnese library. Then the French General Championnet carried off a large number of paintings from Capodimonte. Some of the pictures were brought back from Rome after the Bourbon restoration, and Ferdinand I, on his return from Sicily, created a splendid picture gallery at the Palazzo Altavilla near the Via Chiaia, together with many fascinating, recently excavated classical remains from Pompeii and Herculaneum. He planned to create the finest collection in Europe, but was thwarted when the arrival of French troops caused this Bourbon King to flee again to Sicily. This time he took 66 paintings and much furniture from Capodimonte. However Murat, who became King in 1808, added to the Altavilla collection, mainly with paintings acquired from the suppression of monasteries and churches in the kingdom. Murat wanted to create a museum in Naples along the lines of the Louvre in Paris, or the British Museum in London. When Ferdinand returned in 1815, he recreated a picture gallery in the Museo Archeologico, leaving in Palermo only the paintings he had taken with him as a gesture for the hospitality he had received there. By the time the Bourbons were toppled in 1860, and the kingdom passed to the House of Savoy, there were 900 paintings on display in the picture gallery in the Museo Archeologico.

Meanwhile, Capodimonte had become a favourite court residence. The Murats liked it, and in the palace on the first floor today you can see the royal apartments with some splendid First Empire furniture and china, and pictures of the Bourbon and Murat families enjoying palatial splendour. Ferdinand II redecorated the principal State Rooms, and today they are still striking. See if you can find the door to the secret staircase, up which the royalty used to disappear when they were bored.

The Savoys moved the Royal Armoury to Capodimonte. As would be expected, the Bourbons had a wonderful collection of sporting guns, including an early double-barrelled one, which is still on show. They did not really need double-barrelled guns because the kings always had a loader in the days of muzzle guns; they handed them a primed and loaded gun as soon as they had fired one shot.

In 1866, the Savoys gave up the royal palace at Portico, and the famous porcelain boudoir was moved to a room in the *piano nobile* at Capodimonte; here it can still be seen with all its rococo fantasy. The boudoir had been made for Queen Maria Amalia wife of Charles III, a century earlier, and is the last word in refined Chinoiserie. A fine Roman floor, discovered in 1788 during excavation at a villa in Capri, was also moved to Capodimonte where it can be seen in the 'Cradle Room'.

After 1860, the Savoy family used Capodimonte very little, but their cousin, the Duke of Aosta, established himself here in the 1920s and his family remained there until 1948.

Under the House of Savoy, many of the art treasures and famous paintings of Naples were removed to decorate prestigious ministries in Rome, embassies abroad and public buildings elsewhere. One hundred and thirty-six Farnese paintings were sent back to Parma and Piacenza to replace those taken away by Charles III, and there was only part compensation by State purchases of pictures and transfer of pictures from churches and monasteries in the Kingdom of Naples.

Not until May 1949 was it decided that Capodimonte should house the Neapolitan art treasures, and the pictures were transferred there from the Archeological Museum. Alterations were begun in 1952 and completed in five years, and with a great flourish the National Gallery and Museum of Capodimonte was opened to the public in 1957.

Now, the able and distinguished Director Nicola Spinosa is arranging all the pictures and treasures in strict chronological order, subdivided into schools and incorporating pictures like the *Crucifixion* by Masaglio, which have been bought.

More and more visitors come to Capodimonte Monte each year - mostly Italians, and many school children. But unlike Florence or Venice, where there are long queues for the Uffizi, Pitti, and Academia, at Capodimonte there is quiet, and you will usually find that you have the room to yourself. The Farnese collection is wonderfully augmented by the 19th and 20th century pictures and by pictures from churches and monasteries in the region.

It is a joy to visit one of the most important art collections in Europe without crowds or hassle. Take a bus or taxi uphill to Capodimonte (Buses are R4 and Z4), passing S Genaro church and the entrance to the vast catacombs. Alternatively, if you are energetic enough, walk up from the Sanità quarter. There is quite a walk from the entrance through the grounds to the palace. On the first floor in the Royal Apartment is the famous China

Room, but the picture masterpieces are on the second floor. Do not worry, there are lifts.

I am not qualified to comment on the artistic merits of the pictures, but here in roughly chronological order are some details about those which I have found the most interesting. I recommend visitors to buy the English guidebook, *The National Museum of Capodimonte,* edited by Nicola Spinosa, before you go around the galleries.

There is little from the 13th century, only works on panels showing the local Byzantine tradition; the 14th century produces a notable work by Simone Martini of *S Ludovico di Tolosa,* painted for the Angevin Royal family on the occasion of the canonization of Ludoviso (or Louis), elder brother of Robert of Anjou. This formerly hung in S Lorenzo; there are also some small Tuscan works from the Borgia collection in Velletri, which were bought in 1817 by Ferdinand I.

Good examples from the 15th century are the *Crucifixion* by Masaccio, which was bought in 1901; the *Annunication* by Fillipo Lippi; the *Slaughter of the Innocents* by Pinturicchio; *S Euphemia,* and the portrait of a Gonzaga by Mantegna and the *Transfiguration* by Bellini.

There are interesting altarpieces by Fra Bartolomeo and Sodoma. However, the jewels of the 16th century are the Raphaels and Titians, and a famous *Madonna with a Cat* by Giulio Romano. Raphael painted a *Cardinal Farnese* in 1509-11, and *Pope Leo X with two Cardinals*; while two other pictures from the original Farnese collection are attributed to him. However it is worth coming to Naples just to see the Titians. Titian, a Venetian, came to Rome in 1543 and was commissioned to paint two portraits of the pope Paul III. The Titian of the *Pope with his Nephews* is fascinating; it shows his two nephews Alessandro and Ottavio Farnese, both cardinals, in attitudes that create a wonderful atmosphere of intrigue. This is considered one of Titian's masterpieces, and clearly draws some of its inspiration from Raphael's portrait of *Leo X with two Cardinals*, which is hung nearby.

Titian's *Annunciation* was formerly in S Domenico. At one time it was considered to be a copy by Luca Giordano, painted for the viceroy. It is now accepted that Giordano's copy has gone to Madrid, while the painting at Capodimonte is Titian's original. Two other outstanding Titians are one of *Danae*, the beloved of Zeus, which was painted for Alessandro Farnese's private room, and his *Madelena.* Nearby are two El Grecos; his picture of a young boy blowing on a burning coal is unforgettable; he painted the two pictures for the Farneses on a rare visit to Rome. There is a good painting by Pordenone, and several works by Schiavone, but the two Bruegels are extraordinary. One (*Misanthrope*) shows a hermit shunning the world while a vagabond steals his purse; the other (*The Parable of the Blind*) shows six blind people following one another after the leader has collapsed. They must be amongst the best Bruegels in the world.

In the 16th century part, I particularly liked the room devoted to the paintings of Beuckelaer, a Dutchman, (1576). They show in colours as vivid today, as when they were painted, the costumes of the people, the gestures and the fish, fruit and meat markets of Amsterdam. The cheerful faces are full of life and they leave you feeling you have spent a morning shopping in late 16th century Amsterdam. I do not know any other paintings that so evoke the contemporary everyday life of the period; seeing them is like watching a colour film of life in Amsterdam in those far off times. Not surprisingly, in view of the Farnese connection with Parma, there are several paintings by Parmigianino (1503–1540), the best of which are *Antea* (a famous Roman lady of the court), in elegant clothes with a marten stole, and a portrait of *Galleazo Sanvitale* which is considered to be his masterpiece.

The mysterious Strozzi panel shows Naples from the sea, with the Aragonese fleet returning. Then the hills around and above the city had virtually no buildings upon them. It was purchased from the Palazzo Strozzi in Florence in 1910.

Before leaving the 16th century, pay attention to the many pictures by Annibale and Ludovico Carracci and their two brothers. They painted in Bologna, not Naples. Annibale is the best of the brothers, and he was much inspired by Michelangelo. All the Carracci pictures come from the original Farnese collection.

From the picture galleries, where it must be admitted a number of inferior pictures mingle with the masterpieces, the windows to the south overlooking the terrace give you a wonderful view of the sea and the island of Capri.

In the 16th 17th and 18th century section, there are numerous canvasses by Fra Bartolomeo and Schedoni, much praised in English 19th century guidebooks. In perhaps Schedoni's best known picture *Charity* (1611), the realism and the expressions of the girl and the beggars are remarkable. An Emilian, he never came to Naples but the Farnese family in Rome bought his pictures. Amongst paintings purchased around this time by the Bourbons was the beautiful *Passagio* (Landscape with the Nymph Egeria) (1669) by Claude Lorraine. The landscape is the lake of Nenni on the Colonna property near Rome and this fine picture was part of a series of paintings commissioned by Prince Colonna. As the Colonnas had their own enormous picture gallery in their Rome palace, it is a mystery why this painting was ever sold to the Bourbons.

The most important Neapolitan-painted picture is *The Flagellation* by Caravaggio, one of several masterpieces painted by this artist when he was in Naples. Caravaggio (1571-1610) came to Naples in 1606, having been banished from Rome after a fight in which he was wounded and Ranuccio Tomassoni killed. He delighted in showing figures in extremes of light and shade and this picture is a splendid example of this. *The Flagellation* was originally in the church of St Domenico. For security reasons from 1977 until recently, *The Flagellation* has not been on public show. I was most indebted to the director of the museum, Nicola Spinosa, who kindly allowed my daughter and me to see the picture in the workroom where it was being restored, and who also provided a guide to show us the galleries. Spinosa considers the picture a 'landmark' in Naples painting history, and thinks that this Caravaggio picture was responsible for the rebirth of Naples painting in the 17th century. The Neapolitan painters of the following period— Stanzione, Falcone, Guarino, Gentileschi and Cavellino - certainly owe much to Caravaggio.

There are numerous paintings by these artists at Capodimonte - nearly all of considerable interest. Cavallino's *St Cecilia* (1645) stands out. It has only been returned to Naples recently, having been sold by the Fascists to the Germans in 1941 and bought back in Florence in 1948. It originally hung in the church of St. Antonio delle Monache at Port Alba.

Giuseppe Ribera occupies a special place at Capodimonte with some extraordinary paintings, which include *Sileno Ebbro* (drunken Silenus), with an enormous paunch, and two famous pictures coming from the church of Trinità dei Monti, in Rome, *St Jerome and the Angel*, and *Terrestrial Trinity*, which show how he was influenced by Caravaggio. Ribera himself died in Naples. Alas, several more works painted by Ribera for the Farnese family and mentioned in old catalogues have disappeared without a trace. Near the Riberas are Guido Reni's *Atalante and Hippomenes* (1620-) a dream of movement, and Giovanni Lanfranco's *Assumption of Mary Magdalene* (1605), which was a turning point in landscape painting in the 17th century.

Luca Giordano and Mattia Preti are well represented at Capodimonte and show how new ideas were determining the trend of Neapolitan Baroque painting during their lifetime. Giordano's *Marriage of Cana* (1660) is an intriguing scene of a wedding feast, and although he had the reputation of always being in a hurry there is no sign of it in this painting. Two other pictures by Giordano, *Lucretia and Tarquinio* (1663), *The Madonna and the Rosary* (1686) are noteworthy.

Mattia Preti's sketches for the votive frescoes for the 17[th]century plague (1656 - 1659) are fascinating historically because Preti was commissioned to paint frescoes on all the ancient gates of Naples to invoke divine protection against the plague. Only one incomplete fresco survives on the actual gate, Porta Nolana. (...) Look also at Preti's *San Sebastian* (1657), that comes from the little known church of S Maria dei Sette Dolori. Also most interesting are a considerable number of sketches for the decoration with frescoes of religious buildings made by Solimena and de Mura and some important paintings by de Mura.

Giovanni Pannini, including one piece recording the visit of Charles III to pope Benedict XIV after the victory of Velletri in 1744, has captured significant scenes from court life in the 18th century in paintings.

Ferdinand I as a small boy is skillfully captured by Raphael Mengs; the detailed richness of the Prince's dress vividly evokes the splendour of the Bourbon court. Angelica Kauffmann's picture of Ferdinand I as King with his wife Maria Carolina Hapsburg and six children, plus three dogs and a lovely garden (probably the English garden of Caserta), is another delightful window on the royal life of that period.

The series of late 18th century landscape paintings by native Neapolitan painters should not be missed. They include the dramatic *Eruption of Vesuvius* (1782) by Volaire; but the most interesting is Ferdinand II shooting coots on Lake Fusaro. This shows the delightful hunting pavilion built for him by Vanvitelli on the lake and about twenty boats encircling and closing in on the birds in the centre of the lake. The sky is filled with coots, who must have been fed on barley to be present in such numbers, and in each boat can be seen the figure of a man aiming his gun while an attendant stands by ready to hand him another loaded gun as soon as the first gun has been fired. Nothing gives a better idea of how the King and the royal family enjoyed passing their days in the open air in this delightful climate, untrammeled by cares of state.

Early in the 19th century, Naples developed its own innovative school of painting - the School of Posilippo. The Dutch Anton Pitloo (1791-1837) was an inspired teacher at the Academy and was also with Giacinto Gigante, the best painter. There was a breakaway movement occurring in the second half of the 19th century caused by dissatisfaction with the teaching at the Academy. This is known as the Retsina School. Capodimonte holds an unrivalled collection of paintings from both the Posilippo and the Retsina

School. There are oils, watercolours, and gouaches (colour washes) depicting landscapes, buildings, and everyday life in Naples. This was an era in which British tourists flocked to Naples and many such paintings were eagerly snapped up by British travellers and taken back to Britain. Today, when they come on the British market, rich Neapolitans eagerly buy them back, especially by phone at Christie's and Sotheby's auctions, and thus these paintings are returned to their place of origin.

Pictures by Alexandre Dunouy and Johann Dahl of Portico and Castellamare respectively, show the delightful countryside with its woods and orange groves and only a few buildings in view 175 years ago; now the landscape is unrecognizable. There are many Pitloos and Gigantes. I especially like *Paestum* by Pitloo, and *Amalfi* by Gigante; Gigante's *Duomo at the moment of the melting of the blood of San Gennaro* (1863) colourfully recalls one of the regular dramatic features of Naples life with the church crammed with devout faces. King Victor Emmanuel II commissioned this watercolour. Note the glare of candlelight on the silvers and the bronzes that decorate the chapel. Domenico Morelli (1823-1901) is well represented and his *Lady with Fan* is outstanding. Surprisingly on the second floor is a collection of paintings by Andy Warhol, who had been fascinated by the eruption of Vesuvius, and came for an exhibition held here in 1985.

There are not only pictures to be seen at Capodimonte. In the decorative art collection there is an exceptional number of works from diverse fields - ivories, amber, enamels, small bronzes, jewellery, weapons, pottery, glass, clocks, jewels and furniture. There are also 22,000 prints, nearly all from the original Farnese collection. The most famous are three cartoons (draft sketches). One is by Michelangelo with details of his frescoes for the Sistine Chapel at the Vatican; another is by Raphael for the vault of Stanza di Eliodoro at the Vatican, and the third by an anonymous follower of Michelangelo of *Venus with a Cupid* from a lost original by Michelangelo himself. Ask to see them; they are on the first floor with much space given to them. One day is not enough to see all the art treasures at Capodimonte. I advise one day for the pictures and another day for the rest.

The original Farnese collection, including sculptures and the outstanding 16th century Farnese Coffanato (casket) is the only one in existence made out of gilded silver and rock crystal.

The royal collection of weapons has 4,000 pieces and is one of the most important of its kind in Europe. Several rifles and shotguns of British manufacture are also included.

The pottery collection of both majolica and china is exceptionally rich. Take particular note of the porcelain from the Capodimonte factory founded by Charles I. The Cabinetto di Porcelanna (Porcelain Room) is unique. It was originally designed as a boudoir for Queen Maria Amalia, wife of Charles III, for the palace of Portico. It consists of porcelain slabs fixed with screws to a wooden wall and decorated with festoons, musical trophies and chinoiserie based on French designs by Watteau and Boucher. Birds stand on the panels and fly across the sky. It is breathtaking rococo and the most remarkable surviving monument to the luxury of the Bourbon court in the 18th century. Although designed by a Dresden artist, Neapolitan craftsmen at the Capodimonte factory fabricated it all. The only parallel is Austrian rococo in Vienna. Queen Anna Maria was a princess of Saxony and in the 18th century the art of porcelain was much the province of Meissen and Dresden. It is a tribute to Maria Amalia's good taste. Fascinating too are the little coloured Capodimonte statues; they resemble Dresden but the Neapolitan painters were lighter and more humorous. Look too at a large painted and enamelled porcelain mirror with putti on the apex, and a smaller one with china candlesticks. They are amongst the best artistic work of the Royal Palace of Capodimonte.

Charles III closed down the Royal factory when he moved to Madrid, taking the best trained workmen with him. However a few years later his son Ferdinand I opened another porcelain factory, known as the Royal Porcelain Factory of Naples, whose work in the second half of the 18th century is well shown here, including a lifelike bust of Queen Maria Carolina.

The staterooms on the first floor are much as they were in the days of Murat and the Bourbons with excellent pictures showing the monarchy and their family and their contemporary furniture. These rooms evoke the lives of the various monarchs who preceded the House of Savoy.

A walk through the avenues of the pleasant park is rewarding, although it takes a considerable time. There is a secret garden surrounded by walls with heating systems in them designed for exotic species such as pineapples. Another feature is the English garden. Formerly there were many statues and fountains as well as shooting lodges and the inevitable pheasantry. These are now nearly all in disrepair - although the imposing statue of the Giant or Hercules, which comes from the Farnese collection, remains as does one of the *Twelve Months*, a gift by Carthusian monks to the King in 1762.

4
The National Archaeological Museum of Naples

The National Archaeological Museum of Naples, originally called Museo Bourbonico, is the most important in the world for classical archaeology. It lies just north of Piazza Dante and Piazza Bellini in an old Spanish cavalry barracks, built in 1588 and converted into the University of Naples in the seventeenth century. The museum dates back to the eighteenth century when Naples was one of the most civilized cities in Europe, with many gentlemen scholars and fine practitioners of the arts like Sanfelice, Vaccaro, and Solimena.

Spanish Viceroys had carried out excavations of the classical sites in the 18th century, notably in the Phlegraean Fields, but it was not until the early 1700s that excavations became an industry. Charles III's accession to the throne of Naples in 1734 coincided with thrilling discoveries of classical statues at Herculaneum, which had begun under Prince d'Elboeuf in 1711. Charles and his wife, Maria Amalia of Saxony, came from families with a fine tradition of collecting, and Charles's mother, a Farnese bequeathed to him the foremost collection of antiques in Rome. Fourteen years later in 1748 excavation work began on the newly discovered town of Pompeii and a year later at Gragnano to explore the villas of Stabia. These digs yielded a constant stream of treasures for the royal collection, including the papyrus scrolls, mosaics, objects in daily use, weapons, and precious belongings including glassware. Staggering quantities of paintings emerged from the ground intact, with their colours as striking as the day they were painted.

The royal palace at Portici was, in 1750, adapted as the museum to receive these excavated treasures. A new museum at Capodimonte was proposed by Charles III, but with his departure to become the King of Spain, work on it diminished. As a result, the palace at Portici became filled to overflowing, and there was always the danger there that the collection might be destroyed in a new eruption from Vesuvius. Charles commented that if this happened they would be the joy of excavators 2000 years hereafter. In 1777 it was decided to adapt as a museum the university buildings which were in a bad state of repair and move the university to the former Jesuit College of Il Salvatore. Ambitious plans to enlarge the building amounted to little. Gradually the famous sculptures, which adorned the Roman Palazzo Farnese, such as the famous Hercules, and the Farnese Bull, were brought to Naples.[7]

In 1801 the Farnese collection, together with the bulk of the classical

---

[7] The Farnese Bull was set up as a centre piece of a fountain in the Villa Reale de Chaia and only placed in the Museum in 1826).

remains at Portici, was opened to the public in the new museums known then as the Museo Reale Bourbonico. Fortunately, while Joseph Bonaparte and Giocchino Murat ruled Naples, the collection was spared from the greed of Napoleon I. With the restoration of the Bourbons the museum was finally inaugurated in 1816 and Canova was commissioned to make a marble statue of Ferdinand I as protector of the arts and a latter-day Athena (Greek goddess of wisdom and industry).

With excavations at Pompeii gaining pace, the museum's collection grew rapidly. The most striking objects were the mosaics from the House of the Faun, including the famous Battle of Issus. (This on no account must be missed on a visit to the museum). The museum was much visited by Victorian travellers and occupied many pages in the 1855 John Murray handbook and in the early Baedekers. Baedeker cites the collection as 'the finest in the world' and calls the bronzes from Herculaneum 'unrivalled'.

During the Second World War, the most valuable collections were moved first to the Abbey of Cassino, then to the Vatican Museum only a few days before its bombing The Nazis pilfered the collection of gold work, but this was recovered after the war. Fortunately, Second World War bombs did not hit the museum.

In 1957, the picture collection was moved to Capodimonte and this made more space for the exhibition of classical remains. However, a shortage of staff makes it impossible to open all the rooms at once. One good rule for a student or visitor is always to ask to see a particular exhibit, and in the official guidebook it is stated obligingly that a visitor can always ask the Museum Director to put on display an item 'which is not currently visible'. For this purpose you need to buy the catalogue.

The Director, Stefan de Caro, (whose offices are surrounded by the strictest security), cordially explained to me that the pornographic collection (*Sala Segreta*) has been dispersed, with some objects placed in their historical sequence because there is no reason to exhibit them except in chronological order. However he told me he might put the magnificent bronze from the Villa dei Papiri of a satyr making love with a goat on show shortly. The pornographic collection was popular with Victorians and British visitors until the Second World War. For those interested, I can recommend an excellent well-written book by the British classical scholar Professor Michael Grant, *Eros in Pompeii - the Erotic Collection of the Museum of Naples*, published in English by Mondadori and readily available from British bookshops. This has 160 photographs, mainly of erotic objects, with many murals of the Bacchanalian scenes including some of erotic objects such as two of *Pan and the Goat* and the famous tripod with ithyphallic young Pans. The latter is displayed in one of the galleries alongside other domestic furnishings from Pompeii. The ithyphallic young Pans are a splendid example of the elegance of Greek art. Many other photographs in this book give an insight into the sensual lifestyle of the ancient Roman people.

When Garibaldl was dictator of Naples in 1860, he made Alexandre Dumas curator. He catalogued the pornographic collection, and 206 objects were put on show in a special gallery. Permits to view them were freely granted to men, but not to women. Casual curiosity was, however, discouraged. Under Fascism, the same controls were applied, as can be seen from the permits still filed in de Caro's office. But the collection in its entirety will not be seen again.

Stefan de Caro told me that the current plan is that the Museo Nazionale will house and exhibit all the major works of classical art discovered, and that a series of minor provincial museums at Capua, Baia, Pompeii, and Salerno will exhibit the best of the local finds. Progress has already been made with the new museum in the castle of Baia, from which there are the most magnificent views.

As the exhibits are frequently changed and all the galleries are never open on any one day, I will not attempt, as in the old-fashioned guides, to describe a tour of the museum. I give the inventory numbers so that with a copy of the catalogue in your hand you can always ask to be shown any object.

Anyone who is interested in the original Greek settlement on Ischia should look at the grave goods from S Montano (*Lacco Ameno*). ( ) You will probably have to ask to see them. The later Greek objects from Cuma in the same room are also remarkable. A Greek amphora with a picture of a discus thrower (Inventory 86333) from Curia is renowned for its grace and feeling of movement.

When the Greeks landed on the shores of Campania in the 8th century BC, they found that the Ausonians and Opicians already had some culture. But the Etruscans, who enjoyed the fertility of the Campanian plain and who had become prosperous there, occupied the hinterland. It is remarkable how the Greeks influenced Etruscan culture, although it represented a period of violent conflict between them. There are interesting Greek finds from pre-Roman Cuma and Capua, notably (Inventory 82744 and Inventory 85873) - the first a red amphora with a typical Samnite warrior; the second a lively household scene with much colour. Inventory

25085 is a gold signet ring of the 1st century BC, with an exceptionally fine quality male portrait originating in Capua.

A large part of the Naples museum exhibits comes from Roman Campania and especially the Phlegrean Fields and from the towns around Vesuvius before its AD 79 eruption. The whole area was included in the orbit of Rome, as symbolized by the opening of the Via Appia in 312 BC. There were many potters, masons and mosaicists, together with painters, architects, sculptors, goldsmiths and bronze workers, some of who are known by name. From all this art an enormous and unique collection has developed.

The Naples Museum also contains much material from Magna Grecia, collected both in the time of the Bourbons and after the Unification of Italy. Look particularly at the magnificent collection of Apulian vases from Ruvo and Canosa, (although just as exciting is the collection still housed in a private museum in Ruvo). Also dramatic are the gold ware and the figured terracotta, and the weapons and paintings on tombs. A gold necklace from Ruvo (Inventory 24883), with over a hundred small heads, is unique, as is Inventory 25234 - large gold earrings with pendants from Taranto, and a helmet (Inventory 5691) found at Paestum in 1805. The vases, mostly from Apulia, are colourful, and do not miss the outstanding bronze stag's head from Herculaneum (Inventory 69174) in the form of a drinking vessel. (Inventory 2459) - a Greek marble inscription about Olympic games held in Naples and found below one of the streets of the ancient city - has an inscription of great interest. It states that Marcus Aurelius was a wrestler who won 29 contests and 127 money prizes. The presence of this and other similar inscriptions erected to honour athletes in Naples is due to the celebration of the local Olympic Games, instituted by Augustus in 2 AD, and held every five years with competitions of gymnastics, wrestling, boxing, horse and chariot racing and musical and theatrical contests. The emperors themselves often assisted, and on occasions competed. The list of games on the inscription indicates that during the year athletes went the rounds of a circuit, rather like football players today, taking in Italy, Greece and Asia Minor, in which Olympic-style contests had been instituted alongside the traditional games from the classical age.

The Apollo from Pompeii (Inventory 5629) should not be missed. It is a particularly graceful figure and is presumed to be part of the famous spoils of Corinth when the Romans captured the city in 146 BC. It stood in the Temple of Apollo at Pompeii, and shows the god drawing his bow.

The rooms upstairs, which are given over to finds from Pompeii, are nearly always open. The collection of Roman mosaics, mostly from Pompeii and Herculaneum, is tremendous. The detailed scene of the Battle of Issus in which Alexander the Great defeated the Persian King Darius, and one with a view of the Academy (Inv. 124545) at Athens, which includes a portrait of Plato, are world famous.

Indeed, the most celebrated mosaic of antiquity is this *Battle of Issus* (Inventory 10020). It was discovered in 1831 in the House of the Faun at Pompeii and records the battle between Alexander the Great and Darius. On the left is Alexander at the head of his cavalry, with Darius fleeing in his chariot. Darius was the last of the Persian kings. There are masses of men caught up in armed struggle, with their long lances highlighted against a light sky. It has something like a million tesserae and was made around 100 BC. The same scene was famous in Etruscan times, and has often been reproduced on their urns.

In addition to the mosaics, there is a wonderful collection of Roman mural paintings. Most have come from the walls of Pompeian and Herculaneum villas. Some resemble Renaissance, others Baroque.

Two large-scale paintings of a prince and philosopher and an architectural painting come from the Villa of P Fannius Sinistor at Boscoreale. (....) (Inventory 906). The fine painting of *Europa riding the Bull* (Inventory 11745) comes from the House of Fatal Love at Pompeii. It is a copy of a Greek original of the 4th century BC. *The Punishment of Dirce* (Inventory 9042) is a large striking picture of the unlucky Dirce tied to a bull that is about to be freed. This is typical of the third style, circa 30 AD. *The Three Graces* (daughters of Zeus) from Pompeii (Inventory 9236), is another famous example of the third style showing the skill achieved in painting the female form, symbolizing beauty, grace and wisdom.

An attractive and evocative seascape (Inventory 9514) is alleged to be the port of Pozzuoli, mainly because of the arch on the Quayside. *The Judgement of Solomon* (Inventory 113197) is a moving evocation of the well known tale of Solomon the Wise, King of Israel, directing that the disputed baby should be cut in half so that the true mother would renounce her claim. A piece of history comes to life in the painting of the fight in the amphitheatre of Pompeii in 59 BC in which the Pompeiians and Nucervions (from Nola) came to blows over the gladiatorial combats, rather like football fans today, and as a punishment the Pompeii arena was closed for ten years. (Inventory 112222). It gives a good picture of the amphitheatre and the gymnasium, and ties in with the remains, which can be seen today.

There is an inspired reconstruction of the Temple of Isis in Pompeii, which was excavated in 1764 and found to be decorated with paintings freshly executed after the earthquakes. With fine rooms, it gives a unique realistic idea of the sanctuary as it appeared to the 18th century excavators. If it is closed, ask to be allowed to see it.

Other objects worth seeking or asking after are: the painted frieze depicting life in the Pompeii forum that is a contemporary image of a Roman city in the first century BC. (Inventory 9068); the painting with *Hercules and his young son Telephus being suckled by a Doe* (Inventory 9108); the marble statue of *Aphrodite* from Old Capua (Inventory 6017); the *Isiac Ceremony* from Herculaneum (inventory 8924); the *Prometheus* sarcophagus from Pozzuoli (Inventory 6705); the head of a horse from the theatre of Herculaneum. (Inventory 115391); found in 1739, of remarkable artistic quality and still showing remains of gold leaf, especially if you are going to Capri; the bronze statue of Tiberius in the act of sacrificing from Herculaneum (Inventory 5615). For those who like domestic scenes, look for the large garden ornament of a whole boar being cooked in a cauldron, overseen by a bearded man and a boy. (Inventory 6218).

Amongst the Pompeian mosaics I particularly like the *Cat and Duck* mosaic from Pompeii (Inventory 9993). Both this and T*he Satyr and Nymph* (Inventory 27707) come from the House of the Faun. There is an erotic painting from Pompeii, usually on display, which is of much higher quality than the caricatures that adorn the brothels of Pompeii (Inventory 110569), showing an artistic and vivid contrast of bodies. Also somewhat erotic is a nearby picture of a *Satyr trying to rape Hermaphrodite* (Inventory 110878), and *Pan and Olympus* (Inventory 6329), described in the catalogue as 'erotic - idyllic'. The still life of fish from Pompeii (Inventory 8635), is a fine painting of mullet, cuttle fish, scorpion fish and shellfish that depict the Roman passion for meals based on fish.

The museum contains a splendid collection of furniture, personal belongings, pottery, gold and silver ware, and ornaments from the Vesuvian cities. The houses were cold and dark in winter, which made braziers and warmers and lanterns and candelabra essential. These were made of terracotta or bronze. Most citizens could only afford earthenware or bronze cutlery, but the rich had excellent table silver. In the House of Menander, a complete set of 115 silver pieces of crockery has been found. Many are much the same as would be expected in any well-to-do British household today where they go in for formal lunch and dinner parties.

Remember that the marble sculptures are mostly Roman copies of

Greek originals; in many cases these are the only surviving evidence of masterpieces that otherwise would have been lost forever. Amongst the statues do not miss the *Dancing Faun* from the Villa dei Papiri at Herculaneum (Inventory 5292); or the *Satyr with a Wineskin* from Pompeii, (Inventory 11495). Of remarkable artistic quality is a bronze group of two dogs attacking a boar (Inventory 4899). It is derived from a Greek original, and originally water ran out from the mouth of the boar. A splendid bronze statue of a ram (Inventory 4903) was a garden sculpture and is an excellent work of the early Imperial period. A typical garden ornament in Pompeii is an *oscillum* (circular marble shield bearing mythological figures in relief) (Inventory 65551), from the House of the Githarist; it is a splendid example and probably the best crafted of any of those found in Pompeii so far. On one face a satyr uncovers a cistern from which a serpent emerges; on the other a satyr plays the flute in front of Priapus. This is from the end of the 1st century BC and represents workmanship of an exceptionally high standard. Inventory 124845 is an amusing little statue of an elephant carrying a tower. It comes from Pompeii, and seems to relate to the war against Carthage. The elephant bears on his back a square tower, tied to its belly by three chains, while the driver, a Negro, holds a sickle shaped prod. There are two splendid equestrian statues (Inventory 4996 and Inventory 4999).

The first is Alexander the Great riding his horse and slashing down with his sword against an enemy on foot, while the second is a riding Amazon from Herculaneum with beautiful legs - this is probably a Greek original from the first half of the fourth century BC.

A bronze brazier from Herculaneum (Inventory 73104) has lion paws shaped on the feet and represents a good example of the manner in which the houses were heated, while Inventory 72734 is of mule heads adorning an ancient bed. The faces of the mules are attractive. To remind one of how strict the Romans were about weights and measures, look at the steel yard (Inventory 740), which has a plate on which the object to be weighed is laid and counterbalanced by a moveable weight shaped like a child's head, sliding along a graded shaft. On the short arm of the shaft, a dotted inscription records the consular date of 47 AD, and attests that both the sealings on the weights were the type specified by the decree issued in that year in Rome.

A painting with a scene representing a dyer's workshop is also evocative of Pompeian life (no number). A marble relief (Inventory 6575) shows a boilermaker's workshop; it is realistic, with giant scales, and depicts the beating of hot metal on the anvil. Further indication of Pompeiian activities comes from a painting of cupids at work from the House of the Deer at Herculaneum (Inventory 9179) in which the cupids playfully imitate various activities including perfume making, field measuring, cobbling, and carpentry. Most interesting are the gestures they used in their work on the machines and the cupboards. The surgical instrument (Inventory 78029), with S shaped curved extremities, might well be used by a modern day surgeon; the rattle in the shape of a gladiator at Herculaneum (Inventory 27853), used to be in the pornographic collection. It is the grotesque figure of a gladiator with an enormous penis, which has transformed itself into a panther against whom the gladiator is fighting with swords. This was probably a lucky charm.

In a separate section you will find the blue vase from Pompeii, which was found in 1834 (Inventory 13521). It is a magnificent glass vase representing grape harvesting carried out by cupids under vine stalks harmoniously wound round the body of the vase, while other cupids play music under a bower. A glass vase (Inventory 129404) in the shape of a Negro's head from Pompeii, was almost certainly a perfume container. The gold lamp (Inventory 2500), from the Temple of Venus at Pompeii, is striking. It is one of the gifts of Nero and Pappaea to the city, going back to their stay there in 64 AD.

The Farnese Collection in the National Museum was started in 1534 by Alexander Farnese, who became Pope Paul III. The collection grew considerably through the efforts of the Pope's grandson Alexander, who was made a cardinal at the tender age of 14 and who became one of the leading patrons of the arts in his day. He purchased the Palazzo Farnese in Rome and commissioned Titian to paint two pictures. During his lifetime the Farnese Collection reached its maximum size. It began to be dispersed in 1662 when Ranuchio II, the Farnese Duke of Parma, took part of it to Parma. The Farnese dynasty came to an end in 1731, and the art treasures were passed on to the Bourbons through Elizabeth Farnese, wife of Philip V of Spain, and mother of Charles III King of Naples. On his arrival in Naples in 1754, Charles transferred his Parma collection to his new capital, and in 1770 his son Ferdinand requested permission from the Pope to do the same with the Roman collections. Several years of diplomatic wrangling followed, but in 1787 to the fury of the Romans, its removal to Naples began. This was a trauma for Rome and for the world of culture in general. The Romans were furious because a visit to the Palazzo Farnese was obligatory for all visitors to Rome. Probably it is fortunate it went to Naples because the last Bourbons would almost certainly have sold it off, as they showed no scruples about selling the few pieces still left in Rome.

The crowning glory of the Farnese Collection are the sculptures, the most famous of which were brought out from the quarry that was opened up in 1545-1546 on the Aventine Hill in Rome in the complex of the Baths at Caracalla. The colossal statues of Hercules from the Baths at Caracalla and the Farnese Bull, also from the Baths at Caracalla, are always on show in the principal gallery of the museum (Inventories 6001 and 6002). The thoughtful, almost melancholy figure of Hercules after his latest labour, that of the Apples of the Hesperides, which he holds in his right hand behind his back, is lovely. When the statue was found its left arm was missing, as were the legs, which were re-done by an artist called della Porta. The Farnese Bull represents the punishment of Dirce. Her sons have tied her legs to a mad bull so that she will be dragged to a cruel death. She is being punished for her torments on Antiope.

The impressive group of a *Warrior and Child*, (Inventory 5999), again from the Baths of Caracalla, represents a warrior in the act of hurling away a wounded youth, held by his foot. This is another colossal statue - the head is modern. There are various interpretations of the theme.

Much to be admired is the statue of Atlas carrying the vault of heaven on his shoulders (Inventory 6374); it is a Greek original. Antoninous was a youth loved by Hadrian who died in Egypt in 130 AD and whose death was followed by the inauguration of a cult about him. There are many statues of him, but the Farnesian specimen in Naples, whose origin is unknown, is considered to be the best for the extraordinary softness of its contours (Inventory 6030).

There is plenty more to see, but I hope I have succeeded in drawing the reader's attention to the most important works of art in this unique museum.

Before departing, you should try to go up to the Sala della Meridionalia - an enlargement renovation started in 1777 and opened in 1804, intended to house the library. This fine room is exactly what a museum should be; it is magnificent, with a beautiful painted ceiling, and has almost to be seen to be believed.

The museum leaves many visitors with the strange feeling of having seen the ghosts of AD 79. At Pompeii and Herculaneum you visit ruined temples, baths, house after house, barracks, brothels, theatres and all the array of a Roman city that came to a sudden end almost 2,000 years ago and which has been entombed. In the Museum you see the statues, vivid paintings, mosaics, art treasures and details of daily Roman life in excellent, often perfect condition so that one feels in close contact with the daily life of the ancient Romans. Using slave labour in place of modern technology, the Romans by AD 79 had achieved a sophisticated lifestyle and surrounded themselves with artistic objects. Only towards the end of the 20th century can the West be said to have paralleled some of the standards of luxury and art environment enjoyed at Pompeii and Herculaneum by the free men who had at their disposal armies of slaves.

5

Palazzo Reale and other Museums

The Royal Palace (Palazzo Reale) is a striking feature of Naples; it dominates the harbour and the lower town. To the east is the vast Piazza del Plebiscito, which was until recently just a giant car park but is now thank goodness, a large pedestrian precinct.

The palace closes off the east side of the Piazza del Plebiscito. Domenico Fontana built it for the Spanish Viceroy Conte de Lemnos in 1601. The main difference today is that on the advice of Vanvitelli in the eighteenth century, each alternate arch of the portico was filled in to create a series of niches, with statues representing the eight dynasties that have ruled Naples. They are Roger the Norman, Frederick Barbarossa, Charles I of Anjou, Alfonso I of Aragon, Emperor Charles V, Charles III, Joachim Murat and Victor Emmanuel II. The statue of Murat erected in the days of the Bourbons, does not show him as a dashing cavalry hero; instead he is paunchy and unregal - more a fat, middle-aged businessman. Still, these statues are a nice bit of potted history.

The palace was damaged by fire in 1838, somewhat by World War II bombs. It is open every day. The Staircase of Honour, designed by Francesco Pichiatti in 1651, is magnificent. Blunt describes it as, 'an unusual spacious example of the so-called Imperial Stairway beginning with a short single flight with curved steps and dividing into two long flights which follow round the walls of the cage and lead up to a corridor over the cloister'. This form of staircase was invented in Spain in the 16th century and his is the first example of an imperial staircase in Italy on a large scale. It is richly decorated in marble and lit by large windows and has a spectacular ceiling. Naples, the town of staircases has nothing finer.

Blunt criticizes Fontana for having a limited supply of ideas and claims he simply took the same design he had used for the Sixtus V villa at the Vatican. The appearance of the palace today is certainly marred by the blocking up of so many arches of the loggia, and Blunt is correct in saying the general effect is 'dry'. Still, the effect would have been lighter if Fontana had been allowed to execute a line of obelisks and urns on the roof, which he had designed. After the death of Sixtus V in 1590, Fontana lost the position as papal architect in Rome and was most gratified to be made royal architect in Naples by the Viceroy.

Once up the staircase you find the 30 rooms of the Royal Apartments arranged around a central courtyard. There is a magnificent collection of eighteenth and nineteenth century furniture, Murat contributing much fine First Empire production, especially in his study. However, it is all rather a jumble; the best pictures have been moved to Capodimonte. Still, there are some good pictures, including a Titian in rather poor condition and pictures by de Mura, Corenzio, and Caraccio. The throne room has works by Vaccaro, Giordano and Preti. There is also much good porcelain, watches and clocks, together with tapestries and works of art.

Crown Prince Umberto was the only one of the Savoy Royal Family to like Naples and he spent quite a lot of time here in the 1930s, but can only have used a small fraction of the space. The whole area gives an idea of the splendour with which the Bourbons surrounded themselves. Worth seeing in one of the staterooms is Maria Carolina's remarkable revolving lectern, based on those used in monastery libraries.

To the east at the top of the staircase is the exquisite small eighteenth century court theatre, designed by Fuga, and still in perfect condition. It was built in 1768 for the marriage of Maria Carolina to Ferdinand I and is delightfully decorated with pâpier maché sculpture. Still used frequently for concerts, it is a sheer joy, and pitchforks one back into the middle of the eighteenth century, a model of good taste amid the Bourbon excesses. Note the balcony where the palace servants stood to watch.

On the second floor is the Biblioteca Nazionale (National Library) of Victor Emmanuel III the most important library in south Italy, with two million books and a collection of parchments from Herculaneum. A door to the east of the San Carlo theatre reaches it; and foreigners are allowed to use the library.

On the ground floor of the palace, take a look at the royal chapel with a fine ceiling painting by Morelli and a nineteenth century high altar by Lazzari (1671). Probably more attractive for many than the royal palace is the theatre San Carlo immediately to the east. It stands in all its former glory in tip-top order, and is a magnet for lovers of opera, ballet, and music from all over Europe, although curiously the package tour operators ignore it for their 'opera-goers' trips. Little matter as it is nearly always full, but tickets can usually be obtained from the obliging box office attendants at about £20 for a good seat. They are good at producing 'returns' at short notice.

The theatre was inaugurated in the reign of Charles I (III) in 1737 and named after his patron saint. It seats 3,000, and has outstanding acoustics. The interior is magnificent, with six tiers of boxes surrounding the central royal box with its enormous Bourbon lilies and arms. Anyone attending a performance here must feel Naples is crying out loud to have a monarch again, or at least to be a capital city. Note especially the curtain with its intriguing clock and the painting on the ceiling of Mount Parnassus. Many world premières of operas have been held here over the centuries.

San Carlo has its own opera and ballet company, with as high a standard as anywhere in Europe. The price of admission is a fraction of that charged for ballet or opera in London, and an evening at San Carlo is an unforgettable experience. But you need to have your hair done and to wear something decent or you will feel embarrassed by the elegance surrounding you.

Another elegant theatre in Naples is the nineteenth century Teatro Bellini, close to the Piazza Dante; the Neapolitan Vincenzo Bellini opened it in 1878 with an opera. If you cannot go to San Carlo, book here; you will enjoy this theatre with its rich façade and its elegant statues and paintings and little putti musicians. The ceiling, with a small Gesu carrying Bellini and the titles of his works in triumph, is impressive; this is by a well-known painter of the Posilippo School, Vincenzo Palliotti–a pupil of Pitloo. Closed for many years after the Second World War, this attractive theatre was reopened in 1988.

Walk across the Piazza del Plebiscito to the west of the Palazzo Reale, enjoying the view of the bay and the lack of motor cars, but stop first at the Camprinus café for high quality and much needed refreshment. In the piazza you are faced with the church of S Francesco di Paolo with its semi-circular Doric colonnade - most untypical of Naples. The colonnade was built by Murat in 1810 and clearly imitates Bernini's magnificent colonnade in front of St Peter's in Rome. Ferdinand I built the church in 1817 to fulfill a vow that he would do so if he ever recovered his kingdom of Naples. Inside S Francesco di Paolo is crude neo-classicism, without appeal for most people; it seems more suitable for post Revolution Paris than Naples.

More pleasing are the two statues in the piazza by Canova of Charles III and Ferdinand I. In the attractive baroque church in the adjoining Piazza Trieste Trento, the morganatic wife of the eccentric Ferdinand I, the Duchess of Floridia, is buried. The church was renamed S Ferdinando by the king.

The Certosa S Martino and the castle of Sant' Elmo tower over Naples. In 1325 Carlo, Duke of Calabria, the eldest son of King Robert of Anjou, founded the Certosa for the Carthusians who sent monks from their original monastery of Tours in France. A previous Carthusian monastery near Naples was Certosa di Padula (10 & 222) and it was followed by one at Capri.

The monastery adjoins the castle of St. Elmo, rebuilt for the Viceroy Toledo on the site of an old Angevin fort of 1329 at the same time as S Martino on a six-pointed star plan with deep moats. From Sant' Elmo a wonderful panoramic view is obtained in all directions (360 degrees). For centuries it was a prison, but it has been used more against the city of Naples than to defend it. The Viceroy took refuge here during the revolt of Masaniello, and many of the liberal revolutionaries of 1799 were imprisoned here. A ramp leads to the entrance that has a large heraldic crest of Charles V, and continues inside until you reach the parade ground where you find the little church of S Erasmus with tombs of the Viceroys families and an interesting model of the Certosa from the eighteenth century-otherwise it has little of interest.

Plans for the original structure of the Certosa were under the control of the abbot of SS Severino e Sossio, and the most important architect was the talented Sienese sculptor Tino di Camiano. He and Ferdinand de Vito were sent to find ideas at Charterhouse of Trisurti (Fresinone). The Duke of Calabria died unexpectedly in 1328, and his father Robert of Anjou carried on the construction - by 1337 there was a community of thirteen monks. Work slowed down when Robert of Anjou died in 1345 and his granddaughter Joanna I succeeded to the throne, so the church was not consecrated until 1368. The monastery became rich and acquired a great number of works of art, while lovely frescoes adorned the walls and ceilings of the church, sacristy and chapels. Beauty was considered by these ascetic Carthusians to be equal to the praise of God.

In the seventeenth and eighteenth centuries, the famous architects Dosio and Fanzago embellished the monastery, and it constitutes with the Duomo a spectacular testimonial to Neapolitan baroque. The Carthusians were evicted in 1866, shortly after the unification of Italy, but G. Fiorelli then created in its buildings a magnificent state museum, which is still being restored. Unfortunately much damage was done by the earthquake of 1980; restoration continues and it is not always possible to tour all the collections and rooms.

Take a taxi or bus, or walk from the funicular to the large square in front of S Martino. From here you can enjoy a panoramic view. There is an exceptionally good restaurant with a view and a welcoming café.

The main door to the church is on the left, just after crossing the entrance. A facade by Fanzago masks its fourteenth century appearance. I have never found this door open; it is necessary to go through an arch to the seventeenth century cloister of the Procurators. From here a corridor to the left leads to the Grand Cloister. Turning to the left from this corridor, you can enter the church. The first glimpse is stupendous. Fanzago has created a masterpiece of baroque decoration. The main effect of the interior is due to

Fanzago, but certain parts had been created before he took over from Dosio. Fanzago indulges in the full range of coloured Sicilian marbles and inlaid patterns. Blunt considers the church of S Martino to be one of the few examples in which a Gothic structure has been satisfactorily given a baroque covering. The nave must still have its Gothic proportions because the ceiling is composed of its original Gothic ribs. According to Blunt, 'the proportions of the nave which must have been exceptionally wide for a 14th century church, seem perfectly designed to take baroque decoration - and there is no trace of the conflict so common in Gothic churches clothed in baroque decoration between the tall narrow proportions of the structure and the rich decoration which was conceived for a wider space'. Anyone who has visited other Neapolitan churches is likely to agree with Blunt, and in S Martino we see baroque at its pinnacle of splendour.

The church is a most successful example of contrasting coloured marble decoration with frescoes; the two fuse into each other in rich and perfect unity. The walls are decorated with large rectangular canvasses by Lanfranco (*The Crucifixion*, 1638); Guido Reni (*Nativity* 1624); Stanzione (*Last Supper* 1639); and Ribera (*Communion of the Apostles* 1651).

The magnificent paintings of *Christ in his Glory* on the vaulted ceiling are by Lanfranco (1637). The floor of the choir is simple, but that of the nave is a fantastic inlay of geometric and floral patterns in many colours. Both were almost certainly done by Fanzago.

Decoration of the side chapels had been well advanced before Fanzago took over. Fanzago did the two in the middle, and instructed Stanzione to fresco the ceilings. Then he quarrelled with the monks in 1656, and the works were only completed in the eighteenth century. Around 1700, the two chapels at the west end were redecorated by Vaccaro and two further chapels were added, flanking the entrance portico, but only accessible from the other chapels. Fine marble balustrades and gilt bronze grilles designed by Fanzago close off these chapels. Although Fanzago erected the steps to the high altar, the current ornate rails date from the mid 18th century, while Solimena designed the high altar.

In the ceiling of the Chapel of the Treasure (*Capelle del Tresoro*), Luca Giordano has painted a splendid *Triumph of Judith* (1704) that seems to be a forerunner of Rococo; while Ribera painted a fresco of the Pietà (1637). Giordano is reputed to have painted St Judith in 48 hours! Look also at the canvas in the vestibule of the chapel of another painting by Giordano, the *Apostles Peter and Andrew* (1656). In the chapel of S Martin, look at the fine Solimena painting of Christ appearing in a dream to St Martin. In the chapel of S Bruno there are paintings by Stanzione (1637) and sculpture by Vaccaro (1707), while the floor is a good example of Fanzago's mixing marble with hard stone (1631).

The chapel of San Giuseppe was designed (and painted) by Vaccaro and di Matteo (1719) and the chapel of the Rosary has a painting by Vaccaro (1721). One of the best statues is that of S Bruno by Bottigliera in the chapel of S Ugo, while there is an attractive *Annunication* by de Mura in the chapel of the Annunciation (1757). Do not fail to look at the inlaid wood carvings in the spacious sacristy, and the carved stalls nearby; look also at the immense refectory and the paintings of the monks in it.

Although S Martino is amongst the three most visited museums in Naples,. there is a sense of emptiness; it should be peopled with monks in white habits. One picture by an unknown artist features 60 Carthusians. Their faces are expressive and leave the impression they resent trespassers on their property.

From the church it is an easy walk to the Grand Cloister - made cheerful by the presence of flowers. There are 16 Doric columns and marble arches on each side that are bright and attractive. Opinions vary as to whether Dosio or Fanzago was the architect. The statues on the arcade give a lively impression. In the southwest corner is the marble enclosure of the cemetery of the monks studded with skulls, and designed by Fanzago who was responsible for its simplicity. The dignity of the Grand Cloister makes it a pleasant spot to linger. Gunn describes it as a perfect fusion of Renaissance and baroque.

It is not easy to find your way around in S Martino. There are many custodians and if you ask, you will find them obliging. In the museum there is much majolica, and a rich collection of china from the Royal Factory of Capodimonte with many attractive figures. Look at the Gallery of Historical Records and the history of Naples will come alive for you with pictures of Naples in 1600 and the revolt of Masaniello by Milo Spadaro. Of as much historical interest are the pictures by Antone Juli of the departure of Charles III for Spain in 1759, and by Michele Foscini of Charles III signing his Act of Abdication and of Ferdinand I as a child, swearing his oath before the Barons of Naples in 1762. These contain almost photographic detail. There is also a large canvas by Fischetti showing the taking of Capri from the British by the French by in 1808. It is worth pottering in the gallery and visualizing the history of Naples.

The Prior's Lodgings (*Quarto del Priore*) have a wonderful view and are full of art treasures. In the seventeenth century various writers considered his lodgings 'worthy of a prince'. Recently an effort has been made to bring back to the Prior's Lodgings some of the more important works of art confiscated in the nineteenth century. Now it has many of its former pictures back to match the lovely ceiling paintings from the end of the seventeenth century. These pictures are mostly pastoral scenes. A most striking statue in the Prior's Lodgings is the statue of the *Madonna and Child with St John* by Pietro Bernini (end of sixteenth century).

From the cloister of the Procurators you can walk to the southwest into large gardens - a rare array of pergolas, flowers, shrubs and olive groves preserved in the heart of the city.

The crib section of the museum is much admired with a vast collection of Neapolitan cribs. Here is kept the fifteenth century crib from S Giovanni Carbonara with 180 shepherds, 10 horses, eight dogs, a rabbit and 309 detailed wooden statues. In the art section of the museum there are 'nostalgic' records of famous Neapolitan theatres, actors and other theatrical relics. In an arch leading to the Cloister of the Procurators are some state coaches of the Bourbons, most interesting for anyone who likes pomp as they are even more ornate than their counterparts at Buckingham Palace.

S Martino closes at 2:00 p.m. You will probably want to spend two mornings there. Everything is well kept and such a collection of art in a fabulous Carthusian monastery is unique.

A drive of seven miles to the west, through at first a very built-up area, takes you eventually into chestnut and fruit trees and near the monastery of Camoldi where there is a series of views, possibly the most famous in Italy. The monastery, where there are still a few monks, is interesting and women are not admitted. However most of the monks enjoy talking with visitors. Take a 10 minute stroll along the path from the terrace outside the monastery entrance to the Belvedere Pagiarella and you can see to Gaeta to the north - the whole sweep of the Naples Bay from Ischia and Proclida to Capri, and the Sorrento peninsula with the Cilento mountains behind - while Misenum and Baia and the Bay of Pozzouli are in the foreground to the south. Gunn advises 'sunset' on a clear day as the best time for this magnificent view.

Villa Pignatelli Museum

The Pignatelli museum lies on the Chain Riviera. Built in 1826, it has an imposing Doric arcade and a nice green park. An Englishman Sir Ferdinand Acton, son of Sir John Acton who was Ferdinand II's Prime Minister, built it. The site at the time belonged to another Englishman, Lord William Drummond.

Harold Acton gives a contemporary account of a ball there in February 1840 given by the French ambassador, the Duke of Montebello, who was renting the house and who loved to entertain. '4000 glass lanterns of many colours scattered amongst the trees illuminated the garden, 80 lamps of bronze whose flames were protected by globes of opaque crystal and a thousand candles glittered in the many luxurious halls dazzling the eyes of 500 guests. When the King and Queen appeared, followed by all the princes and princesses of the Royal family, a charming Bengal blaze lit the path for them, which led from the garden entrance to the festive hall. This unexpected vision was accompanied by a burst of melody which seemed magical - not knowing whence it came - an orchestra hidden among the trees was playing the Bourbon anthem.

The splendour of the fête was all the more original in so far as it was not dominated by luxury and gallantry as usual, but rather by science and intellect. The ball ended at 7 o'clock on Sunday morning. The King and Queen withdrew towards 4 o'clock and the other Royal princes at 5.30. The host offered coffee and chocolate to the hundred guests who remained when day was bright.'

The Acton family sold the villa in the 1850s to an Austrian Carl von Rothschild, who played an important role as a Neapolitan banker. He built a second palace to the north facing Via Piscicelli, known as Palazzina Rothschild. After the unity of Italy the Rothschilds, closely associated with the Bourbons, closed down the Naples bank and the villa was sold to the rich Pignatelli family who lived the life of the nobility there, being a very old Naples family. One forebear was the Pope Innocent XII (Pope 1691-1700).

In 1955, the Princess Rosina Pignatelli left in her will the villa and its contents to the state on the understanding that the art collection be preserved intact. A visitor today can admire not only the Pignatelli furniture but also the pictures and china and the enormous library.

The museum was opened in 1960, and is also used frequently for high-class classical concerts. The garden is a jewel of early nineteenth century Neapolitan architecture, forming an oval around the house, and it comprises an English garden together with a splendid collection of rare trees - while in the spring there is a terrific scent of magnolia. Alas, today the villa has a backdrop of high-rise concrete buildings. A picture in the museum, painted by Guiseppe Giordano in 1825, shows the house against a green countryside, topped only by Capodimonte.

Inside there are early 19th century frescoes and statues and some elegant furniture of the same period, but it is largely empty. Look at the busts of the Pope Clement XI (Pope 1700-1721). There is also a lifelike portrait of Queen Maria Carolina, and an especially nice statue of Narcissus by the top nineteenth century Neapolitan sculptor Vincenzo Gemito.

The main feature of the museum is the porcelain collection from the 18th and 19th centuries. There is more Dresden than anything else, but there is excellent Viennese Limoges and late Neapolitan. Especially interesting are the pieces from the short-lived Royal Factory of Capodimonte, with a delightful *Laundress and Young Man*, and *Girl with a puppy*. Note also a later lifelike statue of Queen Caroline Murat, and other attractive Neapolitan pieces of the same period. A nineteenth century Carriage Museum in the old stable was presented by a Neapolitan family in 1960 and recalls the days not so long ago when all traffic in Naples was horse drawn.

Villa Floridiana

The park and Villa Floridiana provide a green belt on the way up to the Vomero, and are much used by the Neapolitans, rather like Kensington Gardens in London. In the long leafy avenues you see plenty of prams and small children and a few well behaved dogs enjoying the shade of exotic trees and pergolas and relief from the Naples traffic. There are plenty of benches in the shade. It is the largest and best preserved of all the villas of the Vomero. In June 1815 at the time of his triumphal return to Naples after its ten years under French domination, Ferdinand I brought back with him from Palermo his second wife Lucia Mighliaccio, Duchess of Floridia. She was good looking and had a gentle character; twenty years younger than him, she took no interest in affairs of state, which was a great contrast to his domineering first wife. Within three months of the death of his first wife Maria Carolina Hapsburg, Ferdinand married her morganatically and although she was not officially his consort, he did everything to flatter her and keep her happy. In September 1817, finding that a suite of rooms in the royal palace was inadequate; Ferdinand bought this palace and the farm above it for Lucia. It was already an elegant and refined nobleman's residence, but Ferdinand enlarged it with the help of a Tuscan architect, Antonio Niccolini, and laid out the beautiful spacious park that surrounds it.

An enjoyable morning can be spent at the Villa Floridiana, both in the lovely grounds and in the museum within the villa. The Duchess loved a zoo of tigers, bears, lions and eighteen kangaroos (bought from London in exchange for precious papyrus from Herculaneum). Remains of the cages and caves where the wild animals lived can still be seen. Ferdinand I died in January 1825 and Lucia fifteen months later. It was a love abode where

Ferdinand was much happier than he had been with his Austrian wife.

The villa passed to the Duke of Martina born in 1829, who was a courtier with Ferdinand II and Francis II; his father too was close to the royal family and shared King Francis II's hardships at Gaeta where he died, leaving his son heavily compromised with the *ancien régime* at the time of the unity of Italy. So the young duke went to live in Paris, where he accumulated a magnificent art collection and became known as one of the foremost collectors in Europe of his time. In 1869 he decided to return to Naples, and went on collecting as enthusiastically as ever - mainly through Paris dealers. In those days, antiques were relatively inexpensive; the collection became richer and richer, initially being housed in the Palazzo Sauro in Piazza del Nilo.

The Villa Floridiana had been acquired by the State in 1919 and when the Duke and Duchess of Martina died in the late twenties they, with enormous generosity left most of their collection to the city of Naples, and it was decided to house it in the elegant Villa Floridiana. But the Martina family never lived in Villa Floridiana. The last duke in 1978 left his remaining great collection of porcelain and other rare objects to Villa Floridiana. As a result, today we can see not only a magnificent house and park, but also a fascinating art collection - which has uniquely the atmosphere of a private family collection, although several pictures and other objects have been added from the Palazzo Reale and Capodimonte.

Of the pictures, look especially at Solimena's *Vision of Pius V;* Vaccaro's *Ipomene receiving Aphrodite's Golden Apples* and de Mura's *Imene.* There is a good collection of ivory, coral, and tortoise shell. There is a cheerful small collection of china from Ferdinand's factory at Capodimonte and some nice pieces from the later Naples factory. The collection of German china is larger, it's about 700 pieces with 60 percent from the Dresden factory. There is also a good collection of Chinese ceramics.

The whole atmosphere of Lucia's palace and its rural situation in the heart of Naples make the Villa Floridiana well worth a visit.

Castel Nuovo

The Castel Nuovo is not wholly a museum. It is used by the local government of Naples, and contains the Museo Civico. It is all open to the public, and should not be missed.

It was called Nuovo (new) to distinguish it from the two earlier castles - dell'Ovo and Capuano, which were not large enough to accommodate the entire Angevin court. Charles I of Anjou began the construction in 1279, but the Cappella Palatina is the only surviving part of his original building. Alfonso V of Aragon who later became Alfonso I, King of Naples and Sicily, ordered it to be rebuilt completely in 1443 upon his triumphant entry into Naples after defeating the Angevins.

He ordered a spectacular white marble triumphal arch (*Arco di Trionfo*) to be built over the main entrance to celebrate his victory over the Angevins and his establishment as King of Naples. This is a superb example of early renaissance of Southern Italy. His first plan was to build a freestanding arch in the middle of the city, but he abandoned this in favour of an arch to form the entrance to the castle. The architects were Onofrio di Giordano and Francesco Laurana. Blunt believes it is modelled on Frederick II's arch at Capua or the arches in the walls of Perugia; he thinks Alfonso's arch far bolder than either of these models, and more impressive, especially because of its display of sculpture. Blunt writes: '... the triumphal Arch of Alfonso I is not merely an example of local ingenuity but is one of the most original inventions of the mid *quattro centro* for which no parallel can be found in Tuscany or Lombardy. Further its carved decoration shows a mature knowledge of classical detail and was executed by a band of artists who ranked with the best to be found in Italy at the time'.

There is the figure of the Archangel St Michael and a bas relief of Alfonso I in his chariot, and allegorical reliefs of the four virtues, looking from left to right - Temperance, Justice, Fortitude, and Magnanimity and also the Coronation of Ferrante, son of Alfonso, at Barletta.[8]

The castle itself is trapezoidal, with fine cylindrical towers facing onto a beautiful central courtyard. From the courtyard you can enter the Sala dei Baroni (Hall of the Barons), now used for the debates of the Town Council. Here was hatched a famous plot by the barons against the Aragonese in 1485. They were all arrested and executed after being lured to a banquet by King Ferrante - who kept up a myth afterwards that they were alive in prison.

It is an elegant and rather grand hall, 85 feet wide and 92 feet high, built by the Spanish architect Guglielmo Sagrera who was summoned by Alfonso from Spain to Naples to carry out the work. Look especially at the Spanish inspired ribbed vault with intersecting ribs shaped like a large star, the monumental fireplace, and the large rectangular cross windows.

Somehow this castle manages to be a real fortress and at the same

---

[8] C. Seymour (Sculpture in Italy 1400–1500) assigns the scupltures to local Neapolitans.

time an elegant palace. Particularly elegant is the Renaissance doorway to the Capella Palatina from the courtyard. Giotto and his workshop once decorated the walls inside this chapel, but only fragments remain. The chapel has high windows resembling S Chiara, and is in the same Gothic style.

Ask a guide to let you into the subterranean chamber, reached by a stair through the sacristy. Twenty steps lead to a little chamber faintly lit by a deep set window. In the dim light, four coffins are visible - two open and two closed. By lifting the lid of one of the closed coffins the guide can show you the mummy of a man distorted in agony, fully clothed probably - strangled. As Arthur Norway writes: 'He is wearing the clothes he wore when he came down that little winding stair; hose, buttons and doublet still intact'.

Each of the other coffins contains the mummified body of a man killed in his clothes, with his separated head lying there. According to Norway, King Alfonso and King Ferrante regularly cut off the heads of their enemies 'and kept them salted in chambers underneath their palace'. It is an eerie sensation to look at these bodies, unmoved for 550 years since their death, and a strange step back into the Middle Ages with a revealing glimpse of the brutality of the Aragon rulers.

Lower down, excavations are proceeding and traces of a Roman villa of the 1st century AD have been found together with a cemetery of the 5th and 6th century AD. Pottery found there indicates that before the castle was built there was a Franciscan monastery on the site, and Charles I moved them out to S. Maria la Nova. The excavations under Castel Nuovo are to be opened to the public.

It is alleged that under Castel Nuovo was a pit into which prisoners were thrown. It was below sea level, and many prisoners mysteriously disappeared. A hole was discovered, out of which an enormous crocodile would emerge in order to drag the wretched prisoners into the sea. The crocodile was stuffed and remained hung over one of the castle gates until the middle of the 19th century.

The Museo Civico (Civic Museum) occupies a large part of the western area of Castel Nuovo. However, before visiting the museum, try to make the steep climb to the upper floors of the castle to enjoy the views of Vesuvius and the Bay of Naples. In the museum are paintings and sculptures from the fourteenth to the nineteenth centuries; the largest section consists of nineteenth century Neapolitan paintings, many of which depict views of parts of the city that no longer exist.

6
Underground Naples

U nderground Naples is seldom visited by tourists, but visitors will find it a unique experience, more rewarding than the catacombs in Rome. There are vast catacombs under Naples. The city is built on a soft light yellow but strong and durable rock (tufa) of volcanic origin, which also makes a strong mortar. Large blocks were easily cut for outside walls, and smaller ones for interior walls. The Greeks brought pure water to Naples with an aqueduct, and dug out cisterns and tunnels under the town to store it so that it could be raised through shafts to houses and streets.

Buckets raised the water to the surface, and in the antique old centre of Naples it is calculated that there were 12,000 holes or wells. Today the marks of the axes can be seen in the catacombs, just as in the cave of the sibyl at Cuma. Unfortunately until shortly before the First World War, the caverns were excessively used as deposits for rubbish.

The Romans made further aqueducts to supply Pozzuoli and Misenum. The Greeks used these underground quarries as cemeteries, and there are many traces of this with inscriptions on the walls of pagan cults. Many fresh Greek tombs were found after the earthquake of 1980; the historian Celano had briefly described some of these. The early Christians hid in the same caverns as the Greeks. Here in vaults often 24 feet high, are the first simple Christian churches and cemeteries.

Belisarius, the Byzantine Imperial General, in the reign of Justinian in AD 549 slipped his troops into the town via aqueducts which ran under the walls, and captured the city which he had failed to reduce by blocking the aqueducts, because the citizens could still get enough water from their wells. In 1442 Diomede Carafa, Alfonso I's General, sent his troops to attack through an aqueduct and defeated the Angevins.

In the 1500s the Spanish Viceroys alarmed at the congestion within the city, forbade any more building; carts with stones or bricks were denied access to the town. Then the Neapolitans excavated further vast underground areas, and with the stone extracted, built upper storeys to their palaces, houses, castles, churches and convents without damaging the water supply. These caverns provided air raid shelters between 1941 and 1944 when over 281,000 bombs fell on Naples.

Around 700 caves have been identified under the old part of Naples. Unexpected secrets are still doubtless to be found within them. The most famous catacombs are those of San Gennaro extra Moenia, and San Gaudiosio under the church of Santa Maria alla Sanità, and lesser ones at San Lorenzo and San Paolo Maggiore.

The catacombs of S Gennaro have a large sign on the hill leading up to Capodimonte in Via Capodimonte at the church of the Madre del Buon Consiglio. There are guided visits each morning from the church. These catacombs go back to the second century AD. Here were found the remains of several bishops, including St Gennaro himself, who gave his name to the whole complex. The Prince of Benevento, who placed them in Duomo where they can still be found, removed the bodies in 831 AD.

Underground there are interesting frescoes, paintings and mosaics of saints and apostles and carvings of Christian symbols. Note especially the frescoes of the oldest image of St Gennaro from the fifth century, with a monogram of Christ and the letters Alpha and Omega; on the floor above are frescoes of Adam and Eve, and after those David and Goliath - and a unique work showing the Construction of the Tower of Babylon. Also, notice that there is an image encircled by a halo (eighth century) of Christ holding a scroll. The height of these catacombs, which are on two levels is impressive - as are the large passageways. In one area is a marble Priapus - evidence that this cult was alive here under the Romans. An eighth century font shows this catacomb was used as a place for normal Christian worship.

The catacombs of S Gaudiosio and San Severo are in the Sanità area that was originally outside the city walls; they were much used for burial in the Graeco-Roman period. Access is gained only on Sunday mornings by guided tours from the church of S Maria delle Sanità. If you have the time do not miss visiting them. Under the Sanità there is a large underground area with communicating underground cemeteries. The main catacombs are developed around the tomb of the Saint Bishop of Bythnia who, persecuted by vandals, came to Naples and died. Here are frescoes and remains and paintings from various periods, amongst which is a jewelled cross, four evangelical symbols, a bust of Christ, a fresco with pictures of St Peter and others and a painting of S Sossio of Miseno. There are numerous interesting mosaics, some in poor condition. In a corridor dug out in 1600 there are macabre sights. Bodies were placed on hollow chairs and allowed to dessicate; when they had dried out the skeletons were walled up with only the skull protruding. Then the wall covering the rest of the skeleton was decorated with frescoes, reminding onlookers of the features of the deceased.

The excavations at S Lorenzo Maggiore are open most mornings (but not Tuesdays). The entrance is in the cloister, and below there are archeological remains from the Greek, Roman and medieval periods. There is a Greek city wall from the fourth century BC, a vast Roman building from the first or second century AD, where the public treasure was housed and some shops (dyers, vase-makers and a bakery) together with a public meeting place from the eighth century AD. These are all evidence of the prosperity of the former Greek and Roman cities on the site of Naples.

The Associazione Culturale of Naples advertise extensively several times a week tours of the 'underground city'. The tours start from the prestigious Gambrinus Café in the Piazza Trieste e Trento, near the Royal Palace. Do not fall for this. They only take you to large caverns used as air raid shelters during the Second World War. No English is spoken, but there are many jokes in Italian. Go for the real thing at S Gaudiso or S Maria della Sanità. Unfortunately the tours from la Sanità are at the moment, confined to Sunday mornings. However a smaller interesting underground area is open every day at S Paolo Maggiore, close to S Lorenzo. This area is not true catacombs but rather a fascinating series of cisterns and water systems in old brick quarries. Greatly expanded by the Romans, they cover several hundred acres and several miles of water canals.

7
From Cuma to Capua

After the endless miles of urbanization from Naples it is a joy to reach Cuma, which stands in its pristine, luxuriant countryside, with vines and fruit trees. To the east is the nearby prominent arch of the Arco Felice, built by the Emperor Domitian to support his road to give easier access to Pozzuoli and Misenium from the Via Appia. Some of Domitian's original paving stones remain. The acropolis of Cuma on a hill rises abruptly from the plain.

Cuma was the oldest Greek settlement in Southern Italy, dating back to around 750 BC. In 421 BC Cuma fell to the Samnites and later like the rest of Campania, to the Romans. However unlike Capua, she stayed faithful to Rome against Hannibal in the Punic war. The town was more or less destroyed by the Saracens in 995 and became a den of criminals and outlaws until the Government of Naples exterminated the place in 1207. The whole locality became forgotten and buried under fallen masonry and dense vegetation until the time of the Bourbons.

An uphill walk from the entrance leads to the much-visited Cave of the Sibyl (described by Virgil) opposite, which is a chasm that is the entrance to the enormous Roman 'crypt.' The Cave of the Sibyl is fascinating; excavated in 1932 it is 144 yards long and 16 feet high. Openings to the west give views of the sea, and galleries to the left were used first as water cisterns and then as Christian tombs. The end room was until recently, considered to be the Holy of Holies where the sibyl possessed by gods uttered her prophecies. However, recent researchers believe her room was not here, but in another gallery below. Still a walk through the so-called Cave of the Sibyl is a moving experience. Latest studies indicate it was built for defense.

The vast Roman crypt is not open to visitors; it was bored right through the Monte di Cuma from west to east - a tremendous work of hand labour. Christian symbols inside show it was used as a catacomb by an early Christian community. A fourth or fifth century baptismal font has been found. It was probably a vast water reservoir.

A pathway from Sibyl's Cave leads up through trees - on Via Sacra to temples on top of the acropolis. Halfway up is the site of the temple of Apollo, built in the Greek Samnite period and made into a Christian church in the sixth century AD.

Continuing up the Via Sacra you come to the site of the Temple of Jupiter - originally also Greek, and later converted into a Christian church. A large circular basin for baptism by total immersion has survived well. Only the bases of the pillars of these temples remain, and to gather what they looked like when they were complete you need to go to Paestum, where similar sixth century Doric temples still stand in all their glory. From the temple of Jupiter the view along the coast is magnificent. You can see the waves breaking on the shore for many miles to the north towards Gaeta, and little of the hideous modern development is visible because of pine trees along the coast, while to the south Ischia and Procida stand out amid a shimmering sea.

In Roman times the grand forum of the city was removed from the top of the acropolis to the plain to facilitate communication with the Roman cities to the north and south. Excavations, which are still going on, have uncovered large sections of the new forum and its principal buildings. On the south side a large square has a fine tufa portico with emblems of arms. There are also the remains of a particularly imposing temple on the western side of the forum, while to the north stand the ruins of a large thermal building. It is uncertain how soon visitors will be admitted to the Roman remains in the plain, but these are evidence of the remaining great importance of Cuma in Roman times after Pozzuoli and Capua had risen and outstripped her.

North from Pozzuoli Via Domizia and Sessa Arunca

An old Roman road Via Campana linked Pozzuoli with Capua, bypassing Naples. On both sides of the road (in a now rather built up area) from Pozzuoli to Quarto there is an almost continuous succession of Roman monumental tombs. The most imposing groups are along the two mile stretch around Celle. Immediately behind the Rome - Naples railway stands the gate that marks the end of the town of Pozzuoli and the beginning of the Via Campana; there is a long well preserved section of the road here clearly indicated by the tombs flanking it. The façades of the tombs are ruined and the plaster stucco and painted decorations have almost completely disappeared. Yet to anyone interested in classical remains this seldom visited area is of exceptional interest. On the left of the road there is a splendid two storey mausoleum with a circular drum upon a square base.

The deep cutting of the Rome - Naples railway crosses the old road and uncovered a 100 metre series of tombs, which can best be seen from the bridge over the railway. Two kilometres further north in the S Vito area the old Via Campana appears in its original width lined with tombs and other structures on both sides; these are most impressive. Particularly look at the fork of Via Campana with a by road for a beautiful mausoleum, partly concealed by a farmhouse. This large area of striking tombs reflects the importance and wealth of Pozzuoli in the time of the Roman Empire. They are well described with photographs in *The Phlegreaen Fields* by Amedeo Maiuri that is available in an English translation. In grandeur and interest they are the equal of the much more famous tombs on the Via Appia Antica in Rome - although less extensive.

However, in 95 AD the much hated Roman Emperor Domitian, shortly before his assassination, constructed a coastal road from Minturno to Pozzuoli and Baia, cutting out the giant staging post of Capua and building bridges over both the wide rivers Volturno and Garigliano - a great engineering achievement in a region of swamps and forests. This is further evidence of the great importance of Pozzuoli as a port and also of Baia as a playground for the Roman aristocracy. With the fall of Rome the Via Domizia was abandoned and the bridges collapsed. After the Second World War the Italian Government reconstructed it, and today it is a convenient alternative route to take into northern Campania. Fifty years ago I recall driving with an Italian friend [the site then was not enclosed] to the top of the acropolis at Cuma and seeing stretching away to the north an unbroken vista of empty sandy beach and pine wood. Revisiting in 1998 I was shocked. Concrete has taken over. For many miles north of Cuma the coast is ruined by an almost unbroken development of houses, hotels and restaurants catering to summer bathers seeking an escape from the burning heat of Naples.

Cuma itself remains a charming oasis, surrounded by most fertile fields, vines, oranges and lemon groves, but within a few miles the concrete jungle begins. There was always a small bathing beach at Marina di Cuma just northwest of the ancient city. Writing in 1947, Maiouri in his *Passegiate Campana* pointed out that Ostia, the bathing resort of modern Romans, had produced the most ugly bathing beach architecture of any capital and that it would be 'intolerable' if anything like this erupted on the unspoiled littoral to the north of Cuma from where 'the most beautiful views in all Campania' were visible. Being a classicist he invoked the goddess Cloacina and implored her to protect 'the religious and deep silence of the Cuman coast.' Alas, his worst fears have been fulfilled. For many miles up the coast there is ribbon development with all the paraphernalia of cheaply built seaside towns - Napoli Maritima, or Naples-by-the-sea. I could hardly believe my own eyes when I saw it.

Still the recently built Via Domizia has its interests. In some places the old paving stones of the Roman Domizian road are visible, and one pillar of the Roman bridge over the Garigliano can be seen in the river. However, the great forest of Silva Gallinara in which Virgil wrote about Aeneas wandering has in recent years almost completely disappeared, and the marshes are now all drained and replaced by farms with modern buildings.

Near Lake Patria, close to the road, stand the ruins of the Roman town of Liternum in an area as hideous as any part of Blackpool. The Victorians loved to visit Liternum by carriage and described it as being within a hamlet. Here Scipio (237-83 BC), the conqueror of Africa and victor of the war over Hannibal, lived out his final days with veterans of his campaigns after being driven out of public life by Cato. Livy and Seneca wrote of visiting Scipio's villa and tomb at Liternum, but today they are lost despite extensive excavations carried out in the 1920s and 1930s. A bust of Scipio was found at Liternum but no trace of his villa or tomb. A tall column from the temple and remains of the theatre and basilica can be seen. These ruins so appreciated by Victorians are neglected today and are often closed to visitors. Byron wrote: 'Scipio buried by the upbraiding shore.' The 'upbraiding shore' can now only be reached through a hideous sprawl of seaside buildings.

When Allied troops reached the Lake of Patria in 1943 they found an important statue of the Roman senator Antona at a farm; they thought it was Mussolini, despite massive moustaches and threw it down a well. In 1824, Lady Blessington complained of the odours at Liternum. These have gone, but I would rather put up with what she called 'the insalubrious smells of the marsh' than with the concrete.

Although in 1939 Maiuri wrote of the Via Domizia around Castel Volturno as an empty countryside with masses of small shrubs and junipers and only a solitary duck shooter with his gun, today it is an unattractive seaside sprawl of buildings that continues over the Volturno and almost to the Garigliano. When you look down on the waters and examine the width of these two rivers close to their exit to the sea, you appreciate how great was the Roman engineering achievement in building them. Not until one reaches Baia di Domizia well north of Mondragone (famous formerly for its wine and Roman remains but today more for its extensive bathing huts), does the coast become attractive with pine woods and lengthy extents of unblemished sand, while the mountains to the north and west are near the coast. Here are some nicely built hotels. Now we are in the heart of the most fertile part of the Campania; there are many buffaloes, which fifty years ago were hand milked in the fields, but nowadays are kept in large compounds to be machine milked to provide the raw material for the popular cheese *mozzarella*.

Taking a road to the right, shortly before the junction of the Via Domizia with the Via Appia at Minturno, brings you in a few miles to the charming unspoiled medieval town of Sessa Arrunca. Curiously, neither Augustus Hare nor Charles Lister (*Between Two Seas - A Walk Down the Appian Way*) liked Sessa. I find Sessa delightful. I first knew the town in the spring of 1944 when I was responsible for 900 Italian soldiers and their 750 mules and horses. They had changed sides and were being used to carry rations, ammunition and post to the front line infantry in the hills around Casino. After nasty experiences in this battle we were sent to Sessa to rest. It was an ideal rest town unscathed by the fighting, although it was in view of the Germans from the high mountains to the north, but fortunately well out of range of their guns. The mules and horses were bivouacked in long lines on the olive terraces adjoining the town and the other officers and I billeted ourselves in medieval houses in the town. I found the inhabitants of Sessa to be most charming and friendly. There were a few of the nobility who owned land in the area and we were glad to stay in their decaying Sessa palaces to escape from the bombing of Naples by the Germans. I remember them as being most hospitable, and how they liked playing bridge. The ordinary people of Sessa were most welcoming, as they still were when I revisited the town 54 years later. In 1944 the ducal castle was the headquarters of General Juin, who came here with his two mountain divisions of Moroccan Goums and created a complete surprise when he attacked through the mountains and cut the road from Rome to Casino - thus being responsible for winning the Battle of Casino, which the Americans and British had lost.

The Goums were difficult troops to control; they would only obey their own French officers, who went straight from St. Cyr to Morocco and never served outside Africa. '*I Goumi*' as the Italians called them, raped young Italians of either sex and caused such chaos that I lent my jeep to a young patrician Neapolitan officer to take the Bishop of Sessa to Naples to complain to the cardinal about the occurrences. I know the cardinal spoke to General Alexander, with whom he was friendly, but I fear it was to little avail.

Some of the olive groves and terraces where I bivouacked my mules and horses, just outside the walls of Sessa, have succumbed to new buildings but the walled town is entirely untainted and very quiet except on market days; rather 'sacrilegiously', you can take a car into the old narrow streets. In front of the cathedral there is a sweet little piazza.

The cathedral of San Pietro dates from 1103, and many Roman remains from the pagan temple of Mercury underneath it were used in its construction; you can see the Roman columns in the nave and crypt and a Roman architrave in the pediment above the main door and other Roman items in the walls of the adjoining Bishop's house. The cathedral portico is studded with interesting animals - wolves, goats, sheep and lions enjoying a meal. I particularly like the two wild boars on each side at the top, and the elephants guarding the main door. Above the main door is a Roman architrave taken from the Roman theatre, with two panthers in front of a large vase from which a vine grows with two masks over the centre of the portico. There are also stone carvings dating from 1300, with the story of St Peter very well preserved.

Inside, the attractive pulpit of 1224 is rich with mosaic. It is a square resting on six columns, propped on six little lions with five looking at the main door and the sixth in the opposite direction. There is also a spectacular paschal candlestick of the same date. The Arabesque majolica floor of the cathedral is magnificent and blazes with colour, as does the baroque decoration of the chapel of the Blessed Sacrament to the right of the altar, above which there is a fine picture by Luca Giordano (1693-1705). There are further interesting Roman columns in the thirteenth century crypt.

The Sessa cathedral is a little gem - seldom visited, but beautifully cared for and surrounded by the early bishop's elegant palace. Look particularly at the lovely Gothic picture of Jonah emerging from the whale - done by a good artist around 1250.

There are plenty of other churches in Sessa but it is best to visit them in the morning; however so obliging are the guardians that polite importuning will usually secure admission. The large church of Sant' Annunciata should not be missed. It is wide and has twin towers with a large pediment broken by a central window. It was originally built in 1489, but elegantly restored by Vaccaro. Note the white marble tomb of the Spanish soldier Don Luigo di Serriera, and the old picture over the altar on the right, which gives a good idea of old Sessa with its panorama of medieval halls and towers. The fine majolica floor has been worn away except for the portions where the confessionals (now removed) must have rested for centuries.

Both inside and outside the walls of the town are clusters of old churches, hospices and convents dating back to between the thirteenth and fifteenth centuries, although many were altered during the baroque period. Try to see the church of S Giacomo and the fine cloisters at San Stefano and San Domenico. As you walk through the narrow streets you see many interesting windows and doorways recalling the existence of many fine medieval houses. The elderly inhabitants of Sessa appear to have forgiven the Goums for some of their misdeeds, and prefer to talk with pride of de Gaulle coming and inspecting his troops there. Little English is spoken but you would not find a friendlier town either now or during the Second World War.

It is rich in Roman remains; its origins go back to the Etruscans of the seventh century BC and she flourished - especially in the time of Augustus (63 BC-14 AD). From the Roman theatre there is a splendid view over the Gulf of Gaeta and to the mountains. This fine Roman theatre, which was excavated and kept beautifully clean thirty years ago, is now overgrown and neglected, but the lovely *crypto portico* (underground gallery) nearby is well maintained and should be visited. There are also Roman baths. Even more impressive is the twenty one arched Roman bridge which links Sessa Arunca with the Via Appia - built in the time of Hadrian (76-138 AD) to bridge a small gorge and a tiny stream (Travolta). It is still in perfect condition and one of the best preserved Roman bridges in south Italy. On the way to the bridge from Sessa you pass interesting Roman tombs and an excellent section of the old Roman road with well-preserved flagstones. The setting of the bridge is idyllic with luxuriant green vegetation and orange and lemon groves - an ideal spot for a picnic. From the bridge you can hear the angelus being rung from many churches in Sessa and see the sun on Sessa's cliffs, towers, majolica domes and walls of yellow tufa stone and at the same time admire the view of the high mountains to the north. Before leaving Sessa look at the ducal castle dating back to the eleventh century. The police, who were delighted to show me the magnificent view of the Gulf of Gaeta and the golden Tyrrhenian Sea from its roof, now occupy it.

Anyone interested in medieval frescoes should go to nearby Carano, Rongolise and Lauro where the twelfth century frescoes are noteworthy, but the brilliant fresco of 1100 at Lauro has recently been moved to the museum in the Royal Palace at Caserta.

From Sessa there is a delightful drive to the east up the hills to Roccamonfina. Roccamonfina, the site of an ancient volcano, stands at 2,000 feet in beautifully wooded hills as high as 3,000 feet. Gorgeous chestnut and acacia woods cover the hills, and there are magnificent views. The air is cool at this height even in summer and this country is ideal for hiking but is little visited by tourists. Indeed at Roccamonfina, as at Sessa Arunca there is no hotel and no restaurant. From Roccamonfina signs show the way to the attractively situated sanctuary of Maria dei Lattari through nice woods and the village of Gallo. To the right of the sanctuary there is a chestnut tree, said to have been planted by San Bernadino of Siena who founded the monastery in the early fifteenth century. The Franciscans here will welcome men but do not, at the time of writing, allow women into the monastery - only into the church. The monastery was restored on Mussolini's orders and you can see the original fifteenth century loggias.

The wooden doors of 1508 have interesting wooden locks. There are remains of fifteenth century frescoes and a very early figure of the Madonna and Child from the tenth century. The road continues through lovely chestnut woods with fine views, especially from the wireless station, of the Volturno Valley past a reconstructed chapel.

Descending to the southwest from the volcanic heights of Roccamonfina through masses of chestnuts heavily coppiced and worked by mainly industrious foresters with small tractors largely to produce pergolas for the vines, we come to Teano in a fertile valley. It is a well populated but peaceful town with nice views, heavily damaged in the Second World War. Here in October 1860, the victorious Garibaldi met King Victor Emmanuel II at the head of the Piedmont army and sealed the fate of the last Bourbon king, then hemmed in his final stronghold at Gaeta.

Just outside Teano through luxuriant gardens and fruit trees lie the unexcavated ruins of a very large Roman amphitheatre. There are rough houses built into the arches and it is a forgotten but impressive relic of the Roman Empire in rural surroundings. There are also relics of four Greek temples. In the early days of the Roman Empire Teano was popular with the Roman nobility who built their luxurious villas on the slopes down to the River Teano. It was at one time the most flourishing inland city of Campania after Capua.

Teano

Teano cathedral was built in 1116 and modernised by Andrea Vaccaro, who also built the Sant' Annunziata here. Sadly apart from the façade it was completely destroyed by bombs in 1943. In the atrium (forecourt) of the cathedral there are two interesting Roman sphinxes in red granite and as usual in this region there are three naves divided by columns with Corinthian capitals. The fine thirteenth century pulpit is largely a reconstruction but it is worth looking at the crucifix painted on wood above the high altar, thought to be by Barrile in 1330 The locals say that the workers used this historic piece of woodwork as a lunch table when they were repairing the bomb damage, but happily it is unharmed. Near the high altar you can see in a marble vessel the water of a spring. St Paride is believed to have cleansed and left pure for his followers. Despite the war damage, the winding narrow streets of old Teano have many relics of medieval churches and palaces including a strange arched building with a waterfall within. Parts of the wall of the Roman acropolis can be seen in the Palazzo Fondi in the Piazza della Vittoria. In the Via San Benedetto is the church of S Benedetto. When the Saracens sacked the abbey of Monte Cassino in 883, the monks fled here bringing with them the original copy of the Rule of St. Benedict.

Going south from Teano on the *autostrada* we find on the left the village of Calvi Vecchia built on the site of the Roman town of Cales, a Roman colony founded in BC 332, and whose wine was much praised by Horace. It contains a small basilica and the remains of an amphitheatre and a theatre. We are now well into the plain of Campania that can yield, in addition to rich plantations of fruit trees and vines, two crops of grain and one of hay each year. Consequently it has always been one of the most densely populated areas of Italy and still is.

Before entering the Capuas from the *autostrada,* it is worth making a visit to San Angelo in Formis to find one of the most fascinating churches in Campania for both architecture and frescoes. You may have to search for the caretaker to gain access. It is a Lombard Romanesque basilica, originally built around 900 on the ruins of a big temple dedicated to the goddess Diana Tifatina, protectress of the forests. It was finished under the supervision of the famous Abbot Desiderius of Monte Cassino in 1073; there is an inscription to him on the architrave of the portico. Alas it was badly damaged in the 1980 earthquake but considerable sums of government money have gone into the restoration of its structure and of the frescoes - and it is now in good condition again.

This is one of the best examples of medieval ecclesiastical architecture in south Italy. There is a delicate portico with five arches held up by Corinthian columns clearly taken from the temple, and the church floor inside is partly ascribed to the temple. The splendid Byzantine style frescoes were finished in the second half of the eleventh century and painted by the same artist who worked on the famous frescoes at Monte Cassino abbey so sadly destroyed by Allied bombing in 1944. Above the arches in the central nave is depicted the life of Jesus; the central apse above the altar has *Christ Giving His Blessing*, and on the back wall opposite is a chilling scene of the Last Judgement. The insides of the arches are also gracefully painted. Their colours, perhaps helped by the 1980s restoration, are brilliant and show what must have been links to the exotic colouring of all the frescoed churches of the Gothic period, of which now so little remains.

The unattached bell tower (campanile) must be as old as the church, and the enormous stone blocks used to construct it have obviously been taken from the spectacular amphitheatre of Capua Vetere. The upper storey has attractive coloured bricks, and it is thought to have been the earliest prototype for the innumerable campaniles of Campania.

Behind the church steps lead to the old temple. Excavation work is in progress and it is shortly to be opened to the public. Pause a moment and look at the spectacular view and take in Campania's green fertility and the charming Monte Roccamonfina to your right. My wartime recollection of the badly bombed S Angelo in Formis is clouded by a horrifying incident, which I did not witness but was told about by distressed Italians. In November 1943 when the front was at Cassino, British soldiers brought 13 young Italian prisoners all from northern Italy in a lorry, together with a priest Dom Guiseppe Ferrier, who was trying to console them. Soon 13 shots rang out, and the young Italians lay dead. They had been accused of passing through the line on a spying mission and sending information back to Mussolini's Republican Army, and of committing acts of sabotage and refusing to give the names of their accomplices. In the cemetery of Santa Maria Caius Vetere there is a tablet, which gives their names and honours their memory. Their execution may have been justified under the rules of the Geneva Convention, but its memory leaves a nasty taste.

If you have time, I would advise a trip to San Leucio before visiting the Capuas. Going south, turn left from the SS87 *autostrada* through Vaccheria and you come to San Leucio with its Piazza della Sete (Silk Square) - more like a roundabout than a square. Go through a Bourbon arch with elegant lions on top, and you come to the old silk factory where they still possess some Bourbon silks and an ancient machine for making silk that is in perfect working order. Adjoining on the street running to either side are the homes for the silk workers - rather like a row of British alms houses, but more elegant. They are the work of Ferdinand I who made a bold social experiment here. He wanted to revive the ancient craft of making damask and brocade not only for his palaces but also to sell to the aristocracy of his kingdom as well as abroad.

King Ferdinand took a great interest in the colony of silk workers at San Leucio. It was a pet project to which he devoted much time although he usually ignored the serious matters of state, leaving them to his wife Maria Carolina. His detractors accused him of founding the colony just for his sexual satisfaction, as it is known he liked sturdy country wenches. This

NAPLES, What most tourists never see

seems unfair. It is true it was his only social experiment but he genuinely wanted to found a model industrial town, and drew up sensible rules and insisted on good wages, free public health and free education. His idea was to call the town Ferdinandopolis, but his model town really remained an arcadian dream because he took fright with the terror of the French Revolution, and with the massacre of the aristocrats in Paris he ceased to be a benevolent dictator at San Leucio. Actually, the colony and the silk works thrived under the French occupation. Ferdinand himself built a huge yellow and white palace as a weekend retreat in 1776 known as the Casino Reale di Belvedere, although it was only four miles away from his own palace in Caserta. Ferdinand liked it because of the wonderful view from the terrace. Today the Casino is in disrepair, and only artificial silk is made in San Leucio. This can be bought in one little shop in the piazza called the Bottega della Tessetura della Arte where they specialize in intricate silk, and their shop has an atmosphere reminiscent of an eighteenth century workshop. At San Leucio there is now a large and well looked after game and wildlife reserve that preserves the atmosphere of the Bourbons when it was a shooting paradise for them.

The 1855 John Murray handbook tells of an Ilex forest at San Leucio 'abounding' in game. Perhaps this is not surprising because the same book states that a few miles south at the Casino Reale Di Carditello near San Tammaro, the king kept a game farm for rearing prodigious numbers of pheasants and wild boar. There is a wall 18 feet high to keep the game in, and a prettily decorated cottage, which can still be seen. Perhaps this rearing of game for shooting is not as out of date as it seems; in state owned woods in Tuscany the government sells licences to individuals to shoot so many pheasants and wild boar. I also came across a farm where intensive artificial rearing of pheasants and wild boar was being carried out in the same way as the Bourbons did in the eighteenth and nineteenth centuries in the Kingdom of Naples.

Turn to the right off the *autostrada* near Caserta, and you come to old and new Capua. Capua (Santa Maria Vetere) was an important and rich town even in the time of the Etruscans (598 BC). Fear of the Samnites caused the Etruscans to make an alliance with Rome in 340 BC. By then it was a wealthy and prosperous city much influenced by Greek culture with its own coinage. After the Battle of Canna (216 BC), the Capuans had a dispute with Rome and treacherously opened their gates to Hannibal (247-182 BC); however the mild climate and the luxury of the city and the allurements of the beautiful young women were fatal to the morale of

Hannibal's army. After five years spent in bliss in Capua, the army was in no fit state to resist the Romans. After a long siege the Romans recaptured it in 211 BC. The Romans then took revenge on Capuan leaders for their betrayal of the city to Hannibal. Livy in his twenty third book describes in considerable detail what happened to the Capuans. The Capuans then lost their civil rights, but under Rome Capua flourished almost incredibly. The population reached 300,000 for it was the great staging post for both the port of Pozzuoli to the south for trade with Africa and Spain, and Brindisi to the east for trade with Greece, Constantinople and all the Middle East. In addition to an enormous amphitheatre, sumptuous temples, baths and gymnasiums were built and there was the largest school for gladiators within the Roman Empire. The Appian Way passed through an arch at the northern end of the city, known as Hadrian's Arch (Arco d'Adriano) (76-138 AD), and the foundations can still be seen. Hadrian did much for Capua, and died at nearby Baia after being an invalid for many years. In 73 BC, the Spartacus revolt began in Capua. The nucleus was a band of 74 gladiators who came from the gladiator school in Capua, and the revolt developed so rapidly that at one time it appeared it would topple the Roman Empire. In 456 AD the city was devastated by the Vandals under Gaiseric, but somehow recovered much of its former prosperity and the Games continued in the amphitheatre until in 840 AD when the Saracens took the city and devastated it - so that the inhabitants fled to found New Capua nearby.

The ruins of the amphitheatre at Old Capua, that was never used after 840, are fantastic. It was taller than it now appears because nearly all the stonework for the upper storey was removed to build new Capua and Caserta. There are no signposts to it (and it is not easy to find in the centre of a large modern town). The amphitheatre is one of the oldest in Italy and second in size only to the Coliseum in Rome. The substructure passages and dens for the wild beasts are especially well preserved and can be visited. There must have been eighty underground passages. Gladiatorial combat is believed to have originated here, and there were awnings to protect the spectators from the sun. In the ruins of the amphitheatre which could seat 100,000 spectators, there is plenty of space and well cared for attractive gardens. A huge area was flagged to accommodate the enormous crowds. Note especially near the center a good Roman axe and fasces, much admired in Mussolini's day but neglected today except by students and fans of Fascism.

In return for a tip the custodian of the amphitheatre will take you to the nearby fascinating temple of Mithraeum, in Piazza Mazzini. This was only discovered in 1922 and is one of the best of its kind in Europe. It is a rectangular room where rituals dedicated to Mithras were practised from the 1st to 3rd centuries. Mithras was a god in Persia and his cult developed tremendously in the first three centuries AD into a widespread religion which became a rival to Christianity. It even reached as far north as York. Roman soldiers brought the cult back from Persia.

The worship of Mithras was always celebrated in similar underground temples of which the one at Capua is probably the best example. A perpetual fire was kept going before the altar. Women were given no place - perhaps just as well because initiates were sprinkled with blood from a bull slain as a sacrifice in front of the altar.

In the Capuan Mithraeum, on a back wall behind the altar is a fine colourful picture of a god killing a bull; there are stone seats for members of the cult. This room is eerie and sinister but nowhere else in Italy can you feel so close to this strange religion. The cult was banned in 395 AD, fortunately for Christianity.

Opposite the Mithraeum is the classical museum full of local relics well worth seeing. It is amusingly and interestingly described by Charles Lister who 45 years ago made great friends with its young director who is long since dead. According to Lister *tombaroli* (robbers of tombs) were having a heyday in Old Capua in the 1950s and 1960s, driving off in their battered cars with sack loads of valuable Etruscan and Roman remains. The director of the museum complained to Lister that he was being assailed with so many officially discovered Etruscan and Roman relics in such quantities that he could not cope with them. This museum is very rewarding although some of the best finds in Capua have been taken to the Naples museum.

Town planning of Capua goes back to the Etruscans in 425 BC - it was their power base in South Italy. According to aerial photographs it was octagonal with six broad east to west avenues with many transverse streets defended by an irregular circuit of walls enclosing about 400 acres. It is an early example of Etruscan town planning only equalled at Marzabotto near Bologna. In its heyday it must have sprawled outside the walls as the transit post between Rome, Pozzuoli and Brindisi. Today there are few Roman remains to be seen above ground. It cries out for excavation however buildings, many very recent and increasing in number, cover almost every bit of ground. Still you can have a wallow in the museum and the giant ruins of the amphitheatre, and imagine what life in the seething heart of the Roman Empire was like.

On the road to Caserta through intensive modern development you come to two large interesting Roman remains in exceptionally good condition, that stand out for their noble architecture in contrast to the modern rubbish which surrounds them. These buildings were much visited by the Victorians; today, they are firmly closed and shuttered. The larger building was a Roman prison. It is worth stopping to look at their exteriors. The church of San Prisio close by on a road to the left, contains sixth century tomb mosaics and according to Lister was once a temple of Priapus where the locals still practised pagan obscenities to the god of fecundity.

William Hamilton in 1781 noted that not fifty miles north of Naples 'devotion is still paid to Priapus, the obscene divinity of the ancients in Catholic churches, and phallic rings were sold. In the place of Priapus St Cosmo was honoured, and the priests collected alms in effect designed for Priapus.' I am informed traces of this pagan cult can still be found not far from Capua.

Three miles north from ancient Capua lies new Capua. You drive along a heavily built up road and find it on the banks of the Volturno. The ancient Via Appia went right through the town of new Capua, which was founded in 856 after the destruction of the old town to the south by the Saracens. A great quantity of giant stone blocks from the amphitheatre at Capua Vetre has been used to build the numerous churches, palaces and other monuments in new Capua.

There had been a Roman town here (Casilinum) at which the Romans had put up a heroic defence against Hannibal in 216 BC, but it became ruined and deserted. Parts of the mantle of old Capua fell on new Capua; the last Bishop of old Capua became the first of new Capua as did their last Count. Capua fell to the Lombards but became a jewel in the crown of the Two Sicilies under the Normans with the enormous fertility of the surrounding land. Frederick II gave it a famous gate in 1247 but it was destroyed in 1557, although paintings and engravings survive in the local museum. Frederick himself fell in love with the town and called it Capua Fidelis. After a bloodthirsty siege the town fell to the French in 1501.

On 24 July 1501 new Capua was burned by the French on the orders of Cesare Borgia son of Pope Sixtus VI, and 5,000 inhabitants were massacred, having been treacherously invited to a banquet after paying a big fine. Each year on that day the bells still toll their lamentations.

Garibaldi fought the Battle of Volturno around Capua in October 1860. For once, the Bourbon army fought gallantly in great contrast to their poor performance in Sicily. Garibaldi came very close to defeat and narrowly escaped capture, but at the last moment his luck turned and the result was a draw - although the battle is often interpreted by historians as yet another Garibaldi victory. The royalist troops had crossed the Tolturno at new Capua over the Roman bridge, and reached old Capua in a fog. There they narrowly failed to capture Garibaldi in a horse carriage killing his coachman, but Garibaldi managed to jump out and run away despite his 'gammy' leg. The railway from Caserta to Capua had recently been opened and Garibaldi saved the day by bringing up reinforcements by train. Soon after the Piedmontese army arrived from the north to save Garibaldi's bacon which according to Sir Henry Elliot, the British Ambassador and author of *Some Revolutions*) got the Garibaldians 'out of their difficulties' - because 'the young King with 40,000 or 50,000 men is still holding his ground,' and 'ugly things are doing here which very much lower one's opinion of Garibaldi.' In the end the Piedmontese army, after defeating the papal troops in the Papal States, arrived at Teano on the 26th of October and immediately proceeded to bombard new Capua very heavily. New Capua then surrendered on the 2nd of November. But this bombardment of Italians earned King Victor Emmanuel II, like his Neapolitan predecessor Ferdinand II, the nickname of 'King Bomba.'

In October 1943 there was another Battle of Volturno between the United States 5th Army and the Germans; fortunately it soon ended in an Allied victory, but the chief damage to the town came from a single American air raid on 9th of September 1943, two days after the Salerno landings. The raid was quite unnecessary. There were no Germans in the town although they were using the bridges over the Volturno to reach the Salerno battlefield.

I first saw Capua a few weeks after the bombardment. It was at very low ebb. Many streets were blocked by rubble and there was a sweet sickly smell of dead bodies emitting from the ruins. A parish priest told me that when the bombers came overhead all the inhabitants cheered, thinking the Americans were allies because of the armistice; instead, the bombs rained down and, according to him, there was not a single German in the town. I believe him.

After having seen the town in such a distressed state over 50 years ago, it was a great joy to find it prosperous in 1998. It is a beautiful medieval town, although the gaps in the streets caused by the bombing have been replaced by modern buildings. Nowadays the town is full of offices of insurance companies. I remember a remount depot there with the mules and horses together with cattle stabled in the courtyards of some big houses. These have all gone and the medieval streets are now thronged with cars.

There is a complicated traffic system that I never fathomed. The best thing is to find a parking space and discover the treasures of Capua on foot.

Soon after her foundation in the ninth century New Capua was surrounded by massive walls and fortifications so that today, once you pass through her narrow gates, you find a peaceful sheltered atmosphere far different from the unsightly modern commercial development which laps her walls. The town is aubergine shaped and fits snugly into the bends of the Volturno, with fine views of the mountains from the gates and towers.

The Via Duomo crosses the town from south to north. Take a look at the Palazzo del Municipio (1561) where you can see seven impressive marble busts taken from the old Capua amphitheatre. Originally these busts ran in a frieze around the whole circumference of the amphitheatre serving as keystones for the arches, but there are only four left in their original positions on the amphitheatre.

The cathedral was built soon after the city was founded but alas, was almost completely destroyed in the atrocious American air raid in 1943 - apart from the atrium that is a square courtyard with 20 classical columns resembling the atrium of Salerno. The old crypt with 22 ancient columns has been restored, but the main cathedral had to be entirely rebuilt. Fortunately the charming tower which dates back to the ninth century was almost undamaged. Its base is built of large stone blocks stolen from the amphitheatre, and the top built of attractive bricks. In the cathedral there is a magnificent thirteenth century paschal candle - one of the most beautiful of its kind.

To the left of the *Duomo* is a colourful market, there since the inception of the city and well designed as goods could be brought into it without crossing the city - while the citizens had easy access by straight roads.

On the further side of the river across the rebuilt Ponte Romano, are the remains of Emperor Frederick II's famous Capuan Gate (1239). In the Museo Campano insist on being shown an early painting of this in its former glory and reflect that the masons and carvers who made it were the direct heirs of those who worked on the ancient amphitheatre.

Crossing back over the Ponte Nuovo, you arrive at the Porto Napoli, a marble archway built at the end of the eleventh century. A few yards from there is the Via Appia and on the right is the Castello delle Pietre, the enormous palace of the Norman princes - so called because it is built of large blocks of stone from the amphitheatre. Begun in the eleventh century the castle was enlarged and embellished by Frederick II. Nearby is the church of San Marcello Maggiore, originally ninth century but rebuilt in 1313 and since restored. But it is symbolic to see one of the original churches from when Capua was founded. It was the scene of a vicious murder in front of the bishop who had just finished saying mass on the 20th of April 993, and still has a haunted feel. Note in the two square door frames a carving showing the story of Abraham - goats, lions and other animals are exquisitely done; this is a good reminder of the caliber of the artist who fled from Old Capua to the new town in the ninth century (Although according to some sources they may have been executed by Lombard sculptors in the twelfth century).

Go back under an arch to the Via Duomo and you find that this part of Capua is full of ancient churches and medieval palaces with a fascinating mix of styles. The Palazzo Fieramosca is thirteenth century and although restored, if you go into the courtyard you get a good idea of its original form; the tower on the right is definitely fourteenth century. There is a tablet in the tower recording that Ettore Fieramosca the hero of Barletta was born here. In 1505 he led his warriors out of Barletta to ignominiously defeat the French. Above the doorway can be seen the lilies of France.

New Capua, being built in one piece and on a cleared site is a town well planned. There are three long streets with the river at both ends and closed by the massive medieval and Renaissance walls and fortifications. It is easy to walk everywhere and enjoy the fascinating atmosphere of this sad, sleeping but unique and beautiful sun filled town. The Corso Appia swells out to form a square in front of the town hall (*Palazzo del Municipio*). Here is the fine church of the Annunziata; it sits on a tremendous stone base of blocks taken from the amphitheatre and is made of black lava stone and white plaster. Roads run to the east and west and piazzas to the north and south, so it is like a great square ship moored within the roads. The dome designed by Fontana soars spectacularly above it, and the campanile is dramatic floating with the other domes and towers against the dreamy blue sky of this ancient town.

The Museo Campano is housed in the fifteenth century palace of the Duke of Antignano. It is a feature of New Capua and is one of the most interesting provincial museums in south Italy. Whereas in the archeological museum in Naples you are overcome by the two treasure houses of Pompeii and Herculaneum, here you feel you are close to the everyday life and art of the people who enjoyed living in this delicious climate and fertile countryside many centuries ago.

The museum, approached through a pretty garden at the end of the

Via Duomo, contains a fine series of sculptures from ancient Capua and an extraordinary collection of mother goddesses and many interesting medieval sculptures. The statues of the mother goddesses came from the sanctuary of Mater Matuta, the early classical goddess of fecundity and maternity, and were found in 1845 near Santa Maria Capua Vetere. These statues span the fifth to first centuries BC. Offerings were made to this goddess in the hope of becoming pregnant or of giving birth to a healthy child. The stone women are seated with swaddled babies up to five or six on each arm. Once seen this votive goddess will never be forgotten, especially by those couples who have had their own problems producing healthy children.

There are also delightful Etruscan bronzes, a good collection of ceramics, excellent examples of Roman mosaics and a fine collection of ancient coins dating back to Magna Grecia. One room is devoted to sculpture from Frederick's Capuan Gate (including the picture of it) and in the picture gallery are good fifteenth century Neapolitan paintings.

In Victorian times, and even 50 years ago, there were no hotels in New Capua and scarcely a restaurant. Today, there are several of varying quality. I was lucky enough to stay in the Agritourist Massima Gia Sole, Via Giardini 31, (Telephone 0039 0823 961 108), a mile from the walls in green fields running along the Volturno river. It is a large baronial style country house that has belonged to the Pasca di Magliano family for four generations. They have a most productive fruit, grape and vegetable farm in a particularly nice angle of the Volturno. Their accommodation is lavish, the welcome most warm and the food excellent. A roaring log fire warms a large comfortable sitting room and there are masses of books about the history of Naples to read. It was a joy to eat their traditional Campanian home cooked food with plenty of vegetables and fruit from their own land - a welcome change from restaurant food, no matter how good it has been. But no English is spoken.

The road from Capua to Caserta is heavily built up and it is a great relief when one sees empty spaces and the Royal Palace and can admire its proportions. The Bourbon King Charles III started building the Caserta Royal palace in 1752, and employed the Dutch Luigi Vanvitelli (1700-1773) as architect. The king wanted to create a rival to Versailles in his kingdom of Naples. The main façade is a semicircle 750 feet long, and is rather monotonous, probably because the original design with arched raised towers at the corners and a tall central cupola were never completed. Originally, Charles wanted Caserta to be his administrative capital as well, but a vast plan for blocks of offices was never put into effect nor were proposed large barracks ever built. In the end, only the south wing was lived in. Behind are four courtyards, the decoration of which was never completed.

Inside the palace is impressive. Entering through a huge atrium you come to a hexagonal vestibule from which a spectacular staircase leads up to the royal apartments. Before attempting the steep staircase, look at the exceptionally well designed and pretty court theatre with tiered boxes in horseshoe shape and twelve beautiful columns from the forum at Pozzuoli. Here Ferdinands I and II delighted their guests with light operas and comedies by Goldoni (1707-1793) and others. The Hamiltons were frequent guests there, and Murat much appreciated the palace and theatre during his reign as King of Naples.

At the top of the stairs the was the first part to be lived in by royalty; look especially at the queen's boudoir and bathroom - the latter that had a gilded bath and gold tap. Ferdinand II (King Bomba) died in 1859 in the king's bedroom. As he was supposed to have died from an infectious disease, all the furniture and his belongings were burned immediately. The throne room was last decorated as late as 1845; however here the main interest is the sumptuous First Empire French furniture brought to Caserta by Murat. There is a splendid king's bathroom with a stone bath decorated with lion heads, and in the alabaster dressing table there is a scent fountain. Ask for or look for the enchanting nineteenth century picture of a duck by J. Tischbein - a fabulous bird painting. Tischbein was a friend and companion of Goethe.

Charles III was made ruler of Spain in 1759 and never lived at Caserta. The palace was completed by his successor Ferdinand I in 1774. In some ways Caserta outrivals Versailles. I find the dramatic staircase, the staterooms, the twelve little waterfalls and the delightful views in the park in many ways more exciting than Versailles. Definitely at Versailles there is nothing like the grand Caserta staircase flanked by its large stone lions. Many consider the ornamentation of the staterooms at Caserta to be overdone. That is not my view. I particularly like the walls lined with silk from the factories at San Leucio in the Appartamento Vecchio, and the three rooms of the library with its conical glass bookcase - although the much-praised *presepio* (crib) with its thousand figures leaves me cold.

Among the pictures on view in the palace are two interesting historical works - the launching of the first steamboat in Naples harbour and the inauguration of the first railway in Italy (Naples to Portici). Look also for the fine portrait of Charles III, a wax mask of Queen Maria Carolina, a group of the family of Ferdinand II and the bust of Queen Maria Cristina of

Savoy. These all bring the days of the Bourbons to life.

The park with its woods, gardens, fountains and waterfalls owes much to a Frenchman (Martin Biancour), who took Versailles as his model. It is a splendid achievement of Italian landscaping. A three mile walk or drive (there are buses and horse carriages for hire) leads to a waterfall and basins with statues of Diana and Actaeon. One with hounds baying at and attacking Actaeon who has sprouted horns on his forehead, while the other is of Diana and her nymphs bathing at the moment Actaeon stumbled upon her. These statues are much photographed and reproduced and were much admired in the nineteenth century. The hounds are lifelike and clearly inspired by pictures of English foxhunting scenes. They date from the late eighteenth century. The water for the waterfall and pools arrives via an aqueduct specially built at Monte Taburno 27 kilometres away. Carlo Vanvitelli the son of Luigi designed the numerous fountains after his father's death.

Ferdinand I and Maria Carolina were so keen to develop the English garden that they imported a British expert botanist Graffer, to lay it out and tend it. Graffer was a friend of Sir William and Emma Hamilton, who had originally suggested this garden to the king and queen. They persuaded the king to procure his services. At first Graffer was unhappy. Not knowing the Italian language he was cheated right and left, and his wife and family had difficulty settling into Italian life. Once he and his family learned Italian, he was ecstatically happy and loved his work, which was made easy by the 50 acre garden being walled in and 80 men provided year round. His first wife died and he was even happier with his second wife. At first the queen was the prime mover but when she discovered how much was being spent she blew cold, wanting to spend the money on her other projects. Then the king waxed enthusiastic and became very friendly with Graffer. William Hamilton noted a camphor tree that had grown to a height of 36 feet in three years, while other 'Botany Bay' plants made spectacular progress so that the garden bloomed with tropical species. Today it is a little paradise of shade and green when the weather is hot, and we must be grateful to Graffer.

Emma, Lady Hamilton noted that the English garden had become William's 'favourite child', and Sir William himself wrote, 'We go on admirably provided Graffer follows my advice and makes H.M. believe that he does it all himself.' Hamilton added, 'I wish you could see the camphor tree in full bloom.' Do look or ask for the camphor tree if you are in the garden, and think of Graffer walking there arm in arm with the king (according to Hamilton).

In gratitude for his return to Naples in 1799, Ferdinand gave Nelson a magnificent estate Brontë, in Sicily, and Graffer also laid out the gardens there but with considerably less success due to lack of money and water.

Near the palace is a sweet miniature mock castle built to entertain the numerous royal children, and beyond it is a fishpond (*peschieria*) half a kilometre long. Ferdinand I was so keen on fishing that he ordered priority to be given to building it; the labour for building the palace was largely drawn from galley slaves and Moslem prisoners of war who were then diverted to dig and build this pond.

I knew the palace well when it was the headquarters of Field Marshal Alexander during the Second World War. Fortunately little damage was done to the palace during this Allied occupation. The State Apartments were sealed off from our gaze at that time. Here in 1945 Alexander received the surrender of the German forces in Italy a few days before the whole German Army surrendered. Nowadays part of the palace is used by the Italian Air Force as a training school, but there is much to be seen inside.

Caserta was linked to Naples by railway as early as 1843; it was not the first railway in the kingdom as one to the Royal Palace at Portici had been opened in 1839. The railway was extended to Capua but as the popes rigidly refused to allow railways in the Papal States, travellers to and from Rome had to go by road between Capua and Rome. The roads were poor and dangerous, so that nearly all travellers to Naples came by sea. At the opening ceremony of the railway the journey of 20 miles between Caserta and Naples took an hour. At first Ferdinand II insisted on chapels at each station being used by passengers to ensure safe journeys. These are now unused and forgotten on this very busy suburban line.

Caserta has a Jolly and other hotels but it is an uninteresting town apart from the Palace. A delightful excursion on a fine day may be made to Caserta Vecchia - an untainted medieval town on a hillside 9 kilometres away, but quarrying has worked havoc on nearby hills. It has cobbled streets and the ruin of a ninth century castle. It was founded by the Lombards in the ninth century after the fall of Old Capua. It prospered under the Normans who built the twelfth century cathedral of San Michele; this is a fine example of Italian Norman architecture. Look at the blind arcades of the facade with projecting animals - horses, centaurs and a bull, rather like those on the cathedral at Sessa but more common in Apulia. Eighteen columns in the nave clearly come from the Temple of Jupiter Tifatino located nearby. Inside you find a good paschal candle and mosaics. The octagonal tower of the cathedral is most interesting, with single column arches rather like the cathedral of Salisbury. The tower and the campanile have a slight Moslem feel about them and it is known that Arab labourers worked at Caserta Vecchia as well as at Salisbury. The Gothic thirteenth century church of the Annunciata is well worth observation as well.

Neapolitans love to drive out to Caserta Vecchie as its height usually ensures certain coolness on a summer evening. The citizens are well catered to with several good restaurants - some of which specialize in wild boar and other traditional delicacies of the region. You do better by sticking to more conventional dishes and on no account fall for the old fashioned wines which some of the restaurants try hard to sell made by romantic but out of date methods..

In Victorian times Aversa on the road back to Naples was considered a compulsory part of the Tour. Then it was situated in very attractive countryside and was quiet. I hesitate to recommend Aversa nowadays as I have heard from one or two people whom I advised to go there that is so overcrowded and full of traffic that they could not enjoy it. However, if you are prepared to put up with all this, there is plenty of interest to see. In 1030 at Aversa the Normans gained their first foothold in south Italy. From the ruins of the Roman town Attela King Rainulf took away much stonework, which he used to build the town walls. Attela two miles from Aversa is hardly worth visiting because so little of it remains. The countryside around Aversa is extremely fertile and produces the strawberry coloured wine known as Asprino, which has a slight natural sparkle and is delicious as an aperitif or at lunchtime. The grapes are grown on vines introduced from France by Murat.

The entry to Aversa is usually by the Porta di Napoli under an arch constructed in the seventeenth century. To the right of this gate is the church of the Annunciata. There is a fine Renaissance doorway with carvings of allegorical figures at the end of the world and the resurrection dated 1518. The church of the Annunciata is Angevin, and the baroque façade is preceded by a portico whose arches are supported by four columns from ancient Attela.

On the other side of the road is a massive campanile dated 1477. The Annunciata church has beautiful fifteenth century paintings that alone make a trip to Aversa worthwhile for some. Sometimes it is necessary to ask the sacristan to unlock the chapels where the paintings are located. To the right of the entrance in the first chapel are two paintings by Angelillo Arcuccio of Naples (1464 -1492). Over the altar the souls in purgatory call on the Virgin who stands on a sickle moon. Another painting is of St. John the Evangelist.

A fine Madonna and Child is the altarpiece in the second chapel. In the space behind the high altar is a beautiful fourteenth century Annunciation.

Brave the traffic and go due north up the main street. You soon come to the church of the Madonna de Casalucia. Shortly before it a dark stone doorway leads into a Gothic courtyard. This is said to be part of the Angevin castle where Queen Giovanna's husband Andrew of Hungary was killed.

From the Corso Umberto turn left up the Strada S Paolo to the *Duomo* dedicated to St Paul that was begun in 1055 and is magnificent. It has been heavily damaged by fire and earthquake so we only see the eastern portion of the original structure. This has a splendid Norman ambulatory and a cupola in the Norman Sicilian style. Inside the *Duomo* the chief interest is in the ambulatory which is pure Gothic. Some of the carving is most impressive. On the inner wall are two remarkable pieces of early medieval carving - one of them showing St George killing the dragon. They must be at least as old as the cathedral.

Leave the Duomo by the Piazza Normanna and take the Strada del Castello to the Piazza Trieste a Trenco, where on the right stands the castle rebuilt by Alfonso I of Aragon after the original one was destroyed by an earthquake. Nowadays, it is an asylum for criminal lunatics. In front of the Castello there is the graceful church of Santa Maria a Piazza, dating back to the fourteenth century. Here look at the beautiful fourteenth century frescoes contemporary with the church, and particularly at the Nativity.

The old town of Aversa consists of a labyrinth of streets with many churches and convents, some of which are clearly Norman - although most have had baroque restoration. There is bustle and squalor in the streets, reminding one of the Middle Ages, but there are no palaces such as one sees in Naples. One word of warning - there are no hotels in Aversa and few in the whole of northern Campania. However all the places described in this chapter are within easy reach of Naples by car, and once you get off the main roads and away from the buildings you luxuriate in some of the richest farmland in Europe.

8
West of Naples –
Phlegraean Fields

To explore west of Naples you need to go on foot, bicycle, motorcycle or as a last resort by car. However there are conducted bus tours to the Phlegraean Fields. Pass the quarter of Santa Lucia en route to Chiaia and Mergellina. Originally, Santa Lucia was a slum area surrounding a small fishing port. At the end of the nineteenth century it was pulled down and rebuilt with luxury hotels and high class residences. Along the coastal road there are plenty of signs 'No bathing' but despite this as soon as it is warm enough, many Neapolitans much enjoy bathing from the concrete slabs of the embankment and diving into not very clean water. The little fishing port at Santa Lucia (Borgo Marinaro) has been taken over by expensive yachts. It is dominated by the Castel dell'Ovo (Castle of the Egg) that juts out into the sea. This is the oldest castle in Naples and was strongly fortified even before the Normans came. Frederick II used it as a royal residence. The medieval shape of the castle bristling with towers as shown in the old pictures was lost after the siege of 1503, and it is an odd shape today. It is used as city offices and there is no official access to the public although I got inside by asking permission. Within is a Hall of Columns with four aisles divided by arches set on columns that may have come from the nearby Villa Lucullus. The Borgo Marinaro is full of character with its own style of bars and restaurants. It is a picturesque piece of Naples.

Look too at the attractive Fontana dell' Immacolatella by Bernini on the seafront above the little port, which was formerly at the Palazzo Reale. It was executed in 1601.

Proceeding along the Via Chiaia you come to the aquarium one of the largest and oldest in Europe. It only houses fish from the Gulf of Naples. On the left before you come to the aquarium there is an interesting Roman column, taken from Via Anticaglia in the antique centre. It is dedicated to those who have died at sea. Follow the Via Caracciolo to Mergellina. When I first knew Mergellina 50 years ago, it was a charming, quiet fishermen's port filled with rowboats. It was a delight to hire a boat on a hot day and dive into the clear deep water just outside the harbour. Today it is a teeming yacht harbour and the terminus for the many hydrofoils from Ischia and Capri. The water all around the little bay is so dirty that no one would dream of bathing today. Its charm has disappeared. Nevertheless masses of fish are sold on the quayside at Mergellina especially to the many neighbouring restaurants where they are so beautifully cooked.

Next to Mergellina is Piedigrotta. Fuorigrotta and Piedigrotta are the names given to the places immediately east and west of the grotto or tunnel, dug in the first century BC through the Hill of Posillipo to ease travel from

124

NAPLES, What most tourists never see

Naples to Pozzuoli. The old tunnel is filled in and there are new tunnels full of fast traffic in several lanes. There is an interesting church at Piedigrotta - Santa Maria de Piedigrotta. It was rebuilt in 1453 with handsome columned cloisters in the adjoining monastery hat is now a hospital (Ospedale della Marina). Gaetano Gigante painted the vaulted ceilings of the church in 1818. It was one of the important shrines of the Virgin Mary with a celebration held on the 7th of September that used to attract the participation of the royal family in a procession. Next to it and behind is the Parco Virgiliano that was very popular with the Grand Tour as it is the reputed tomb of Virgil. We know that at Virgil's request his ashes were deposited in a tomb outside Naples on the Via Puteolana between the first and second milestone; however it is by no means certain that the current tomb is genuine. Virgil's *Georgics* were written in Naples and he describes in them the beautiful Campania countryside, which he loved - writing of, 'weaving the elms with the gorgeous vines.' He fell ill in Greece and died at Brindisi on his way back to Naples in 19 BC. His burial place at first was much visited by pilgrims but in later years it was forgotten and subsequently demolished.

After going through the gateway to the Parco Virgiliano walk up through gardens to a Roman *columbaria* next to the original tunnel. Near it is a monument to the Italian poet Giacomo Leopardi who died in Naples and whose body was only narrowly saved from being thrown into a pit for cholera victims. This is a pretty spot and well worth visiting, but there is seething traffic outside it.

Just beyond Mergellina is the Parco Sannazaro, where Neapolitans love to walk along the seafront in the evenings. Many smart cafés and restaurants have sprung up, they all have a jolly atmosphere and flourish. It is still a pleasure to walk there and savour the excellent ice creams and fruit and look at the view and the sea.

A short distance from Grotta Fuori take a road to the right and after two miles you come to Lake Agnano that was once a crater, then a lake and is now drained. Here is the famous 'dog grotto' much visited by Victorians. The name comes from Anauni meaning snakes that used to abound in the area. A tubular passage leads to the 'dog grotto', which is a cave like cellar where a misty exhalation rises from the floor. It is carbonic acid that is heavier than air and stays at ground level so that dogs suffer - but humans are unaffected. The upper part is free from the gas, but the floor is completely covered by it. In the eighteenth and nineteenth centuries numerous guides, described by Augustus Hare as 'wretches', used to swarm around with dogs waiting for tourists. They would suspend the dogs by their heels until they became unconscious in the toxic vapour. According to Dumas the dog would jump around trying to get above the obnoxious vapour until a convulsion rendered him unconscious. His master then pulled him out of the cave by his tail and he lay on the sand as if dead. Soon outside in the fresh air he recovered first the use of his front legs then his back legs, then shaking on four legs he stood for a moment collecting his strength. He then set off like an arrow and sat 100 yards away on a mound, looking around himself with scrupulous care. Fortunately suffocating the dogs fell into disrepute at the end of the nineteenth century, and it is strange how such a barbarous practice ever appealed to British visitors. There are tales of Victorian spinsters who after seeing the plaster casts of dead dogs at Pompeii and the 'dog grotto' had to curtail their tour in order to make sure their pets were safe and well at home. It is not easy now to obtain access to the dog grotto.

It is alleged that Turkish captives were executed by asphyxiation here and that Don Pedro de Toledo tried the dog experiment upon two galley slaves with fatal effects. Under the Bourbons this area now built-up, was a large game preserve and anyone who fired a gun was liable to be punished by the galleys for life. These waters at Agnano have been used for health spas continuously from Roman times and there is a thriving modern spa (Terme Agnano) hotel there today. Opposite the main entrance to the modern baths are the six storey ruins of Roman baths used until the fifteenth century. Nearby is the famous Agnano horse racing track, one of the most important in Italy. A very valuable race is held each year in conjunction with the lottery. Half a mile beyond the racecourse is an attractive public park called the Wood of the Astroni. It is a volcanic crater, with its bottom covered with marshy vegetation and its sides with holm oaks, chestnuts, oaks, elms and poplars. It must have been an ideal place for deer, pheasant, and wild boars and much appreciated by the Bourbon kings who loved shooting. They even built a wall around it to prevent escape of the wild animals. A walk in this wood is still an enchanting experience and makes one wish that the Neapolitans had created more such 'green' areas. Efforts towards this end are now being made.

A peninsula known as Posillipo juts out into the sea separating the Bay of Naples from Pozzuoli. It was called Pausilypon (meaning respite from pain) by the ancient Greeks because of its great beauty. A huge Roman settlement developed especially along its western edge, as evidenced by the many ruins all along the coast. In the seventeenth century it became the favourite holiday resort of the Spanish aristocracy when many luxurious villas were built, some of which can still be seen. The nineteenth century brought another era of great popularity to Posillipo after Joachim Murat began a new coastal road in 1812 and is still in use. Alas in the 1950s and 1960s many of these beautiful hills were covered with unplanned hideous property development, so that nowadays one has to search for the delightful old villas amid a rash of modern concrete. Sadly this area has been ruined. Fifty years ago it was an area of unsurpassed scenic and historic beauty.

Still from the road a beautiful view at first of the Bay of Naples, Vesuvius and Capri can be seen at intervals. Once over the peak delightful glimpses can be had of Ischia, Procida and the Gulf of Baia. In the nineteenth century many villas were British owned and a number of English names can still be seen on the entrances. But today the English have gone. Norman Douglas lived for several years in the Villa Maya built in 1820 and no work of art. The Neapolitans are apt to confuse him with Lord Alfred Douglas who stayed with Oscar Wilde in a borrowed English villa after Wilde was released from prison, until Wilde's wife threatened to cut off the money unless they split up.

Most of the interesting villas are privately owned and often hidden from view; only a few can be seen from the road. You pass the seventeenth century fountain of Serato and the neoclassical villa Doria d'Angri with a little chinoiserie pagoda (now a hospital). Then the Palazzo Donn'Anna comes into sight much as it appears in many Neapolitan paintings and fitting in well with the natural grottos and remains of the adjacent Roman villas. It was built in 1642 by Fanzago for Donn'Anna Carafa, the powerful wife of the Viceroy Medina. It has never been finished which accounts for its strange ghostly look today. Neapolitans delight in the story that the disreputable Queen Joanna II used the villa for amorous sessions with muscular fishermen and when they had served her purpose she drowned them in the cavernous flooded cellars beneath the house.

Donn'Anna is right on the sea and looks at its best from a boat. Its appearance is dilapidated but inside are some modern elegant apartments. Access is not easy, but do try. From its partially ruined state it seems still shrouded in mystery.

Beyond the point of Posillipo lies the Villa Rosebery, 26 Via Russo now the seaside residence of the President of Italy. King Edward VII was entertained here by the British Ambassador in 1903 when he came to Naples in the Royal Yacht. He was the first English sovereign to visit Naples since Richard Coeur de Lion in 1190. Edward's grandson King George VI, stayed in the villa in 1944 as the guest of Harold Macmillan (Minister for the

Mediterranean) and also with Field Marshal Alexander (Commander in Chief, Mediterranean). While King George VI was staying in the villa, his fellow king Victor Emmanuel II came fishing in the sea outside from a small boat. As the king of a defeated nation he was not admitted to the Allied Councils, nor to social intercourse with his fellow king. However Victor Emmanuel later was allowed to use the villa for his abdication in favour of his son King Roberto II.

Villa Rosebery was built in 1820 for Prince Luigi Bourbon brother of King Ferdinand II. The British Prime Minister the Earl of Rosebery (1847-1929) bought it and designed the grounds. He eventually found Naples too far away to live there, so he presented it to the British Government for the use of the British ambassador in Rome. Tiled floors within and tiled terraces outside are a feature of this sumptuous palace, that is surrounded by orange and lemon groves and a splendid garden shaded by dark pines and holm oaks and overlooking the sea and the view over the point of Posillipo. It is state property and thus not open to the public.

Two hundred yards to the east of Villa Rosebery was the seaside villa (Villa Emma) of Sir William Hamilton. There is a picture of it on a porcelain plate at Capodimonte. His main residence was at the Palazzo Sessa near the Piazza dei Martiri. Hamilton wrote to his nephew Charles Greville in 1780: 'Each day we sail delightfully down to our casino at Posillipo where we lunch in air as fresh as in England.' The villa was cool because it went into shade at 2 pm as the sun became hidden by the hill of the point of Posillipo. Lord Herbert wrote: 'Sir William lunched on the terrace at 2 pm and it is already shady and while everyone roasts in Naples he enjoys the cool.' While Emma wrote: 'We lunch every day at the Villa Emma at Posillipo, and I paint two or three pictures.' In 1787 the painter Tischbein wrote to Goethe: 'The day before yesterday I was with Sir William at his Posillipo villa. It is not possible to find anything more splendid. After lunch 12 boys dived into the sea and played games in it. Their Cavaliere pays them to do this every afternoon - they are a most beautiful sight.'

From this spot there is a wonderful view of the whole bay of Naples. Today the Villa Emma reduced in size is known as the Casa de Mapinulla - 15 Via Posillipo - and is divided into two small houses. The remains of a tunnel that led to the Villa Rosebery, can be seen as can the semi-circular terrace, which figures in a number of paintings. It is worth lingering here to drink in one of the most painted views of Naples and ponder on all the distinguished personalities who came here in Hamilton's day.

Sir Eustace Neville Rolfe the Victorian and Edwardian Consul

General in Naples, also had a villa here. He wrote a book about Naples that degraded the inhabitants, and at one time there were posters all over Naples protesting against his insinuations. He was knighted in 1903 for his strenuous efforts to keep King Edward VII happy here.

Close by is the Villa Galotta, right on the water's edge where a fringe of palm trees produces a tropical effect. Continuing to the west take a curving road which between villas and gardens leads to the old fishing village of Marechiaro (calm water), now full of restaurants selling fish fresh from the sea. It's where in the summer evenings the Neapolitans love to eat and be serenaded by tenors accompanied by mandolins and guitars.

There are plenty of Roman remains here, and at Marechiaro you can hire a boat to see the remains of Pollio's villa. Just outside Marechiaro partly under water are the ruins of a large three storey Roman villa known as Polizzo dei Spiriti - a ghost in white is reputed to have been seen here frequently. This villa is best seen from the sea.

At the extreme southern point of the promontory, excavations have revealed ancient buildings including a well preserved theatre. Other ruins are known as the School of Virgil in the belief that the poet taught there. Around the point are the Isle of Nisida and a high cliff face known as the Cava de Trenta Remi. Contrary to superstition, this had nothing to do with Roman triremes. Carlo Knight believes the name is due to the spot being sold for 30 tareni (an old Neapolitan coin of Egyptian origin).

In passing it is worth looking at the Grotto de Seiano discovered in 1840. It was dug at the end of the first century BC to connect Villa Pausylipon with Pozzuoli and is 800 metres long, 5 metres wide and 7 metres high. The ventilation shafts open on to the cliff of Trenta Remi. It is open to the public.

The tiny island of Gaiola lies on the road to Nisida. Here there are many Roman remains which have led scholars to believe there was once a whole Roman city there. Trenta Remi, Marechiaro and Gaiola have good bathing beaches which get very crowded. Despite the widespread modern buildings, these spots still have charm and beauty. The best way to enjoy them is to hire a boat at Mergellina - but keep away on weekends.

The old Angevin castle now a boys reformatory dominates the small island of Nisida joined to the mainland by a causeway. Here Brutus and Cassius plotted Caesar's assassination and Brutus returned there afterwards and was visited by Cicero. Then he said goodbye to his wife Portia and departed for Greece and the battle of Philippi.

Returning to Via Posillipo we quickly come to the pillared entrance to the Parco de Posillipo. It has one of the most magnificent views of the sea and islands which can be found in the area. It is a fine sports centre. From here the road runs through dreary industrial suburbs to Pozzuoli.

Pozzuoli is a fascinating town but is clogged with traffic and on weekends becomes one big traffic jam. Greek political refugees from Samnos founded it in 529 BC. Like nearby Cuma it fell in 421 BC to the Samnites. The Romans named it Puteoli and it became the chief port for trade between Rome and Greece and the Near East until Claudius and Nero built the port of Ostia near Rome. A vast system of Roman docks was built and the town became very prosperous, remaining the chief port for Campania until the barbarians overran Italy in the 5th century. Its importance and wealth are reflected by the size of the baths, the amphitheatre and the *macellum (marketplace)*. In the old centre nearly all the houses have first storeys of Roman origin. Here St Paul landed and found Christians and Christianity spread all over Italy.

Pozzuoli is most easily reached by the Cumaean railway which I found very easy to do. From the station it is best to walk (it is downhill into the town) and perhaps take a taxi back. Now you are in the heart of the Phlegrean Fields (from the ancient Greek word Phlegraios meaning 'burning fields'). The Roman city was built on terraces sloping down to the sea with a vast marketplace (*macellum*) next to the harbour. Interesting evidence of the topography of ancient Pozzuoli is revealed in small glass flasks produced between the third and fourth century AD depicting views of the bay of Pozzuoli, with a schematic plan of the main buildings.

A short walk from the railway station is the volcano of Solfatara. It is part white desert sand with rocks and part vivid green with a swimming pool and caravan park - much loved by Germans who love the heat. The volcano is said to be dormant but hot sulphur fumes rise continuously from the rocky desert parts. Perhaps better than the tiring walk around is to look down on it from the road on the cliff above. Solfaterra has probably changed little in several hundred years.

At the same level is the vast amphitheatre of Pozzuoli - one of two. The large public baths nearby adjoin it. The ruins of the smaller older amphitheatre were only discovered recently during the laying of a railway line although it was shown on the previously mentioned glass vases. Not much can be seen of it today. On the other hand the large Flavian Amphitheatre is as well preserved as the one at Old Capua or the Coliseum in Rome. It is second in size in Campania only to Capua and is the third largest in Italy accommodating 35-40,000 spectators.

The underground structures are the chief interest. No other ancient amphitheatre has underground works in such a good state of preservation. Their grandeur is most evocative with the shades of light and shadow from ancient wells in the floor of the arena. There is a walkway (*ambularium*) all the way around; off it are forty cells on two levels. In front of each upper cell is a trapdoor opening on the arena. The animals must have been kept in cages that were run on wheels and then lifted into the arena by pulleys or a counterweight. Levers would then open the door of the cage and the animal would spring from the underground gloom into the bright light of the arena where often sand hills and palms simulated the African landscape. The large amphitheatre at Pozzuoli is one of the most important Roman remains still standing in Italy.

An underground chapel to the north of the amphitheatre built in 1689 commemorates the imprisonment here of St Gennaro and other Christian leaders who were beheaded in 505 AD under the edict of Constantinople. Originally they were to have been thrown to the wild beasts but then were committed to beheading because the governor could not be present. St Gennaro's body was moved to Naples so that he became its patron saint.

Follow the attractive and very well kept remains of the Roman baths downhill towards the sea until you come to the *macellum*, known mistakenly as the Temple of Serapis, because in a small temple was found a statue of Serapis, who was a Graeco-Egyptian deity from the time of Ptolemy I. Forty two temples were erected to him in Egypt in the Graeco-Roman period and his head appears on many Roman coins. The Alexandrians who brought glass making from Egypt to Pozzuoli, must have brought the cult of Serapis with them to Pozzuoli.

Ancient Puteoli as a huge trading post was a most cosmopolitan city inhabited by Syrians, Jews, Greeks and Romans. This *macellum* is one of the largest and most complete surviving examples of a Roman marketplace. It has been preserved because the sea level rose by 18 feet as shown by holes bored by mollusks in the columns, probably around the sixteenth century. Today a pump has been installed and it is always either dry or covered with only a thin layer of clear water. It is a rectangular area with a porticoed court and rows of shops recalling an oriental bazaar. There were also open-air fish and meat markets. At the northern end is a surprisingly luxurious public lavatory well worth a glance. Preceded by vestibules are two fine halls with marble walls, pavements and hollowed marble seats with channels for flushing and drainage. They are the most perfect sanitary arrangements left to us by the Romans.

Under the sea in the harbour can be seen the remains of the great quay (ripa) which sheltered the Roman harbour. An inscription of the fourth century AD refers to strengthening the ripa, and from the Via Vecchia about 75 feet from the shore can be seen a row of column bases underneath the sea - all that remains of the seaside part of the rich city. Cicero recorded that one of these porticoes was dedicated to Neptune (Porticus Neptune) and another to Hercules (Porticus Hercules).

The main residential quarter of Puteoli with rich villas and many monuments lay high up on the hillside overlooking the open bay. Cicero himself inhabited a villa in 45 BC. The seaside villas have all disappeared under the sea.

Baia is a short distance to the west of Pozzuoli and easily reached by bus or train. Alas the beautiful countryside between these two places has been heavily developed. En route you pass the Lake Lucrino and then turning to the north to Cuma. The lake is surrounded by restaurants and was renowned for its oysters.

Baia was famous for its sumptuous imperial villas while Puteoli was a commercial port. Baia with its lovely greenery and terraces, was a place of residence chosen by many rich Romans because during the heat of the 'dog days' (cani cerlares dies) in Rome there was usually a sea breeze there. Coupled with this was a fine beach and copious hot springs for the warm baths so beloved by the Romans. Classical writers describe the beach life at Baia as lascivious and degenerate; there are such references in Livy, Cicero and Seneca. It was not only the favourite health and bathing resort during the last period of Republican Rome, but also the largest spa of ancient Italy. The hills and coast of Baia were crammed with the luxurious villas of rich Roman citizens and patricians. When one notes its sheltered position, sandy beach and the protection given by the surrounding hills, it is not difficult to understand how the wealthy sybaritic Romans flocked to it. Horace wrote 'No bay in the world outshines delightful Baia (*Nullus in orbe sinus Baiis*)'.

Nero created an immense porticoed swimming pool to collect all the thermal waters springing on the beach. Dredging operations along the shore in the 1920s reaped a rich harvest of sculptures and marbles, which must have belonged to some of the imperial villas that sank below the sea. Recently many statues have been dredged from the sea.

The Edwardian travel writer Arthur Norway comments that in view of what Vesuvius preserved at Pompeii and Herculaneum it was a pity 'the ashes had not rained down a trifle harder at Misenium and Baia. What noble Roman buildings might have survived until today'. Anyone disregarding human suffering should echo Norway's words. According to Pliny, Baia and Misenium were plunged into darkness by the ashes but there were not enough to kill or bury the buildings.

A staircase beside the railway line to the left reaches the very extensive Roman baths of Baia as you face the station. It is a grand complex with a frontage of 450 metres from the foot of the hill to the top. It was a thermal 'city,' with several hot water mineral springs and vapour spouts. The buildings were in large rectangular blocks facing the sea, housed baths or residential or leisure quarters. They were spanned by porticoes and flat terraces and were separated from each other. Access was by long staircases with ramps that led up to the top of the hill and offering far below a fine vista of the whole establishment.

There are four main baths: 1) The Temple of Diana, 2) The Temple of Mercury, 3) The Temple of Sosandra, and 4) The Temple of Venus. These are well documented in Amedeo Maiuri's little book *Phlegraean Fields* published in English. They are massive buildings with domed roofs and are most impressive. There is also a good description in the *Touring Club of Italy: Guide to Naples* - also in English.

The gulf of Pozzuoli ends spectacularly in the castle of Baia, built in the Aragon era on the ruins of a villa belonging to Caesar. It contains the Museo Archeologeo dei Campi Flegrei from whose rooms there are marvellous views. This collection, at the moment of writing, is being considerably enlarged by acquisitions from the Museo Nazionale in Naples where there is no space to exhibit them. There is a fine temple front from Miseno.

Bacoli used to be a charming small town a few kilometres south of Baia. Although heavily developed it retains some of its charm, especially on the sea front where there is a small bathing beach and the so-called tomb of Agrippina, the mother of the Roman Emperor Nero. This is a semi circular ruin just above the waves. According to Maiuri, the identification is false and it is the remains of a small theatre; the tomb of Agrippina was swept away when Don Pedro of Toledo built the grandiose Castle of Baia. Tacitus vividly describes the murder of the imperious Empress Agrippina by her degenerate son Nero. Nero resented his mother's domineering role, and when she came to dine with him in his palace (now half-buried in the sea at the point of the bay), he plotted to sink the boat taking her home. Agrippina fell into the water but was rescued by a fishing boat that took her home to her villa at Lake Lucrino. After consulting with Seneca, Nero sent sailors to Agrippina's house under Anicetus, who killed her with his sword. The coast at Bacoli is crying out for more excavations as Roman remains protrude everywhere. Perhaps the real tomb of Agrippina will be revealed. Tacitus describes it as a humble sepulchre on the road to Misenium, near the 'Villa of Julius Caesar, which is on a great height'. Caesar's villa was the site of the Castle of Baia.

On the promontory to the east of Bacoli is an interesting two storey Roman building known as the Cento Camerelle or Carceri di Nerone, and sometimes the Labyrinth. The upper storey was definitely a water reservoir and the basement part of a large villa. Artificial light is needed to see it and the chief attraction is the view from it. Remains of the ancient villa are strewn along the hill.

On the summit of the hill to the south of Bacoli between the Bay of Bacoli and the Mare Morto, is the immense Piscina Mirabilis - a triumph of Roman engineering in an exceptional state of preservation. It is 230 feet long and 85 feet wide with a vaulted ceiling supported by 48 massive pillars and is like a cathedral with five aisles. Misenium was the main base for the Roman fleet in Southern Italy, and great quantities of fresh water were needed for the ships. The Piscina Mirabilis is a superb example of a Roman reservoir, the like of which cannot be found elsewhere. It is in as good condition as when it first supplied water to the Roman fleet. Note the sink for extracting sediment from the water. The water must have been raised by a series of water wheels. It is more like an underground temple than a reservoir.

Going south to Miseno the road is on a causeway separating the lake Mare Morto from the sea in the Bay of Misenium. Here was the naval port built by Agrippa in 41 BC and comprising a port in the bay and a sheltered anchorage in the lake Mare Morto, into which ships could enter by an artificial canal that is now covered over. Both Pliny the Elder and Aricetus who murdered Agrippina, were fleet commanders at Misenium.

Misenium was an important Roman military town and it remained prosperous until the ninth century when the Lombards sacked it in 836 and a few years later in 890 the Saracens destroyed it. Little remains of the Roman port works, which made Misenium such a formidable naval base. At the mouth of the port on a fair day from above on a boat can be seen the line of great piles (as at Pozzuoli), that were the foundations of the two moles built to protect the entrance of the port from the breakers. The shore is very steep so the repairs and servicing of the ships must have been carried out in the inner basin of Mare Morto. Nothing survives of the arsenal and barracks that must have surrounded the inner port except the name Miliscolo, still given to a bathing establishment. This is a corruption of *Militum Schola,* signifying the drill area for the troops and crews of the ships. A fourth century inscription found here bears the title Schola Armatur. Still the great legacy of the Roman fleet lies on the magnificent Piscina Mirabilis.

An unsurpassed view of the islands of Procida and Ischia and the whole Bay of Naples can be had from the little hill of Punto di Miseno, the extreme southern tip of the Campi Flegrei. It is very popular with the locals and you may have difficulty in parking your car at the top of the hill.

Fifty years ago the western coast from Miseno to Cuma was a delightful area. Today like the rest of the Campi Flegrei it is built up without much apparent taste, although there are still vineyards and orchards amid the concrete. Proceeding westward we pass Capella and come to the seaside place of Torrevegata, the terminus of the Cumana railway. It used to be attractive but I cannot recommend it as a bathing place nowadays. From Torrevegata a winding road leads up through modern houses, a few vineyards and Roman ruins to the small town of Monte di Procida from where there are splendid views of Procida and Ischia.

Countless Roman tombs have been discovered at Capella and along the slopes of the hills surrounding Mare Morto. These have yielded over 400 inscriptions relating to officers, non-commissioned officers, and veterans of the fleet at Misenium. They give the names of ships ranging from the massive h*exeres* with six banks of oars, *quinqueremes*, *quadriremes* and *triremes* down to the *liburnae,* with two banks of oars. They show that when the seat of Empire was transferred to Constantinople the port of Misenum still existed, although diminished in importance.

If you take a right hand fork before Torrevegata you come to the western shore of the pretty Lake Fusaro, renowned through the ages for shellfish. King Ferdinand I instructed Vanvitteli to build a delightful new classical villa on the east shore in 1782. This has been painted frequently. It can only be reached by a bridge. To the east of the bridge are the less attractive stables and living quarters for Ferdinand's numerous attendants. These always included a large retinue of cooks, grooms, personal servants, gatekeepers and beaters. The picture at Capodimonte (...) of the 'battle' in progress on Lake Fusaro, with the birds in the sky and the boats encircling them, is like a colourful film of a day's shooting at Fusaro. On land around the lakeshores were great quantities of pheasants, quails and partridges - all carefully preserved for the king's amusement in the same fashion as many large country estates in England today provide game for the super rich.

Cuma itself to the north of Fusaro lies in an oasis of unspoiled countryside with peach orchards and vineyards, and the Royal hunting grounds have been turned into luxuriant gardens.

Revisiting the Phlegraean Fields after nearly fifty years filled me with nostalgia for what used to be one of the most attractive countrysides in Europe, so extolled by Virgil and other ancient poets. Only this sporadic trace remains amid the ever present tasteless building development. One wrings one's hands at the devastation Neapolitans inflicted in the 1960s and 1970s on their precious heritage. Yet for the avid sightseer the Campi Flegrei are still a must.

9
Pompeii

ompeii is easily reached from Naples. There are frequent buses from the Piazza Municipio and there is a good train service on the CircumVesuvian railway whose city terminus is ¼ mile south of the main station near Porta Nolana. There are two stations for Pompeii. Villa dei Misteri is nearer to the excavations than Pompeii Scavi.

Pompeii like Herculaneum is unique because it is a time capsule and vital evidence of the way of life of Roman times. Pompeii is so dramatic that it is no wonder there are over 1.5 million visitors each year and this number is increasing. The site of the whole town covered 163 acres. Three fifths, or 1l0 acres have been excavated, but the part open to the public is diminishing. So much excavation was done in the 1950s and 1960s that the funds are insufficient for it all to be maintained today. A large part is closed to the public because the walls are unsafe; after restoration all the walls have to be propped. Many frescoes are fading rapidly and paintings have been stolen off the walls. The custodians dare not leave bronzes or statues on their sites. For example thieves stole the bronze statues from the House of Vettii and these turned up on the German art market. There is no museum at Pompeii although one is proposed. Therefore it is better to go to the National Archaeological Museum (Museo Nazionale) in Naples before visiting Pompeii because there you see her finest treasures.

Excavation is nearly at a standstill. The elements soon start to destroy any remains uncovered, but the major problem is to stop the vandals. As a result, there is doubt whether our grandchildren will be able to enjoy the whole of Pompeii. One hundred years ago you could explore almost all the excavated city, and even forty years ago it was in better condition. Somehow it must be saved from a second death because it is part of mankind's world heritage.

The original town was Greek being a colony of Cumae in the sixth century BC. At that time it covered twenty four acres and had a population of 2500; on the south and west side the walls followed the cliffs over the river Sarno and faced out towards the saddle of land adjoining the sea that carried the road to Stabiae and Sorrento. The town was laid out in the Greek manner with long narrow residential blocks in a rectangular pattern separated by narrow access streets. The town prospered and in the fifth century BC was greatly enlarged to the north and east. Of the Greek architecture we have only the scanty remains of two Greek temples and bits of gaily painted terracotta ornamentation.

After the Greeks from Cumae defeated the Etruscans in 474 BC the city expanded very quickly and the walls enclosed 160 acres. However the

Samnites, a warlike people from the central Appenines, captured the entire coast from Pompeii to Paestum in the fourth century BC and only Naples remained Greek. The Samnite wars ended in 290 BC with the establishment of Roman rule over Pompeii. By now it was an important provincial town acting as a harbour for the surrounding towns, and it became even more prosperous as its monuments depict. As part of the Roman Empire there were great architectural developments at Pompeii. The forum up to then an open space was paved with a great colonnaded basilica added. Public baths were built as was the temple of Isis. Houses became larger, with a central hall (*atrium*) and garden court (*peristyle*); these can be seen everywhere in Pompeii today. But Pompeii was a Samnite and not a Roman town and used the Oscan language. The large part of the buildings was begun in the second century BC under the Samnites.

In 90 BC Pompeii joined the rebels against Rome. Lucius Cornelius Sulla on his return from the Middle East besieged Pompeii; the walls and towers had been hurriedly strengthened and although Herculaneum and Stabiae fell, Sulla failed to take the town by assault. Interesting relics of the siege have survived - painted notices on house fronts directing the garrison to various sections of the walls, the name of Sulla scratched on a tower wall, damage from missiles to stone work and missiles preserved as souvenirs. Sulla restored Roman rule over the whole of Southern Campania and established two or three thousand loyal Roman veteran soldiers on the lands of Pompeii as a revenge for their opposition. In 73-71 BC, Spartacus' slave army camped near Pompeii as can be seen in the famous film of that name, but Pompeii became a Roman town. A riot took place in 59 AD in the amphitheatre in which a number of visiting spectators from Nuceria were killed. The upshot was that the Senate in Rome banned all spectacles in the amphitheatre for ten years - equivalent in modern times to a ten year closure of a football stadium. The scene is well portrayed in a contemporary picture now in the Naples museum.

Then on 5 February 62 AD there was a severe earthquake that badly damaged the town's monuments so that by the time of the eruption seventeen years later, only the amphitheatre and the Temple of Isis had been fully restored. On some buildings work had not yet begun and some experts believe the whole forum was a gigantic builder's yard. It was a major disaster, and the havoc caused can still be seen in many of the houses and buildings.

On 24 August 79 AD came the great eruption of Vesuvius. Pliny described the great cloud above Vesuvius as like 'a great pine tree.' I recognized the description when as a soldier in 1944 I saw a similar cloud above Vesuvius - it was nature's equivalent of the mushroom cloud soon to be triggered by the atom bombs at Hiroshima and Nagasaki.

The best account of the eruption comes in a letter to Tacitus from Pliny the Younger. He does not mention Pompeii or Herculaneum, although he writes of the 'destruction of so many populous cities.' His uncle the elder Pliny had been sunbathing at Misenum where he commanded the Roman naval base when they saw 'A cloud (from which mountain was uncertain at this distance, but it was found afterwards to come from Mount Vesuvius) was ascending, the appearance of which I cannot give you a more exact description than by likening it to that of a pine tree - for it shot up to a great height in the form of a very tall trunk which spread itself out at the top like branches occasioned I imagine either by sudden gusts of air that impelled it, the force of which decreased as it advanced upwards or the cloud itself being pressed back again by its own weight expanded in the manner I have mentioned. It appeared sometimes bright and sometimes dark and spotted according to whether it was more or less impregnated with earth and cinders.'

A letter came to the Plinys from Rectina wife of Cascus who was in great fear for her villa lying at the foot of Mount Vesuvius. There was no way of escape but by sea - she therefore earnestly entreated him to come to their assistance. He ordered the galleys to be put to sea and went on board himself with the intention of assisting not only Rectina, but also others who lived in towns that 'lay thickly strewn along that beautiful coast.' When he arrived at the seashore near Pompeii, he found cinders, which grew hotter and thicker the nearer he approached. They fell onto the ships together with pumice stones and black pieces of burning rock.

The ships reached Stabiae, the modern Castellamare. By now black flames were pouring out of Vesuvius and the court, which led to Pliny's bedroom for the night, became almost filled with stones. The houses were rocking from side to side so they went out into the countryside, having tied pillows upon their heads with napkins. Pliny died having succumbed to the sulphur gas in the air. He was an old man with poor respiratory function. His companions including the younger Pliny survived.

Many Pompeiians reached the seashore but then probably found the waves too high to escape by boats because quantities of skeletons have been found under the sea. However those who lingered in Pompeii were all lost. Interestingly no skeletons of horses were found in Pompeii, which indicates that many may have ridden to safety. Eventually the younger Pliny returned to Misenum and safety. Misenum was experiencing earthquake shocks and when the wind shifted to the east there was a cloud of darkness and falling ash so that the whole population took to the open countryside. The eruption started between 10 and 11 on the morning of 24 August 79 AD and by the evening of that day six feet of ash had fallen on Pompeii. The first eight feet of deposit consisted of a scatter of lava pebbles (*lapilli*) that comprised the debris from the plug of solidified basalt which had for many years sealed the volcano and this was followed by successive layers of almost pure pumice. Within 24 hours the city of Pompeii had ceased to exist, buried to a depth of twelve feet by ash. At the same time there was a deadly rain of lethal gas and red hot cinders as the amount of actual solid material diminished - under this deadly hail no one could survive.

The bodies of the victims found during the excavations all lay above a deep carpet of pumice ash. During the second part of the eruption there was a red hot hail of different material, and the victims all died of asphyxiation or exposure to intolerable heat during the second stage.

The number of casualties cannot be estimated, but in the town and neighbouring countryside, there must have been many thousands. Those who escaped must have done so in the first few hours before the roads became blocked and the air became unbreathable. Those who stayed to collect their belongings or who took shelter in houses and cellars, died miserable deaths as the upper storeys collapsed upon them or the sulphurous fumes suffocated them. The ash solidified around their bodies leaving them for posterity.

When conditions returned to normal a commission was sent by the Emperor Titus from Rome to Campania to report. Herculaneum and the numerous villas along the coast near Vesuvius had vanished, although some of the taller buildings at Stabiae and Pompeii were visible above the ash. The Forum area was ransacked for its bronze statues and some homeowners together with robbers, tried to dig their way in, hunting for valuables in their former houses - with little success. A Jew or a Christian scratched the words, 'Sodom and Gommorah' on a wall.

Another such inscription is, 'The cup from which the whore poured her libation is now covered by stones and ashes,' probably by another Jew or even a Christian visiting the site and hoping to recover some of his possessions. Survivors drifted away amid the knowledge that there had once been a town there lingering on in folk memory. In the eighteenth century the area was still known as *Civitá* (city) but the site disappeared and became unknown as the rich soil was farmed. Oblivion took over.

Pompeii remained buried for almost seventeen centuries. In the late sixteenth century workmen excavating for a conduit for a water supply to the barracks at Torre el Greco found interesting remains. It was not until 1748 after a well had yielded exciting statues, that the archeologist Mazzochi suggested to King Charles III that extensive excavation should be carried out. Charles already enthusiastic about the finds at Herculaneum readily agreed. Prince d'Elbouef, the king's cavalry commander, was already in charge of Herculaneum and was entrusted with Pompeii as well. Hordes of galley slaves mostly chained in pairs were put to work - and the results were spectacular.

Unfortunately excavation and classification were not carried out systematically, the only records being in the diary of a man called Alcubierre. The early 1760s saw many important discoveries at Pompeii. The German Johann Winckelmann came to Naples in 1762 and strongly criticized the way in which the treasures were being handled. According to him they were being shoved piecemeal into a museum at the king's palace at Portici. He published an open letter of criticism that he sent all over Europe to scholars and collectors, including Sir William Hamilton.

The most important discovery was the Temple of Isis in June 1765. The decorations and furniture were in near perfect condition and included the celebrated tripod of the winged sphinxes, which had an important influence on European design. An inscription showed that the temple had been almost entirely rebuilt since the 62 BC earthquake. Hamilton was present when the Temple of Isis was being uncovered, and saw the paintings being removed to the palace of Portico. He began what became a famous collection of vases and other antiques many of which came from Herculaneum and Pompeii, and published a lavish illustrated catalogue in four volumes, that provided inspiration for the Wedgwood ceramics factory. Charles III left Naples to become King of Spain and his son Ferdinand I came of age in 1767.

The new king found the excavations excessively boring, but his wife Maria Carolina Hapsburg was far more interested. Hamilton was called on to escort her father, the Emperor of Austria around the ruins, and he also conducted Duke Albert of Saxony and the Grand Duke Paul of Russia.

William Beckford arrived in Naples from England in November 1780, and found that the gladiators' barracks at Pompeii had just been uncovered - and was enthralled by the Temple of Isis. Meanwhile a black market in antiques flourished and Lady Holland even brought back a statue of Caligula to London as a present for Walpole. Hamilton himself was not above helping himself, and two magnificent candelabra 'found their way' from Pompeii to his secret treasure vault in Naples. Goethe with the painters Tischbein and Hackert went with Hamilton to Pompeii in March 1787. They thought the houses very small and Goethe wrote, 'This mummified city left us with rather a disagreeable impression.'

Around one hundred years later (in 1883), when a great deal more had been excavated, Augustus Hare wrote, 'One's first impression on entering the mummified city is one of disappointment. Its streets are straight narrow alleys in which the ruts worn by wagon wheels... the stepping stones for the use of foot passengers in the wet weather which turned these streets into water courses. The windowless houses are without outside ornaments and look more like ruined cow sheds and pig stys than anything else.'

In 1777 the treasures at Portico began to be removed to the new Museo Borbonico (now the Museo Nazionale) in the centre of Naples in a cavalry barracks built in 1585. Ferdinand II took more interest in Pompeii and excavations continued at a fast pace under him and also when Murat was king. When Garibaldi occupied Naples in 1869 he made the French writer Alexandre Dumas Director of Pompeii, Herculaneum and the museum. Dumas planned great things. In the last years of Ferdinand II's reign there had been the sensational unearthing in the House of the Faun of the *Alexander Mosaic* (....), perhaps the most outstanding mosaic of the ancient world and the bronze of the *Dancing Faun* itself. Dumas hoped to bring French experts to Naples but popular feeling welled against him. The Neapolitans did not want a foreign director; after all, the *Risorgimento* was about Italy for the Italians. Fortunately King Vittorio Emmanuelle appointed in his place an able Director Guiseppe Fiorelli and then began really systematic and scientific excavation.

Today in Pompeii we find Roman life embalmed. There are crowds of tourists but no cars, only walkers and there is a feeling of peace, even solitude. Walter Scott standing amid the ruins could only utter several times, 'A city of the dead', 'a city of the dead'. Yet the life of the citizens, so suddenly ended nineteen hundred years ago, seems to persist in the silent streets and houses laid bare by excavation. It is one of the wonders of the world. No one can imagine it until he or she has seen the size and effect of the ruins. Street after street stretches from gateway to gateway and can be traversed just as the inhabitants did on that fatal day in 79 AD.

Rows and rows of ruined houses reveal the domestic architecture of a typical Roman Greek town. Facing the street are small shops, much like an Eastern bazaar. Then there is a narrow entrance often dividing two shops; it was sometimes paved in mosaic, such as the image of the watchdog and the warning *cave canem*. There were no house windows facing on to the street, rather like the kasbah in an Arab town.

Fascinating details of ancient life are revealed in around 20,000 graffiti painted or scratched on the walls. Schoolboys, prostitutes, soldiers, travellers, slaves and lovers had commented. Penises carved or painted are much in evidence, and they were regarded as charms to ward off the evil eye as they still are in Naples. Many drawings on the walls show commercial life and scenes of gladiatorial combat. One poster painted on the wall of a house advertises gladiatorial games to be held at the expense of Lucretius Satrius. There are many posters for election to the council; some identified the names and careers of the candidates and from which a *Who's Who* of personalities in public life could be created. A great deal of our information about life in Pompeii is derived from inscriptions in stone or bronze on tombs and houses and inscriptions on certain goods to denote provenance or ownership. Thus with the aid also of wax surfaced wooden tablets, we know a lot about people involved in public and commercial affairs in Pompeii. For example, the whole body of free citizens elected magistrates annually.

However, the economy depended on unpleasant slavery, which was often brutal although household slaves were well treated and could accumulate property and become free men. The slaves came from the east as prisoners of war or as the result of a flourishing slave trade along the frontiers of the Roman Empire. Many of the middle class, the professional people, craftsmen, tradesmen and technicians would have been slaves or descendants of slaves. However the vast majority of slaves were treated as a labour force without rights, and made to do the work now executed by bulldozers, tractors and navvies.

The houses were small although they became larger in the last hundred years. The following diagrams show how larger peristyles (inner colonnaded garden courtyard) occupied more space in later years. However the really large luxurious villas with terraces looking out to sea, were built outside the town on nearby farms with wine and olive oil presses. Scope for large villas was obviously limited in the congested, developed area of the town. It is interesting that window glass was coming into increasing use before the eruption in Pompeii. This must have added greatly to the comfort of the houses. The townhouse windows always looked inwards towards internal gardens, while country villas could look outwards to the mountains and the sea. However the gardens of the town houses were lavishly planted with trees and shrubs - also lemons, soft fruit, figs, walnuts and vines in trellises. The finest town garden was in the House of Loreius Tibertinus. Here the rear of the house opened onto a terrace with a marble lined water channel and a large fountain, while the garden sloped downhill from the Via dell'Abondanza towards open ground within the south walls of the city.

The greatest improvement to the town's amenities was the introduction of a piped water supply that replaced the wells; water troughs and fountains became a feature of Pompeii. The water came in a long aqueduct from the mountains and was stored in reservoirs (castelli) raised on columns and then distributed to public fountains, baths and private houses by lead pipes, nearly all of which are still in place. The fountains were adorned with heads of gods and goddesses or wild animals. Lamps hung from the shops and the public altars lighted the streets after dark.

All visitors to Pompeii are struck by the small size of the houses and the rooms within them. In fact the population lived largely out of doors in the forum and the baths and in the theatre, while guests for meals hardly ever exceeded nine. The bedrooms were tiny and have been described as 'Lilliputian or pigeon holes'. The Pompeiians were considerably smaller than the ordinary Europeans of today. Their houses were built for coolness with shade and shelter from the oppressive heat and glare of the sun, but they must have been very cold in winter.

There were a great number of inns (*hospitia*), taverns (*cauponae*), bars (*thermopolia*) and large stables near the main gates. One inn has the sign of an elephant. Their walls are often covered with graffiti giving the names of the guests and views about the fare. One charges the innkeeper with serving water and drinking the wine himself. Look at the tavern in the Via del Mercurio where warm drinks were kept in terracotta vases, and bottles and glasses show how wine and orange and lemon drinks were provided from behind a bar. On one wall are splendid wall paintings showing typical scenes from everyday life in a pub. The guests are shown drinking and ordering drinks, quarrelling and playing games, while the pub food is displayed with representations of hams, sausages etc. In some bakeries loaves of bread have been found stamped with the baker's name. There were many tanners and makers of cloth, and a series of paintings from the fullery in Via del Mercurio showing how cloth was worked are in the Museo Nazionale.

The richness of the decoration of the houses and the number of baths, theatres and gladiators quarters reveal how prosperous this provincial town was. The Pompeiians frequently chose decorations with a love theme (*Amorini*). Most charming is the fresco in the House of Cupids depicting a

145

seller of cupids. He holds a cupid by its wings to sell to a young lady, who already has a cupid upon her lap.

There is a strange contrast between the noisy petrol smelling streets of Naples and the silent streets of Pompeii, where the air is fragrant with untainted sea and mountain breezes. You walk along the narrow pavements past shop after shop but there are shopkeepers no more; the bakery ovens are cold, and the containers once filled with wine and fruit juices lie empty and broken. Yet this dead ancient city still seems alive as countless visitors pace its streets each day fantasizing about its former life.

Since the start of the excavations in 1748 four styles of wall decoration have been identified. The first dating from 150 to 80 BC was mainly an imitation of marble but included small architectural features as in the House of the Faun. The "second" or "architectural" style, occupied most of the first century BC. Based on stage scenery it gave the illusion of depth and space. Pastoral scenes, still life and religious scenes were painted during this period and can be seen spectacularly at the Villa of Mysteries. The third or Egyptian style lasted almost until the 62 AD earthquake. This was a reaction from bold architectural designs to slender columns or bronzes, with minute decorative details and miniature landscapes. The fourth or ornamental style covered the years between the 62 AD earthquake and the end. It was back to architecture but fantastic and blatantly theatrical. Carried out during the time of reconstruction, it has been termed 'decadent'. Examples can be found in the House of Castor and Pollux and in the later works in the House of Vettii.

Although only a few original Greek statues and paintings have been found, numerous copies of Greek art have been preserved for us in a way which could not have survived the era of Goths, Vandals and Turks. Not only does the Museo Nazionale overflow with copies of Greek works, but there is also a plethora on the walls of Pompeiian houses. Enjoy them while you can - many are decaying. Unfortunately, the early excavations only aimed at finding statues and works of art for removal and not at the systematic uncovering of the ancient city. A great number of frescoes unveiled then have now faded away

Most visitors arrive at Pompeii at the Porta Marina where there is the main ticket office and a good bookstall. Arm yourself with a good guidebook containing a plan with the most important sites well marked. Also a stout stick is useful as the going is rough over the large road paving stones and footsteps. I particularly recommend the book *Pompeii Guide with Maps* in the series 'Cities of Italy', published by Plurigraf. There are a good number of personal guides who ply for hire; Augustus Hare dismissed them writing, 'they were all imposters'. Today they are knowledgeable and polite and speak English surprisingly well, and if there are several of you they can provide relatively inexpensive direction. The custodians it should be noted, will nearly always unlock any house that is closed - but they expect a gratuity in return.

An incline and steep steps lead you under the Porta Marina to the Basilica on the right. It has thirty Ionic brick columns covered with stucco in imitation of marble, and at the west end there is a raised tribunal for judges because the Basilica was used both as a meeting place and as a Hall of Justice. It was almost certainly formerly covered with a roof. You are now in the Forum area - the religious and economic heart of the city. At the time of the eruption this area was still badly damaged by the 62 BC earthquake, but was much in use as a food market. The Temple of Apollo antedates the rest of the Forum but is part of it. It was begun in the sixth century BC and extended by the Samnites, and was finally enlarged and embellished in the time of Nero. The inner altar, reached by a long flight of thirteen steps, is raised on a podium. It adjoins a brick triumphal arch in perfect condition. Just beyond to the north are the baths of the Forum - almost the best preserved remains. A remarkable feature is the *tepidarium* (warm bath), which was used as a changing room by those entering the *caldarium* (hot bath). The low round vaulting of the *tepidarium* with stucco designs is carried on a row of splendid statues.

In ancient days the Forum area was a pedestrian precinct. Pass over the obstacles to the chariots and carts into the Via dell'Abbondanza, the fashionable street of old Pompeii, and you come to the brothel (*lupaniarium*) in Via Lupina, much appreciated by visitors. It contains wall pictures of various sexual positions and numerous interesting graffiti by customers. The brothel is on two storeys; this is the largest brothel currently uncovered in Pompeii. Included are a waiting room and a latrine. The rooms are small, gloomy and with stone beds doubtless formerly covered with mattresses. It is a realistic evocation of the various aspects of life in Pompeii.

On the left are the extensive Stabian baths; these are further evidence of Pompeii's prosperity. They are the city's largest public baths. They contain many plastic casts of the bodies of victims found during the excavations. Note especially the stuccoes of cupids and trophies that decorate the men's dressing room. Around the large pool were areas where men wrestled according to the Greek custom, and smeared their bodies with oil and sand.

A road to the right of Via dell'Abbondanza brings you to the Triangular Forum, a picturesque spot much favoured for picnics and usually crowded with visitors. Here were concentrated the leisure activities of the town. A graceful portico of fluted columns gives access to two gates, which open upon the Triangular Forum. This fascinating place is the oldest part of Pompeii. There were an astonishing 95 Doric columns, of which twenty five remain. There are fragments of a Greek Doric temple of the sixth century BC and one is instantly reminded of the Temple of Neptune at Paestum.

The neighbouring Temple of Isis, built in the second century BC, was one of the few buildings in Pompeii to be rebuilt completely after the earthquake of 62 AD. Note the underground chamber where the holy waters of the Nile were stored for rites of purification. The temple was uncovered during the Bourbon excavations with all its furnishings and pictorial decorations almost intact. Isis was an Egyptian goddess and the cult came down to the Romans through the Greeks. The cult even reached England. The Goddess Isis was a universal mother. Some claim Isis worship influenced South European conceptions of the Virgin Mary and that the Madonna in South Italy is Isis renamed. Certainly Isis is frequently depicted with a child in her arms like the Madonna. In the Museo Nazionale is a complete illustration of the Temple of Isis with the story of its discovery. This should be viewed either before or after a visit to Pompeii. It is one of the most fascinating monuments in Pompeii, recalling her Greek founders. It is a real jewel of their architecture and is in surprisingly good condition.

Nearby are the large and small theatres; the smaller also known as the Odeon was built in the age of Sulla. It is well preserved and has the typical design of a Greek theatre. It could hold 1000, and was covered with a permanent canopy. It was used for concerts and especially for mime - comical and often bawdy performances inspired by incidents of contemporary life.

On the eastern side of the Triangular Forum is the uncovered theatre (*teatro scoperto*), built in the second century BC in typical Greek style. It could hold 5000, and had a wonderful scenic background with a panoramic view of the ring of mountains, which stand behind Pompeii. The seats in a horseshoe shape were cut out of the lava rocks and covered in marble. Still visible are remains of devices for spreading an awning over the spectators and sprinkling the air with cooling showers.

The Gladiators' Barracks are in a very old building originally providing a meeting place for theatregoers during performances. In the time of Nero, it was converted into gladiators' quarters. Around the perimeter there is a fine colonnaded court with 74 columns, which must have provided a delightful promenade for theatregoers and a shelter from the rain. Traces of a second storey still exist. A great quantity of weapons found during its excavation are in the Museo Nazionale. There was an arena for mock combats before the gladiators went into the amphitheatre for the real thing. Sixty three skeletons were found here, some in chains including one of a woman with rich jewellery clearly on an amorous visit to a gladiator.

Here you are close to the Albergo di Hermes, the most characteristic inn of Pompeii near the Stabian Gate. There are two large bars and a staircase to the upper floor where there were many rooms. The kitchen and the stables can also be seen. Proceed west and you come to the enormous Palaestra, or Gymnasium, which had a large open space for young men to exercise, including a swimming pool. There is a large latrine on the southwest.

Beyond the Palaestrina but still within the walls is the amphitheatre dating from 80 BC when Pompeii fell under Rome. It is one of the oldest and also one of the largest of Roman amphitheatres. It could hold 20,000 spectators, almost the entire adult population of Pompeii

The most common games in the amphitheatre were fights between gladiators and wild beasts (feroces), and battles between the various gladiator schools. Gladiators were usually prisoners of war and slaves who were hoping for their freedom. Christians were tragically slaughtered here by wild beasts, in what was the most popular form of entertainment in Pompeii. Unlike the even larger amphitheatres at Capua and Pozzuoli, there are no underground passages. Despite its great size, it had a cover that could be stretched over the entire area when there was rain, and the rings to which the apparatus was attached can still be seen.

At the Amphitheatre you are at the extreme west end of the walled town between the Sarno Gate and the Nocera Gate.

Roman laws forbade burial within the City Walls. If you stroll back to the west passing through the Nocera Gate from the Amphitheatre outside the walls, you are in the Necropolis (burial ground). Here you are away from the crowds of tourists who throng the area around the Forum and you can enjoy the luxurious tombs in peace, which the Pompeiians built for their forebears. The contrast between the close packed houses and the spacious area around these tombs in the Necropolis is striking. When I came here during the war I was much moved by the peace of this timeless Roman cemetery. That seemed far away from the devastation of so much of southern Italy, although a few German or American bombs had fallen on

Pompeii itself. This large cemetery area is impressive. The sepulchers are of various types – there are many small temples and mausoleums with extensive decoration of a high artistic standard.

The other similar burial area - also outside the walls - Via dei Sepolori is some distance away. You have to walk half a mile to the northwest past the Porta Marina and through the Porta Ercolano to reach it. Here again you find a peaceful area with few tourists and the same lines of tombs as in the necropolis, but this cemetery is much larger. Here there are also scattered dwellings, villas and workshops in addition to the tombs. The sepulchers are of various types - many small temples and mausoleums with much funeral decoration of high artistic merit. In one tomb, that of Terentius Major, the famous 'blue vase' was found. It is now in the Museo Nazioale. Ask to be admitted to the tomb of Umbricius Scaurus where there are most interesting pictures of gladiatorial games. Each tomb bears the name of the deceased's family, and frequently their business is indicated. All in all the necropolis and Via Dei Sepocri are a fascinating contribution towards understanding the Roman way of life.

You pass the Villa of the Mosaics so called because of the columns covered with mosaics uncovered during the excavations, which can now be admired only in the Museo Nazionale. Still there is a beautiful mosaic fountain in the garden - Bulwer Lytton's tale about it is poignant - telling of a blind girl guiding the man she loves and his betrothed through the pitch dark caused by the sea of ashes. She is the only one who can find the way out of the doomed city.

Continuing to the west you come to the Villa of Diomedes just outside the walls and close to the Via dei Sepolori. This was excavated as early as 1771. Both Goethe and Dickens mention it, and Dickens pointed out that eighteen skeletons of women and children had been found in it. They had food with them and they had wrapped clothes around their faces while a man, probably the owner, was discovered near the garden door holding the key - with a slave behind him with a bag of money. Bulwer Lytton, in *Last Days of Pompeii* (1834), describes the owner as a rich, fat and vulgar man who was very hospitable. I highly recommend *The Last Days of Pompeii* to anyone who has fallen for the lure of Pompeii. It is available in a light and readable modern paperback. Bulwer Lytton describes Diomedes as begging for help from passersby saying: 'I am Diomedes - ten thousand sesterces to him who helps me.'

The villa has a wide view of the sea and coast. The garden over one hundred feet square was surrounded by colonnades; in the centre were a fish pool and an arbour for a summer dining room. It is nicely replanted with palm trees. There was also a private bath, unusual in Pompeii, with its four public baths. All the frescoes have been transported to the museum at Naples. This villa is a masterpiece of Pompeiian architecture and of unusual design. Built into the side of a small hill and being on several floors, it catches all the light. The rooms are on one side of the garden and arranged around a peristyle with direct communication with the outside. Look especially at the large apsed room, which is unusually airy for Pompeii and has a wide ranging view. A staircase leads to the underground room where the eighteen bodies were found. It was titled Villa of Diomedes rather arbitrarily as it is opposite the tomb of the Diomedes family.

Further to the west and well beyond the Porta Maritima is the Villa of Mysteries. This was excavated between 1909 and 1929 and so was not visible to Dickens, Lytton or Goethe. The original owner gave up the Villa after the earthquake of 62 AD and the new owner a Greek freedman, must have had different tastes.

The building has a long colonnade and a series of gardens and a bright verandah, which make it still an attractive spot. In the house are two ovens and rooms for wine making, and there are bathing facilities.

The Villa of the Mysteries is famous for its magnificent frescoes portraying the rites of the ancient Dionysian religious cult that existed into the Roman Empire alongside the official religion. The villa was built in the second century BC but renovated and embellished in the years before 62 AD. Quite amazing is the room with the famous frescoes. The walls are covered with well executed paintings; life size figures tower up the frescoes and the famous Pompeiian red unifies the various scenes. Experts assert that the scenes represent the initiation rites to the cult of Dionysius, which came to be forbidden by the Romans. It was especially deep rooted in southern Italy, and the paintings are not only important pictorial Roman art, but evidence of the survival of the outlawed cult of Dionysius in this area. Here is the usual reconstruction of the narrative of the pictures:

- First Scene: Young Dionysius reads the sacred ritual while seated and a standing woman listens.
- Second Scene: A young woman brings offerings while a seated woman purifies herself, assisted by two young men.
- Third Scene: A woman gives some milk to a faun while a gross Silenus plays the lyre.
- Fourth Scene: A frightened girl takes flight while her cloak billows up, owing to her haste.

- Fifth Scene: Silenus offers one young Satyr water - another holds a theatrical mask above him.
- Sixth Scene: Wedding ceremony of Dionysius and Ariadne.
- Seventh Scene: A woman hides the symbol of fertility behind a cloth while a winged figure whips a young girl who leans her head on another woman's lap. Flagellation was known to be part of the initiation rite.
- Eighth Scene: The dance of a Bacchus.
- Ninth Scene: The bride-to-be gets ready for the rite.
- Tenth Scene: A seated woman thought to be the owner of the house looks on. She may be a priestess of the Dionysian rite.

It should be kept in mind that Dionysius (the modern Dennis) was the Greek god of wine and also known as Bacchus - the god worshipped by loud cries because of the boisterous nature of his rituals. He was a nature god of trees and fruitfulness and associated with the seasonal death and rebirth of vegetation in Greek drama. Dionysius was always attended by many minor deities as in these pictures - satyrs (grotesque little creatures with horses tails or sometimes half men and half goats) and Sileni (similar to the satyrs but older), and nymphs who haunted trees, rivers, springs and mountains. Knowledge of the cult comes from Greek drama but the House of Mysteries is unique. The cult of Dionysius spread to Rome by way of Etruria and replaced that of the national Italian god of the vintage.

Although not all is clear from the paintings there is a fascinating air of mystery created by the unknown artist who with bold strokes, has created what many regard as one of the masterpieces of the classical world. The worshippers are known to have tried to reach ecstasy by wild dancing.

The rest of the rooms are decorated with paintings of the second style. Many corpses were found in this villa that by 79 AD had probably become only a farmhouse.

The private houses of Pompeii are a wonderful series of monuments - apart from Herculaneum - unique in what they reveal of Roman times. I am writing of course, of the upper and middle class dwellings, those of the poor were humble. The more prosperous Pompeiians typically lived in single storey houses, although later more storeys were added. The houses had no windows onto the streets and as in Arab towns, consisted of a number of inward looking rooms surrounding a sky lit atrium (central hall). Behind there were commonly one or more gardens enclosed in a colonnade or peristyle (inner garden around which the main rooms of the house were grouped). They must have been uncomfortable although elegant. The rooms were small, the kitchen and lavatories cramped and overall lighting and heating was inadequate. The windows were often unglazed although there were some windowpanes made of selinite (gypsum), so unless the shutters were closed they must have been miserably cold in winter. The Pompeiians complained of odours and sometimes countered them by burning bread.

However these small and sometimes mean looking rooms were covered with wall paintings, floor mosaics and stucco bas reliefs which overall have produced the most exquisite interior decoration the world has known. They did not hang pictures on the walls; they painted them with murals, the best of which are in the Museo Nazionale in Naples. The subjects are mythology, idyllic landscapes, fantastic architecture, still life on the lines of the Dutch masters, together with many depictions of sex and love. Many are copies of the Greek works - others are original. They are cheerful, light and graceful and show a high standard of technique and taste.

There were some Eastern carpets in Italy, but the preferred mosaics of the floor decoration are outstanding. The mosaics were either like rugs, with a central panel in a frame of plain mosaic, or carpet design over the whole floor, sometimes reproducing famous paintings such as the battle between Alexander and Darius at Issus. Furniture was sparse but elegant, and not mass produced. There are enough surviving bronze tables, tripods, lamps and the metal of wooden beds and couches to show its typical style

The Pompeiians loved their gardens, and used a subtle blend of shrubs, flowers, and trees with statues, reliefs, fountains and *oscilla* (masks often hung from a sacred tree, which spun in the wind). Goethe looked on the gardens as one of the principal characteristics of Pompeii. In the grander mansions there was usually a larger garden painted with landscapes to make them look larger - as in the House of Vettii. The garden of the House of Loreius Tibertinus has been reconstructed to show its exotic shrubs, plants and plum trees identified from the roots found in the ashes. The central feature of the garden is a T-shaped trellised pond forerunner of many later Italian gardens.

Outside the town were large patrician villas usually with farms. There families including the Vettii, produced various brands of wine for sale in Pompeii. The Romans like the Greeks, mixed water with their wine. Twenty taverns and over a hundred bars have been identified in Pompeii.

I will not attempt to explain in detail how various ruined houses in Pompeii differ from each other, or what funny names the guides have given to so many, nor what works of art found in each has been taken to Naples. I will concentrate instead on a few houses. A map showing their positions is a necessity and easily procurable at the bookstall. Here are details of some of the most revealing. To see all these houses and all the monuments described above would take several days, but even those you see in a few hours can provide a wonderful experience.

The House of Vettii, a five minute walk from the Forum to the northeast, is a must for its size, state of preservation and the charm and variety of its wall paintings. The artists have harmonized the colours beautifully, and faithfully followed the designs of ancient Greek masterpieces. Quite enchanting are the cupids, psyches, and *amorini* playing, racing and practising crafts like winemaking, in effective contrast to the serious scenes from Greek mythology. Especially good are those in black and vermilion. It is all in Greek style.

The tinted stucco pillars in the peristyle if rather ornate are charming. The shaded colonnade surrounds a delightful garden with statues, vases, basins, marble chairs and tripod tables amid the flowers - while bronze urchins holding ducks pour jets of cooling water into the garden that has been replanted with the flowers identified from the pictures on the walls of the house. The whole pictorial decoration is a dazzling exhibition of fourth style painting after the 62 AD earthquake.

The House of Vettii is in such good repair that it provides striking evidence of the magnificence attained by the well to do of Pompeii and their luxurious way of life. The dwelling is almost intact and this gives a unique impression of stepping back into the past. In the entrance is an enormous penis or Priapus, which symbolized fertility and warded off evil spirits. In the bedrooms are erotic frescoed scenes that aroused much laughter from a party of Australian tourists who accompanied me there. My grandson was much amused to hear one say to his wife, 'Hi Bella, learned anything fresh?' The kitchens and servants' quarters allow one to reconstruct domestic life.

You will probably pass the House of the Faun on the way from the Forum. It is elegantly decorated and well proportioned. The original structure dates back to fifth century BC (Samnites), but its current condition is due to second century BC transformations. Its name derives from the small bronze of the bearded *Dancing Faun*, which is a masterpiece, and stands in a pool in the garden. From the house comes the large and splendid mosaic of the *Battle of Alexander*, now in the Museo Nazionale, but the Faun is still here. In one of the peristyles is a magnificent mosaic, with flora and fauna from the Nile Region. In front of the house is the salutation,

154

HAVE, 'a welcome'.

Close to the Vettii is the House of the Golden Cupids. This sumptuous building belonged to the rich Poppaeus family. It takes its name from the cupids (*amorini*) - graceful figures painted in gold leaf in one of the bedrooms. Many theatrical masks were found in the house and the peristyle is raised almost into a stage up a flight of steps with three entrances. It must have been designed for theatrical performances. There is a small temple dedicated to Isis —such a thing is rare in a private house. There is fine decoration in several of the rooms in the third style; the subject is 'Mythological episodes and characters.'

In the same area are the Houses of the Small and Large Fountains. Both have fountains that are masterpieces of mosaic art. The fountain in the House of the Large Fountain consists of a niche completely covered with polychrome tesserae and embellished with a bronze statue and theatrical masks. Both are made of glass paste stones and are two of the wonders of Pompeii. In the House of the Small Fountain there are delightful small landscape pictures.

The House of Adonis, also nearby, takes its name from a splendid painting called *Adonis Wounded* - one of the finest and most interesting pieces from the ancient world. It is on one of the garden walls in the middle of landscape paintings. Look also at 'The Toilet of Hermaphroditus' in one of the rooms looking out into the garden.

While here it is worth taking a dive into the House of Castor and Pollux, and the bar restaurant Caupona, in Via Mercurio. In the House of Castor a splendid colonnade with Corinthian columns stands out, as does the series of pictures of mythological scenes depicting *Apollo and Daphne, Adonis, Silenus and Scylla*. Some other pictures have been moved to the Museo Nazionale. The main room in the Caupona bar brings back to life the bustle of a bar like so many in Naples today, because of the freshness and spontaneity of the small pictures to be seen both inside and out. These represent a wagon with a wine skin, players and drinkers, food etc., and graffiti with allusions to drinking. It must have been like a tavola calda in Naples today. On the corner to the left is a scribbled *da fridum pusillum* (pour in some fresh water). In an adjoining room is a painting of Venus fishing. Opposite the tavern is a fountain with a head of Mercury - hence the name of the street.

If you go west from the Forum towards Porta Ercolano you soon come to the House of the Tragic Poet, so called because of a mosaic depicting a *Master of the Theatre*. It is a luxurious villa with very fine decoration in some of the rooms. It was the dwelling of Glaucus in the *Last Days of Pompeii* and best known because of *Cave Canem* (Beware of the Dog) on the threshold. A few yards further and you come to the House of Pansa, which is vast. It was subdivided into small rooms for letting, as indicated by an inscription. There is a beautiful atrium, fine columns and a pool. Unfortunately the original decoration has been lost. A few yards further and you come to the House of the Surgeon where the fascinating series of surgical instruments now in the Museo Nazionale were found.

Along the Via dell'Abbondanza are many houses of the rich. The House of the Crypto-Porticus takes its name from a surprising room where shafts of light filter in. It was an underground cellar used for storing wine, and contains plaster casts of people who died during the eruption. In the house are also good pictorial decorations of the second style showing episodes of the *Iliad* incorporated into a frieze in the colonnade.

However if time is short make a beeline for the House of Menander a short way south of the Via dell'Abbondanza. This is one of the largest and most elegant houses in Pompeii, very rich in decoration and containing many rooms. It is sometimes known as the House of the Silverware because the fine collection of 118 pieces of silver, now in the Museo Nazionale, were found here together with silver cups, gold pieces and coins. This also belonged to the Poppei family. It dates back to the third century BC, and was being decorated and rebuilt at the time of the 79 AD eruption.

The atrium has well preserved fourth style decoration. In one corner is a charming little temple with the original jutting out wooden roof open at the centre to give light and allow water to be collected. Rooms to the left of the entrance have paintings showing episodes of the *Iliad*, and on the left of the triclinium are two rooms with lovely frescoed walls. Other rooms have mythological and theatre paintings of masks and the portrait of Menander which gives the house its name.

Nearby is the House of the Priest Amandus where there is a fine triclinium with an excellent series of mythological paintings - *Hercules, Polyphemus, Perseus, Daedalus and Icarus*. The colours are still brilliant.

Both the Houses of Loreius Tiburtinus and the House of Venus have walls covered with fine paintings. Of exceptional interest in the House of Venus is Venus fishing with cupids riding on dolphins. It is full of Greek models and is typical of middle class taste in Pompeii. Obviously Botticelli used it as a model for his Venus.

The private houses of Pompeii are a wonderful series of monuments. I have described more than can be seen in one day. If you are holidaying in the area you will find several visits rewarding. Details of many of the interesting houses such as the House of the Ancient Hunt, the House of Sallust and the House of the Fugitives can be found in the English guide books in the bookstall.

The House of Sallust features in Bulwer Lytton - it dates back to the Samnite period with paintings of the first style. The best known is a fresco of Actaeon assaulted by a dog. The House of the Hunt has delightful pictures of hunting scenes although its important mythological paintings have been removed to the Museo Archaeolico. In the garden of the House of the Fugitives were found many corpses of Pompeiians who had died as they tried to leave the city. Plaster casts were made of the corpses, which faithfully reproduced their features and the shape of their bodies. Their terror stricken faces are haunting. Several were carrying money and valuables when they died.

There is no museum nowadays at Pompeii but a mile to the north there is the interesting small Antiquarium of Boscoreale (open all day). Opened in 1991 near the site of numerous classical villas and farms it has two sections. The first concentrates on finds which help one to recreate what life was like in Roman times before 79 AD around Pompeii, Herculaneum, Oplontis and Stabia. The second contains the main finds from adjoining Roman villas and farms.

In the first section many finds show how the Romans exploited the sea with hooks and fishing nets and a fragment of a vase contains garum - the famous fish sauce so much loved by the Pompeiians. The ancient scene is brought to life by a pictorial reconstruction of the coast with a particularly striking picture of the old mouth of the River Sarno. A good fresco from Pompeii shows Venus in a boat.

The second section - with interesting exhibits such as farm and land agents' tools, together with various jugs, glass containers, and pictures recalls the pleasant spacious life of rich Romans in their villas in the country with supporting farms. But remember this lifestyle depended on numerous slaves many of whom led very hard lives. Five villas adjoin the Antiquarium; some have been recently excavated and the finds reveal that some of them were reinhabited in the third and fourth centuries. The villa of P. Fannius Synistor excavated around 1900, is renowned for its wall paintings, which are now held in Italian and American museums. A trip to Boscoreale is rewarding as it evokes features of Roman country life - very different to those experienced by the urban dwellers.

Were Christians present in Pompeii in 79 AD? St Paul found some at

Pozzuoli when he arrived by ship. Undoubtedly there were a few and it is known that Christians were sacrificed to the lions and other wild animals in the amphitheatre to satisfy the sadism of the Pompeiians. But no firm evidence of their presence has come to light. Probably it must await the excavation of the large districts inhabited by the less well off that have been neglected in favour of the rich. Christians of that time did not belong to the moneyed class. Lytton's description of a sect of Nazarenes has no historical foundation. However an intriguing inscription in the form of an anagram has been found on a pillar in the Palestra (sports ground) next to the amphitheatre. A patio surrounded this area 450 feet square and in the centre there was a large swimming pool with rows of plane trees. One hundred skeletons including those of many youths have been found there. The inscription reads:

ROTAS
OPERA
TENET
AREPO
SATOR

In this puzzling anagram the word TENET is repeated in the shape of a cross. No sense can be made of the anagram. Interestingly, an identical inscription has been found scratched on a tile at Cirencester in England. Perhaps shortly before the eruption, a Christian scratched it on a column to encourage other believers.

10
Herculaneum

Herculaneum (like Pompeii) can best be reached in twenty five minutes on the Ferrovia Circumvesuviano. One journey is no more than 25 minutes long with trains leaving every half hour from the Corso Garibaldi terminus. Alight at the station of Pugliano in Resina and take the wide avenue to the left down a ramp to the Nuovi Scavi, about a ten minute walk away. The ruins open at 9 am until one hour before sunset. There are also bus services from Piazza Municipio and Piazza Carlo 111. It is 4½ miles by motorway from Naples centre and cars can be parked within the entrance. Remember this is a very dangerous area for thievery.

It is a strangely intact ruin, once a favourite Roman holiday resort and now many metres below the current street level. In Roman times Herculaneum was a small city of Campania to the east of Naples on the lower slopes of Vesuvius. It was situated on a promontory of the coastline flanked by two torrents. In antiquity as today the great coast road that leads to Stabia and Nocera crossed it. The eruption of 79 AD sent a large flow of mud lava into the town, which levelled out the land, and completely changed the physiognomy of the area. Unfortunately for archeologists the greater part of the old city is submerged under the modern town of Resina - while over its former suburbs are the Bourbon villas of Portici and La Favorita. These villas situated on the 'golden mile' can be visited conveniently if going by car or taxi to Herculaneum, as can the Villa Poppea at Oplontis. It was numbered by Cicero as being among the most important centres of Campania. Its celebrity today is due to the wonderful art treasures excavated there that in the eighteenth century, made it the richest centre of excavation under the Bourbons. Originally a Greek city it was considered to have been founded by Hercules after his return from Spain and is first mentioned in Theophastus (314 BC) as Heraklios.

The city was almost certainly founded by settlers from Cuma but the remains brought to light so far tell nothing of its most ancient period apart from a section of the town wall that recalls the plan of Naples towards the end of the fifth century BC. There is no record of which side Herculaneum was on in the second Samnite war but it is known that like Pompeii, it rebelled against Rome and was conquered by Sulla in 89 BC. The earthquake of 62 AD must have had similar devastating effects as at Pompeii, and similarly the inhabitants of Herculaneum had not finished repairing the damage when they were engulfed by the eruption in 79 AD.

What happened at Herculaneum was very different from that at Pompeii. At Pompeii there are layers of ash and lava about 20 feet deep that had rained down from the sky. Over Herculaneum there flowed

160

accompanied by an enormous volume of water, a shapeless mass of volcanic material, which had assembled around the crater and rushed upon the city in the form of an immense torrent of mud. It overturned and submerged everything in its path so that the whole aspect of the district was transformed. The mud lava in a liquid state filled every crevice and void, then it solidified and became tufa. The depth of tufa above the city varies from 36 to a maximum estimated at 80 feet. Vaulted localities have been found, filled up to the top by the fluid mass that entered through holes in the roof or through skylights. This has rendered excavation difficult but has preserved the city from rough handling by treasure seekers, and strangely has preserved much of the wood.

The Austrian Prince d'Elbouef made the first important discovery of works of art. Having purchased a villa there in 1709, he was sinking a well when in 1711 he encountered the stage of the theatre. From then until 1716, d'Elbouef in effect vandalized the best preserved monuments of Herculaneum. The marble of the theatre and a large group of statues were removed, some going to the Dresden Museum, but many others were widely dispersed. However methodical excavations began in 1738 after the Bourbons came to power, and were well supported by King Charles III of Naples. The site was not cleared and investigations proceeded by way of underground tunnels. During this time the exploration of the theatre was completed. The Forum and so called Basilica and several temples were traced and between 1750 and 1765 the fabulous Villa of the Papyri was explored, and its famous sculpture, treasures and papyri recovered. No attempt was made at complete clearance and the shafts and tunnels were refilled with soft earth.

Focus began to shift from Herculaneum with the mid eighteenth century discovery of Pompeii and by 1780 work had ceased altogether and was not resumed until 1828. Then some areas were completely cleared and work continued perfunctorily for seven years. Two blocks of houses were found including the House of Argus. In 1869 after the unification of Italy, King Victor Emmanuel III became interested in the excavations. For six years more work continued and the thermae were totally uncovered - but work was stopped because further excavations would have undermined the town of Resina.

Attempts to restart the work came to nothing until 1927 when the Fascist government became determined to uncover as much as they could without undermining Resina. Excavations have continued until today revealing many houses and villas and four great blocks in the southern part of the city. In 1960 part of Resina was pulled down so that the Forum quarter could be exposed. Excavations continue today. It is a dramatic moment when you look up at the jumble of cheap new buildings of the modern town of Resina, and you note that they are built on top of Roman houses that are almost complete, with upper storeys intact (sometimes under modern roofs). However at Pompeii the remains of the houses seem from outside little more than hovels. The narrow roads at Herculaneum are paved in marble with high pavements, and the gardens have been cultivated again so that they are green and full of nice fruit bearing trees as in Roman times. Unlike Pompeii there are no stepping stones, but both cities appear to have had pedestrian centers. Seldom are there crowds today and there is usually an air of peace in contrast to Pompeii. At Herculaneum where 2000 years ago the air was filled with the chatter of Romans, there is only birdsong today amidst the stillness of the Roman houses.

Serious difficulties have been caused by the presence of many Bourbon tunnels. Then the only aim of excavation was to bring to the surface art treasures for exhibition elsewhere, and to leave the buildings buried in the bowels of the earth. These underground tunnels crossing roads, houses and public buildings mean that many walls are found perforated, as are pavements, lofts and vaults. Some of these have fallen and are ruined.

Entering the excavations one walks directly above the palestra. It is a fine building over 260 feet long and the remains reach a height of 33 feet. The ground floor consisted of shops and workshops with residents accommodation above reached by staircases, traces of which can still be seen. Originally, it was thought to be a temple or a palace, but it resembles the Greek style palestra or gymnasium at Pompeii. As at Pompeii the palestra consisted of a large open area surrounded by colonnades, in the centre of which was a swimming bath building and a large hall for meetings. New excavations prove it was not a sacred zone, but a splendid public area. There are large vaulted rooms with striking decorations that have nearly all fallen but their remains are ranged around the walls. The magnificent swimming pool is a cruciform shape, and close to it there is a paved area where the Herculaneum youth performed their gymnastic exercises before spectators. An interesting bronze fountain representing a large serpent spirally entwined around the trunk of a tree, stands next to the swimming pool and water would flow from the viper like heads of this dragon serpent.

The theatre is probably the most impressive surviving remain at Herculaneum. It is the only building still accessed through the original excavation tunnels and is now lit by electricity. When first discovered dark tunnels and shafts could only dimly light it. It is smaller than the great theatre of Pompeii (159 feet instead of 186), and probably held as many as 3,000 spectators. Today you have to wander and turn among the eighteenth century tunnels and you cannot see the building as a whole. It would have taken less time and work to dig out the whole building and restore it to the light of the sun than to create what, in effect is a glorified coal mine.

d'Elbouef removed magnificent bronze statues and wonderful marbles from the theatre in the early eighteenth century. The stage wall must have been a splendid example of marble work and would probably have looked similar to some of the magnificent baroque that can be seen today in Naples churches. In the external gallery to the right of the stage, on one pilaster there is beautiful painting and stucco, which allows a glimpse of the original magnificence of the theatre. There are two interesting statue bases with inscriptions to a Roman Balbons and another to Pulcher. The actual statues were removed by d'Elbouef and cannot be traced. There are other finely carved columns and it repays a wander around. Ask the guides to point out the curiosities.

No one should spend less than two hours at Herculaneum. I will not attempt to describe everything worth seeing, but here is a list of the more interesting houses. Arm yourself with a plan and keep asking the guides. Most of the buildings will be locked but the guides have all the keys and are happy to show them, especially in return for a tip[9].

The House of Argus was one of the most beautiful to be brought to light during the 1828–1835 excavations. Some of it can only be seen from the Bourbon tunnels. It has fine stuccoed columns and there must have been remains of the wonderful furniture of the Roman patrician occupiers, but Bourbon excavators removed them all and no trace remains. Today you see its lovely garden renewed with palm trees.

The House of the Albergo was the biggest and probably the most affluent household of the southern quarter of the city. It was not a hotel as previously thought, but a patrician private house enjoying a wide view of the gulf and a large garden, with shady colonnades towards the inner part of the habitation. Unfortunately it has been greatly damaged over the centuries, much of which may have already been caused by the earthquake in 62 AD, after which it appears to have been changed from a patrician dwelling into shops and small houses. There are remains of second style painting on the

---

[9] Very recent visitors tell me there are now fewer guides because of economy and most buildings are open; consequently the mosaics, etc. are at risk.

walls and in the pavements and delicate foliation in white tesserae.

The House of the Mosaic takes its name from a singular chess board mosaic in the entrance. There is a pleasant windowed portico in which intercolumned spaces were walled in with windows cut into them, plus two garden entrances. The windows were made of glass and there are clear traces of the sashes. You find four pleasant bedrooms with red walls and in another room little landscape paintings. The atrium floor has become corrugated under the weight of the mud and the force of the 62 AD earthquake, and the terrace must once have had wonderful views of the sea that has now far receded. These three villas were built above the sea wall on high ground overlooking the port in an idyllic situation.

Away from the old sea front is the House of Graticcio, which is an interesting example of a humble Samnite house in contrast to those three previously described that were Samnite patrician houses. The internal partitions are not of stone but of wood with brick pillars. It is the clearest example either in Pompeii or Herculaneum of a house rented out to various families, who have in common only the light of the courtyard and the well. The building actually comprises two independent flats, one being on the ground floor, the other on the first floor. It is the germ of the idea of modern blocks of flats tenanted by various families. Interestingly the upper floor is reached by a staircase that also retains several of its original steps. The upper storey bedroom is painted a lively red, and in another bedroom are the remains of the furniture - a cupboard, wooden beds, little statues of the gods and a marble table that evoke the life of its early inhabitants. The bed is almost perfectly carbonized.

Nearby is the House of the Tramezzo di Legno (House of the Wooden Partition). It has its front preserved up to the second storey and with its doorway, windows and small openings is the most complete private house of either Pompeii or Herculaneum. It is unmistakenly a patrician house. The entrance is grandiose on the roof of which some of the beautiful dogs head spouts are original. There is a fine mosaic pavement in a geometrical design and a good marble table. Upstairs are two bedrooms that contain the carbonized frames of wooden beds. However the most exceptional feature is the wooden partition with three double leaved doors, of which the central one is missing. They have been reconstructed on the site with the wooden doors rehung on their original hinges and fixed again on their upright posts. Glass cases in the house contain objects found there including identifiable remains of vegetables. There is a small and charming garden surrounded by a little portico with rest rooms around it. In the central room the decoration was bright when it was uncovered but it has deteriorated. On the south wall there is a pleasing painting of a garden view with trellises, bushes, an urn and ducks feeding.

In the Insula V there is a beautiful series of houses. The SANNITICA house shows more than any other the best of domestic Samnite architecture in Herculaneum. An open gallery overhangs the porch and runs along the white façade, as in the case of the neighbouring Casa del Tramezzo di Legno. This is due to a later extension of the upper storey whereby the rooms above the main doorway were detached and converted into a tiny tenant apartment. There is a beautiful inner courtyard (the atrium), with a quaint covered gallery above, with diminutive Ionic columns. The house has one room on the ground floor delicately decorated in pale sea green with architectural detail shadowed in and a picture of the Rape of Europa in the centre. Some objects found during the excavations are exhibited, including fragments of table legs carved in the form of a running dog.

At the nearby House of Neptune and Amphitheatre a large shop flanks the entrance, and on the upper floor there are living quarters overlooking the street with the partition walls still well decorated. Of all the many shops discovered at Pompeii and Herculaneum, this is the best example of what a classical shop was like, and is also the best preserved. The goods of the last hours of business lie on the great counter, and on shelves behind there are wine amphoras in upright and lying positions as required. Some were sold full, others emptied in the shop into the customers' containers. Judging by the sumptuousness of several rooms and small bronzes and painted marble panels, the unknown owner must have delighted in taking refuge from his wine selling counter by enjoying his works of art.

The internal courtyard is particularly beautiful with mosaics including a hunting scene of hounds chasing a deer. There are theatrical masks in marble and a superb head of Silenus. On the other wall of the courtyard, facing the entrance to the house, is a mosaic panel of the mythological Neptune and Amphitheatre in an impressionistic style. This is an eloquent testimony to the art of mosaics in the Classical age.

The House of the Bicentenary owes its name to the fact that it was uncovered in 1938, two hundred years after the beginning of the original excavation at Herculaneum. It is the wealthiest household in the Insula V. The walls are painted beautiful red porphyry and there is a fine mosaic pavement. There are frescoes and a frieze with cupids. The house was probably abandoned by its rich owner to become a modest rented lodging house for a family - as the subdivided upper storey would suggest. Its most intriguing feature is a big wooden cross inserted in a stuccoed panel. There seems to have been a footstool for worshippers to kneel on, and a lively controversy has developed as to whether or not the room was an early Christian oratory. There are few Christian monuments predating 79 AD, the time of St Paul's preaching. It may be (and one can go no further), a precious testimony to the early history of the Church. Certainly the room has a devotional feel to it

The House of the Deer (*Cervi*) in Insula IV is a distinguished house with a façade 129 feet long. Originally from the great open portico one would have had a view across the garden to the sea. It is renowned for the marble statuary; two groups of deer being attacked by hounds were found here - though the sculptures currently exhibited are copies. The exquisite sensitivity of the modelling puts them among the most beautiful animal groups of Pompeii and Herculaneum although they must be anathema to anti blood sports activists. Here charming little pictures of cupids playing were discovered - which can now be seen in the Naples museum. In a room on the east side there is a powerful and vigorous statue of the drunken Hercules. He has obviously overindulged and the god who is supposed to have founded this city is not shown in a heroic light. His stomach is dilated like a wine skin; he has a stupefied expression, unsteady legs, with his club slung carelessly over his shoulder and the hero is caught in his least heroic act - that of passing water. If your visit happens to coincide with a gaggle of Italian children, the statue will evoke shrieks of childish laughter. Perhaps that is what the sculptor intended. There is also an intriguing statue of Satyr with a wine skin, revealing the owner's taste for the bizarre.

The House of the Gem almost next door to the House of the Deer, is so called because a gem with a female head of the Claudian period was discovered in it. There is an Etruscan style entrance hall with fine decorations in red and black, and a large mosaic pavement with a magnificent geometrical design imitating a Persian carpet.

Next door the House of the Relief of Telefus was one of the finest houses of the southern quarter of the city. Marble Oscilla was used as in the Casa dei Amorini in Pompeii and satyrical figures and theatre masks suspended between the columns standing out well from the glossy red background of the walls and columns. Household objects including an amulet necklace, several lamps and remains of food are displayed. There are richly decorated rooms with the remains of paintings and magnificent marbles showing the opulence of the owners. In a similar room there is a charming relief of the late Greek school, of the myth of Telephus, son of Hercules being suckled by a deer. Other rooms have sumptuous marble walls, pavements and paintings.

There are other houses worth visiting if you have time, but do not miss the thermae, which occupy most of Insula VI. Smaller than the Pompeii baths, with less sophisticated heating apparatus, yet they have the same divisions and strict separation of men's and women's baths. They date from 50 BC and were decorated at the time of Claudius or Nero. Two glass cases contain the remains of two skeletons - victims of the mudflow. They were probably the custodians of the thermae.

In the men's baths a small square room leads to the round tank of the frigidarium painted marine blue with red walls, and a domed ceiling (with a skylight) upon which is painted a fish pond on a blue ground with fat eels, mullet, and eagles together with a large polyp holding a lamprey. The vault reflected in the clear water of the bath, must have created the illusion of an aquarium, and bathers would have felt themselves immersed between the sky and the sea.

The great tepidarium, with a hollow floor (largely caved in) has a mosaic pavement with a galloping Triton surrounded by four dolphins (repeated in the women's quarters). In the caldarium you can see the smoke vents and hot air pipes. Outside we find the service quarters. The vestibule wall is still encrusted with smoke and soot stains from the large furnaces. On the left there is a part stone and part wood staircase, which leads to attics and terraces and further ahead there is a deep circular well. Water was raised from the well by means of a chain with little buckets - they were then pulleyed over to the water storage tanks. Donkeys, whose bones have been found, drove these. The large furnace and boilers were removed in Bourbon times but you can still see the large iron door of one furnace and a great iron poker that indicates the baths were functioning up until the last moment before the eruption.

There is no evidence of a town aqueduct as at Pompeii. Slaves or donkeys must have pressurized water for the numerous fountains from water towers or cisterns on top of houses that were filled by pumps.

The Forum and most of the public buildings of Herculaneum (apart from the theatre) lie to the north in the area surmounted by the town of Resina. Still a four faced arch at the extreme end of the fortifications is a tantalizing foretaste of the former splendour of the Forum.

D'Elbouef's discovery of the Villa of the Papyri was sensational. Alas it cannot be seen today. Excavation stopped in 1765; the shafts and tunnels had become dangerous with toxic gases and they were all filled in with soft earth. The villa had a frontage of 820 feet with a superb view of the bay. It consisted of an older rather small house to which had been added a large colonnaded area and an oblong pool. Between each of the 64 pillars of the colonnade there were undamaged statues. Some were copies of well known Greek figures while others were original. All were of artistic importance and included many figures to be seen in the Naples Museum today, such as the naked wrestler, the drunken faun, the drunken Silenus, the sleepy satyr, the jumping pig and Hermes in repose (fourth century BC). In addition the celebrated or infamous picture of Pan copulating with a goat was found here. Charles III thought it too explicit for exhibition and had it locked up at Caserta, but in Victorian times it was the prize exhibit of the pornographic collection of the Naples Museum.

A sensation was the discovery in 1700 in a small room - some on shelves and others on two sides of a central bookstand - of papyrus rolls. It was the biggest library discovery of classical times. The rolls were fragile but means were found of unrolling and reading them. They were all written in Greek and their content is disappointing. No new classical writings of importance were discovered.

A detailed plan of the villa was made in 1765. It had its own aqueduct and was of gigantic proportions with a large garden and terraces. Yet not all was uncovered. Perhaps one day this wealthiest and most precious villa of the ancient world, will be totally excavated. The unexcavated area (the living quarters) should yield furniture and more statues, which in a house of such distinction would be likely to have great artistic value. The Villa of the Papyri must have been the most sumptuous of all the Roman villas on the slopes of Vesuvius and even to reveal the wall decoration of the unknown part would be a triumph.

Back in the heart of the excavated site of Herculaneum a poignant sight in the House of the Beautiful Courtyard is a cast of the skeletons of three young people huddling together trying to escape from the deadly fumes that accompanied the lava flow. Far fewer skeletons have been found at Herculaneum than Pompeii, and no skeletons of horses.

The people of Herculaneum were richer than the Pompeiians but as Raleigh Trevelyan points out, no more reticent about sex. There is no brothel but plenty of phalluses. On the wall of the wineshop there is a rough phallic drawing and Trevelyan found a graffiti in the House of the Gem saying: *The Emperor Titus's doctor had a good shit here*, and in a back room of the Baths, *Apellis the waiter had fun with Dexter, the slave of*

Caesar. The House of the Deer has an enormous mural of a naked woman clasped by a bronzed male, with a ram wandering nonchalantly by.

Looking up at the steep rocky cliffs surrounding the town one can understand why Herculaneum was hidden for so long. What treasures must still lie buried beneath the modern town of Resina! Still what has been unveiled is one of the wonders of modern Europe.

From Herculaneum a trip may easily be made to the top of Vesuvius. In Victorian times a visit to Vesuvius was considered to be a 'must' and Thomas Cook then built a funicular railway almost to the top - long since destroyed by the volcano in 1906. Nowadays a road makes the trip simple. Buses leave the forecourt of Herculaneum station roughly every hour and climb up past orchards, lemon and orange groves, and vineyards, all growing in black volcanic soil, to a large car park. From the car park a steep 30 minute zig zag path leads to the lip of the crater the interior of which plunges down hundreds of feet with walls of red and grey rock to the volcano itself. The crater is plugged by enormous rocks, but underneath Vesuvius is seething away. Sometime during the next hundred years Vesuvius will erupt again with terrible consequences. The last time Vesuvius erupted was in 1944. I recall the horrendous damage that the flow of red hot lava did to the villages in its path. Since 1944 great numbers of new houses have been incautiously built far too close to the crater of Vesuvius, and hundreds of houses are on the danger list from the next lava flow. Indeed seismologists consider the next eruption may be as disastrous as the one of 79 AD. Naples itself is far enough away to be safe but the local authority has made contingency plans for the safety of thousands of people.

In the Georgian and Victorian eras the volcano was more active with frequent lava flows, and many British tourists, and especially Sir William Hamilton, have recorded that as soon as there were signs of an eruption, they made a dash to the mountain top to witness what was occurring - braving the rocks and debris thrown out and streams of red hot lava. With Vesuvius dormant for so long, interest in the mountain has dwindled, and today Vesuvius is overlooked by tourists. From the peak often covered by snow in winter, there is a magnificent view over the whole Gulf of Naples, from Ischia to the Sorrento peninsula and Capri. A half hour visit to the crater is enough. It is a trip only for good walkers.

11
East of Naples -
Portici and Oplontis

Bosocio wrote that the area east of Naples was the 'most beautiful corner of Italy' and 'full of little cities, gardens, fountains and of rich men.' In the eighteenth century the sea coast here and the foothills of Vesuvius were covered with charming villas whose owners had been attracted by the beauty of the countryside. In 1738 King Charles visited the Prince of Elbouef at his charming villa (built in 1711) on the seashore at Portici, and was so enraptured by the surroundings that he ordered architects Antonio Canevari and Antonio Medrano to build him a palace upon the most attractive site they could find nearby. When it was pointed out to him the likely dangers from Vesuvius he replied, 'God, Mary Immaculate and San Gennaro will see to that.' Yet only a hundred years before in 1631, Portici had been devastated by a terrible eruption and had to be rebuilt, while his new palace was only five miles from Herculaneum, destroyed by Vesuvius in 79AD. Yet his palace has remained safe for over 250 years thanks either to luck or God.

Today the worst type of unplanned Neapolitan development blights this formerly beautiful area. Nearly all the charming farms and gardens in soil of exceptional fertility, that surrounded Portici when I first knew of them over fifty years ago, have disappeared under a rash of concrete. It is now difficult to find the villas and identify the viewpoints of former days. Still for those interested in architecture it is worth making the effort, either by bus or car. The traffic is dense and parking difficult.

You must follow the old coast road past the docks and over the Ponte Maddelena to Portici. Around Portici you are in what Emma Louise Reilly correctly described in an important article in *Country Life* (27.2.1986), as 'the greatest concentration of historic villas in all Italy.' The Royal Palace of Portici where King Charles III originally stored the fruits of his digging from Pompeii and Herculaneum, is most interesting although situated in an unattractive urban environment. It is an impressive classical style in some ways more pleasing than Caserta. Built around an octagonal piazza, curiously, the main road runs through three arches right in the middle of the palace; the only other palace in Europe with this peculiarity is I believe the Queen's House at Greenwich. From both the front and the garden façade you get a magnificent view of the sea with only the foreground today spoiled by modern buildings.

Since 1873 the palace has been the School of Agriculture for the University of Naples. If you apply politely you will be shown around. A fine staircase has interesting wall and ceiling paintings with false perspectives. The State Apartments have good baroque paintings and King Joaquin Murat,

Napoleon 1's brother in law, redecorated the lesser rooms in good taste. When King Ferdinand returned to his capital after his exile in Sicily, he said he was delighted with the improvements Murat had made at Portici and that Murat's furnishings were perfectly to his taste.

Charles built a menagerie in the park, a mock medieval castle and a real tennis court. These along with statues and other remains from Herculaneum and Pompeii can still be seen in the precincts. Pope Pius IX, who fled from Rome in 1848 to Gaeta while the Garibaldi - Mazzini Republic governed Rome, lived in this palace from September 1849 to April 1850 and was warmly welcomed by the Bourbons and the local population.

The park and surroundings are run down but the palace is being restored by funds provided by the Ente per le Ville Vesuviane - the equivalent of being a listed building in Britain as are the other villas referred to hereafter.

The decline of the palace and the neighbouring villas began with the fall of the Bourbons. Caserta and the Palazzo Reale were enough for the House of Savoy in a region they despised. Then as the area grew squalid with the post Second World War building explosion, most of the well to do owners moved out and the villas became multi occupied tenements. Beyond Resina, the road was known as the golden mile because of the magnificence of the villas. It no longer deserves this title.

It is still worth searching through the concrete jungle to find the remaining gems. Villa d'Elboeuf originally baroque but remodelled in classical style has a superb position on the sea shore at Portici. There is a splendid picture of Pope Pius IX arriving by sea surrounded by boats and a cheering population. The Villa de Gregorio Barra retains the eighteenth century plantings in the garden and has camelias, which are internationally famous. Uniquely it remains in the same family ownership as for generations. Still a showpiece is Villa Campolieto built by Vanvitelli in 1755. It is the most spectacular of the Vesuvian Villas. The road front faces Vesuvius; the garden façade gives onto an elliptical courtyard through whose arches you can look down through the gardens to the sea. If you are allowed in you will see a magnificent staircase and frescoed rooms by Crescenzo among others with Pompeiian scenes recalling the tremendous enthusiasm of the nobility for the excavations in the second half of the eighteenth century. Fortunately more than £½ million has been provided for its restoration.

The Villa Pignatelli di Monte Calvo at S Georgioa Cremano that was in an appalling state, is being converted into a magnificent youth hostel.

This remarkable villa has a huge saloon looking out on to a dramatic flying staircase leading to the former garden now, alas mostly covered by hideous blocks of flats.

To my mind, the gem of the villas being restored is the Villa Prota at Torre del Greco. This is a Rococo villa of exceptional elegance and appeal - fortunately, the owners are restoring it. Also try to see Villa Favorita at Resina designed by Ferdinando Fuga, now a military training college. Unfortunately more new development is proceeding in this area, but you can still have the thrill of gazing through large but decaying coach entrance arches and glimpsing the old courtyards and dilapidated gardens and beyond the sea to Capri, the Sorrento coast and the whole bay of Naples.

Fifty years ago, Pompeii and Herculaneum were surrounded by gardens of olive vines, lemons and oranges. Today buildings hem them in and their charm is confined to the old monuments. Train or bus from Naples easily reaches both. There are car parks but both sites are situated in the worst possible areas for thieves. There are notices reading, 'beware of robbers', and the drivers of taxis and hired cars will not leave their vehicles unattended in the car parks of the nearby garages and roadhouses for fear of robbery. Bassolino, the Mayor of Naples, has to a certain extent cleared up the centre of Naples. The 'bad characters' have mostly gone and are now concentrated in Castela Mare and Torre del Greco. At Torre del Greco coral fishing still continues, and in family workshops they make pretty ornaments including many with shells, mother of pearl and tortoiseshell. If you are prepared to risk the pickpockets bargains may be obtained.

Castelamare must today be one of the ugliest towns in Europe. It has a remarkable history - badly damaged by the eruption which destroyed Pompeii, yet within ten years it rose from the ashes, and rich Romans built villas there because they liked the hot water springs. It suffered from Saracen raids and in the sixth century AD, the whole population together with their bishop sought refuge in the nearby mountains. The castle was built in the ninth century, and King Charles started extensive diggings for Roman remains in 1738. Many of his digs have been covered over and the remains are best seen in the National Museum in Naples. It still has some good hotels that are used by those seeking cures in the thermal waters, and by some package-tour operators - mainly because Pompeii and Herculaneum are so close. In my view the best advice to give to travellers is to be very careful around Castelamare and Torre del Greco because of the unsavoury population. Beautiful excursions into hills and woods from there, much loved by the Victorians and still delightful even fifty years ago, are now mostly horrid tarmac tracks through a wilderness of modern tasteless development.

Oplontis

If you head inland from Castelamare you soon come to Gragnano. In the 1960s Gathorne Hardy described it as having 'a quiet nobility'. This has largely disappeared with new development although the wine is as good as Gathorne Hardy records. Here you are almost in the old Roman town of Stabiae. In the 1950s and 1960s an archeologist Libero d'Orso, became convinced that Stabiae lay in this area and made successful digs.

Some renowned frescoes now in the Naples Museum, discovered between 1738 and 1782 in a building known as the Villa of Ariadne or San Martino in the Passegiata Archaeologia at Varano. Libero d'Orso unearthed two other big villas - the Villa of Poseidon and the Villa of the Obsidon Vases or spiral columns. The Villa of Poseidon is unique and comparable to anything in Pompeii.

Nearby also in the centre of highly populated Torre Annunziata, and very close to Pompeii and the *autostrada* lies the lost site of Oplontis, discovered in 1964 by d'Orso amid many roads and intensive building development. He cleared a very large villa probably belonging to Poppea, Nero's wife, whose family owned the houses of Menander and the Golden Cupids at Pompeii. The villa is now known as the Villa Poppea. It may be difficult to find your way so ask for the Scavi di Oplontis (telephone 081-8621755). There are over fifty rooms and it is one of the archaeological sensations of recent years. Originally built around 50 BC it was later altered and completely surrounded by a shady portico with two enormous pillars at the main garden entrance. It gives a vivid idea of the architecture of a very wealthy Roman's country house. Inside the decoration of the walls is fantastic - weird, richly coloured, with exceptionally good *trompe-l'oeuil* details of bowls of fruit and birds.

Half of the villa is still under the road, which is evidence of its enormous size. Currently one enters via a portico at the back of the villa through the garden. This saloon has walls painted with ?? and looks through to the atrium, decorated with dark red walls and painted yellow fluted columns - false doors with figures like angels, sea monsters, birds, and garlands while fantastic shields give an illusion of depth.

The *frigidarium* to the west is frescoed with gymnasts, fighting cupids, and a resting boxer. Then a *caldarium* follows where Nereid can be seen riding a (hippocampus??). To the east is a magnificent colonnade of thirty white columns and a thirty metre long swimming pool. Beyond are bas reliefs and many paintings before you come to the famous spiral columns with fluting going in alternate directions giving the illusion of movement. Alas they were damaged in the earthquake of 1980.

The dining room has amazing paintings with a mock gate surrounded by winged sea horses and flanked by garlanded pillars surmounted by crouched two winged centaurs. The house was being redecorated when five feet of stones and dust from Vesuvius and 15 feet of mud overwhelmed it in 79 AD - thus enduring the fate of both Pompeii and Herculaneum. The only dead body found there was that of a cat. Because the Romans loved the warm springs Stabiae, unlike Pompeii, was soon rebuilt.

Oplontis is an oasis of Roman excavations well removed from the tourist crowds that besiege Pompeii and Herculaneum. Although hard to find and in an unattractive area, I thoroughly recommend visiting them. Here you imbibe in tranquility the atmosphere of the luxurious sybaritic life of rich Romans who made this part a Mecca for the rich - away from the noise and bustle of town life. Moreover you can congratulate yourself on tracking down a wonderful but little known classical site. Normally the villa is open to the public from 9 am until 1 hour before sunset, but check first.

There is an antiquarium founded by d'Orso in the Liceo Plinio Senior, Via Marco Mario and it is usually open to the public. Here are fascinating objects found in various villas by the dedicated excavator Libero d'Orso, who was responsible for nearly all the excavations. Thirty years ago one could have enjoyed a chat with him when it was his own private museum as he was often present.

There was obviously a complex of big villas at Oplontis. The richest Romans liked to build their super luxury houses in groups outside the towns especially where there were thermal springs. A second Villa (Crassus) is at the moment being excavated. No domestic utensils have been found in the Villa Poppea but a considerable amount of building material ready for use has come to light. Poppea died in 62 AD from a kick in the womb from Nero while she was pregnant with their second child, and her death may have delayed the repairs after the extensive damage from the earthquake of 72 AD. Obviously the new owner was planning to renovate the property when disaster struck once more – meaning that the villa was buried in its damaged state.

As mentioned, Poppea's villa goes back to the first century BC. The paintings are largely of the second and third style (80 BC to 63 AD), which allows us to date the villa. Probably the same artists painted here as in the

Villa of Mysteries (...) and at Boscoreale

The rich colours of the wall paintings are unique and they have not had time to fade. Let us hope modern technology will find a way of preserving them in their original condition indefinitely. When the eighteenth century excavators uncovered the wall paintings at Pompeii they were staggered by the brilliance of the colours - at Oplontis we experience the same vividness. It is a unique sensation.

When I visited Oplontis, we were the only visitors to this amazing site. One feels strongly that if Poppea had lived, she could have moved back in provided the roof had been replaced.

The deep red detailed murals with remarkable still lives of figs, other fruit, peacocks, other birds and animals are in astonishingly good condition. It makes one wonder why nowadays so few murals are painted for the decoration of our own house walls.

In Poppea's day the villa was on the sea but today it is a mile inland. Her wonderful large swimming pool (120 feet by 45) with gleaming white marble slabs around could easily be restored to its original condition. Along one side is the covered terrace with small decorative plaques – it is spectacular with fine views of the bay.

Capri

Capri is easily reached from Naples by helicopter from the Caporichino airport, though it is the most expensive means of travel. More reasonable is a 40 minute hydrofoil from the central quay of Molo Beverillo in Naples or from Mergellina to the west end of the bay. From Sorrento a hydrofoil takes 20 minutes, leaving from Marina Piccolo. The port on Capri is Marina Grande a landing place since Greek times - that has nothing very attractive about it. From there you go up by bus, taxi or funicular to the Piazetta of Capri, which is the focal point of the island. The funicular is to be preferred. As soon as you enter the Piazetta you are struck by the charm of the island. It is small almost like a drawing room from a musical comedy, set with cafés and glistening white houses dominated by the old cathedral. It is a fairytale square where the rich and great mix with day-trippers and working Capriots.

This is an ideal holiday island, full of old fashioned charm. Unlike the mainland there is no urban sprawl and the island is quite the most beautiful in Italy. It seems almost a type of garden perched on a rugged rock. Whereas at Positano the white houses too close together look like white sheets hanging on a washing line, the same type of white house on Capri mixed with Pompeiian red, peeps out from terraces of vines, oranges, lemons, gardens and well wooded slopes. One hundred years ago Norman Douglas warned that Capri was becoming deforested and fortunately his warning was heeded.

In my view it is better to stay a few nights than to come for the day. The excursions take too long being mostly long walks, and during the day the island is overcrowded with day trippers. Once the day trippers take the boat back to the mainland, those staying on have the island to themselves and there are no crowds. The Capriots themselves are polite, cheerful and welcoming - all are anxious for visitors to enjoy their island to the full. They have none of the brashness of the Neapolitans and show their Greek origin.

Trees and flowers flourish everywhere. There are more than 800 species of plants with magnificent wild flowers, among which the wild orchids have to be seen to be believed. The air of Capri is always filled with delicate the scents of the wild flowers, pines, oranges and lemons, while the deep blue of the sea and sky are tremendously exhilarating.

Capri is small and hilly and only 5½ square miles. There are palaeological remains, and the Greeks settled there - although there are not as many traces of them here as on Ischia. The Roman Emperor Augustus exchanged the larger and more prosperous island of Ischia with he Neapolitans for Capri in 26 BC.

According to Suetonius, Augustus was much attracted by the Greek appearance of the island and its inhabitants, and also by the lucky omen that a withered holm oak burst into leaf on his arrival as he was returning from the Macedonian wars in 29 BC. After the death of Augustus in 14 AD, his successor Tiberius made Capri his home during the last years of his life. (27 AD - 37 AD). Both Augustus and Tiberius (known locally as Timberio) built aqueducts and palaces and developed the island. Tacitus and Suetonius have accused Tiberius of all sorts of cruelty and crimes, including unnatural vicious orgies. The truth of their accusations is open to doubt.

In later centuries Capri was much damaged by raids from Saracens. One known as Barbarossa, destroyed the castle now named after him. The streets of the medieval town were made very narrow so that at a moment's notice they could be barred and garrisoned against a Saracen raid. Where the Saracens dined they slept - this explains the few Arab-looking Capriots one sees today. However the vast majority show their descent from the Greeks.

In the eighteenth and early nineteenth centuries the Bourbons loved Capri for its woodcock and quail shooting. Great numbers were found on the island and there are still plenty today. It is recorded that when King

Ferdinand II went shooting on Capri in 1826, Neapolitan warships cruised around the island because of the risk of Saracens carrying him off.

During the Napoleonic wars it was the scene of several engagements between the British and the French - which caused considerable damage. In May 1806 the British overpowered the French garrison and proceeded to fortify the island. Two attempts by Joseph Bonaparte (then King of Naples) failed to retake it.

The British Governor was Sir Hudson Lowe who later was to be Napoleon's jailer on St Helena. Lowe was warned of an impending attack in October 1808 by the troops of King Murat who had succeeded Joseph as King of Naples. According to Norman Douglas he ignored the warning, and one week before the attack began he ordered considerable quantities of the best French wine. Then on 6 October Lowe was taken completely by surprise when the French under General Lamarque attacked. Lowe had assumed the island was impregnable. The Commander of his forces Captain Hamill let him down badly not deploying his artillery. Hamill was killed and there is a memorial to him in the church of St Constanzo. Lowe once the French had secured a bridgehead, withdrew to the town of Capri where he surrendered on 17 October 1808.

Douglas is very critical of the behaviour of the British fleet, which should have cut off supplies of food and ammunition from the French landing force. He believes Genoese captains were bribed by large gifts from Murat and 'only hove in sight two hours after the capitulation had been signed'.

In the middle of the nineteenth century Capri began to be the home of writers, artists and musicians. The first hotel in Capri was the Hotel Pagano (today La Palma). From here a German Herr Kopisch rediscovered the Blue Grotto in 1826. It had been known to the Romans but forgotten in the eighteenth century.

Carriage roads for Anacapri, Marina Grande and Marina Piccola were opened and the second half of the nineteenth century saw many new hotels being built, including the Grand Hotel Quisisana. This became very popular with the British and until the Second World War had a predominantly British clientele. Their prices now are sky high and it is only for the very rich. Until 1939 British visitors with moderate wealth loved the Quisisana. The following letter from a middle income British family in 1922 evokes this era. Strangely in those days the steamers did not tie up at Sorrento or Marina Grande, and passengers had to bob around in small boats to land:

178

'*Thursday 2.3.22. Hotel Quisisana Capri.*

Capri, the Haven - I can't begin to describe it - words are such inadequate things. The getting here was most exciting - we left Naples harbour at 3:30 - there were clouds above and mysterious dark shadows over the hills, but there was blue sky behind them and for most of the time the sun shone kindly down upon us. The coastline was ragged and of precipitous rock and when we came to little villages the houses seemed to almost overhang above the sea - clinging to the crevices in the rock. From three of the villages little boats pulled out to sea - our engines were stopped and they came alongside and people were landed by them. At Sorrento it was amusing to watch five different hotel boats trying to grasp the passengers - like buses at a station - it was about 6:30 when we pushed off from there and Capri appeared dark and forbidding against the cloudy sky, but soon we saw the little twinkling lights of the harbour and little boats rowing out to meet us being tossed about on the waves. I can't quite think how we got safely into them but we found ourselves there. Mother was very frightened and two old nuns whimpered and prayed all the time as we swayed this way and that until we were hauled out at the harbour. The little town is on a higher level, so we were all pushed into a funicular by the hotel porter and arrived at a quaint little town with narrow streets - and steps up the main street and cobbles. The hotel is awfully nice and we soon forgot the billowing waves and our tossing in the little boat as we sat down to a good dinner to the strains of an orchestra. When we were safely in our beds the storm came crashing in with thunder and lightning and torrents of rain.

Friday 3.3.22. Awoke to a clear blue sky, bright sunshine and air that felt like a cool drink. We spent the morning entranced while wandering up and down the little cobbled pathways. Climbing onto rocks and gazing down into the many coloured sea. I've never seen such wonderful clear blue sea with greens and purples split into the depths anywhere. The island is gay now with oranges and lemons, blue iris and anemones, geraniums and here and there a rose - the almond blossom is out too and all the place and people look sunny and happy.

We sat in the hotel garden after lunch and read and wrote some letters, and went for another walk in the cool of the evening - the colours at sunset were even more wonderful than in the morning'.

This is a fair description of Capri in winter when the weather is often perfect. The blue of the sky and sea is as intense in winter as in summer.

In 1838 Lady Blessington found no inn on Capri. Instead her party rented three houses which 'by whitewashing and thorough cleaning were rendered habitable abodes'. She thought the fish on the island good enough to satisfy 'even the fastidious palate of a Lucullus'. Neither did she find an inn at Sorrento but instead, 'excellent lodging houses'. She found the inhabitants of Capri very good looking, in contrast with the Empress Marie Louise (wife of Napoleon I), who was staying in Naples and thought by Blessington to be very plain.[10]

The list of foreigners who made Capri their home or who stayed there for some time is impressive. They include Gorky the Russian writer, who after the abortive St Petersburg rising in 1905 brought a colony of Russian revolutionaries, including the musicians Chaliapin and Tchaikovsky. Other well known writers came as well: Axel Munthe, Joseph Conrad, R.M. Rilke, D.H. Lawrence and Compton Mackenzie. Norman Douglas stayed for long periods on the island and has written much about it, while the well known Italian writers Curzio Malaparte and Alberto Moravia also spent time here.

Capri was not always an island. It shook loose from the Sorrento Peninsula around 10,000 years ago when the ice caps melted.

There is plenty to see on Capri - enough for several days if you intersperse sightseeing with bathing and reading in the elegant hotel gardens. Capri itself consists of the charming little piazza and a picturesque maze of narrow streets and alleys of the ancient medieval quarter. Here are many famous names of shops that together with the locally owned ones make it a shoppers' Mecca. One entrepreneur called Rosso inherited two shops from his father and grandfathers and now has twelve to cater to all ages. The clothes are smart with lovely colours. The famous Capri pants and Capri sandals of the 1950s are as fashionable as ever. The shop assistants are exceptionally polite and not 'pushy'.

The piazza is on the site used by the first Greek colonists and Greek masonry from the fifth and sixth centuries BC can be seen. During the day it is full of day trippers but in the evenings it becomes peaceful. The church of St Stephen (the former cathedral) with its cupola and clock tower (of uncertain date) frame the north side of the piazza. It is late seventeenth

---

[10] During the Anglo–American occupation (1943–1945) Capri and its hotels were reserved as a rest centre for US soldiers, and the British were not allowed to use the island. From 1940–1943 the Germans had held several Capri hotels as leave centres for German officers from North Africa. As a result post war visitors have tended to be more American and German than British, although until 1939 British visitors were dominant.

century and is the work of Pichiatti whose Misercordia in Naples is so much admired. Inside the church there are remarkable coloured tile floors from the Villa Jovis. The tombs of the Arucci the rulers of Capri for centuries are here. Just to the north of the church there is a splendid viewpoint.

The most popular excursion is on foot to Tiberius's palace, the Villa Jovis. This is a fairly steep 45 minute walk from the piazza, which is most enjoyable with glimpses of gardens and the sea, and occupies the majority of the day trippers. The narrow paths are typical of Capri - from them you see the Capriots greeting each other and hear a subdued chatter from house to house. At the Villa Jovis you find the substantial remains of a magnificent Roman Villa of Imperial times. According to Tacitus, Tiberius built a total of twelve palaces on Capri of which the Villa Jovis was the largest. Just before you reach the Villa Jovis on the right stands the remains of a Roman lighthouse tower. From here Tiberius could send smoke signals to the mainland to keep in contact with Rome.

Surprisingly Tiberius was 68 when he retired to Capri having lived a life of strict morality. This leads one to doubt the tales of his sexual excesses. Living until the age of 79 on Capri he was a solitary old man and the tired ruler of an ungrateful world. It seems unlikely he threw his victims down the cliffs from his palace.

Villa Jovis is a scene of indescribable beauty, with a view of the whole island and an almost endless horizon sweeping from far off Ischia to the Gulf of Naples, the characteristic profile of Vesuvius, and the nearby Gulf of Sorrento. The main parts of the Imperial construction are around the magnificent water tanks, that have a total surface area of 7000 square metres. Another conspicuous feature are the baths showing the usual hot and cold rooms and a complex heating system. Above the ruin is the small church of S Maria dei Soccorso – that is not very attractive.

The Blue Grotto is attraction number two for tourists. The traditional route is by motorboat from Marina Grande. However the entrance is so low you can only enter when the sea is calm or your head will be bashed by the rock. Sometimes there are long queues of boats. Once inside you will be seduced by the magic sky blue reflections of the beams of light coming through the narrow access hole. No one visits the Blue Grotto more than once. There are other grottoes for those interested.[11]

---

[11] Murray's 1855 handbook gives the best description of the Blue Grotto. It is unchanged today: 'The traveller finds himself in a fairy scene which justifies the poetical creations of the Arabian nights. The smooth water and the walls and roof of the grotto assume a most beautiful ultramarine colour which no doubt is produced by the light from without entering

Anacapri has great charm and peace and is set amongst gardens and vineyards on the flattish edge of Monte Solar. It is more oriental than Capri itself, and was a favourite haunt of patrician Roman families and much loved by Tiberius, who built himself the Villa of Damecuta here. The Fenician steps were the only way of getting to Anacapri until the carriageway was built in 1877. They are not Phoenician steps at all although there is evidence the Phoenicians came to the island. They are Greek and have recently been restored so you can make the tiring ascent of 400 steps from Augustus' sea palace, the Palazzo del Mare, where there is better than usual sea bathing, to Anacapri. Only a few of the steps are the original Greek ones..

Close to the Fenician steps at Anacapri is the Villa san Michele built by Axel Munthe in 1896. Born in 1857, Munthe worked as a doctor in Rome where he was much admired and sought after by the upper classes. He spent long periods on Capri and wrote his famous autobiography *The Story of San Michele* there in 1929. Perhaps his most notable work was in Naples during the cholera epidemic in the hospitals where he risked his life several times daily. The villa was left in his will to the Swedish State that allows Swedish scholars to stay there while many cultural events are held during the summer. It is a magnificent villa full of Roman remains and beautiful furniture, with a loggia looking out over the whole Gulf of Naples. There are Roman ruins in the grounds. From Villa San Michele you can see the Castle of Barbarossa, so called because he captured and destroyed it in 1535 during the worst pillage the island ever suffered.

Do not miss the church of St Michael at Anacapri, which has a splendid baroque façade designed by Antonio Vaccaro and completed in 1719. This is a delightful small baroque church with very good pictures by Solimena and de Matteis well lit and in good condition. The church was built at the request of an unusual Carmelite nun, Mother Serafina di Dio, who had already founded the convent of S Teresa. Serafina has a tremendous reputation on Capri, although is little known outside the island. She inherited a house and a large legacy from an uncle who was a priest, and

---

the water, and being refracted upwards into the grotto. The light is not diminished and the blue assumes a deeper hue when the entrance is half blocked by a boat coming in. A man swimming in it appears of a silvery hue. The best hour to see it is between 10 and 1 o'clock; but the traveller should remain at least 20 minutes to accustom his eye to the colour and appreciate it in all its beauty.' The same book describes the Capri Emerald grotto: '... roofs and sides assume a dazzling green colour as if they were made of emeralds. The rocks below the water assume on the contrary the appearance of dark polished brass.'

after some legal trouble was able to use it to endow the Convent of S Teresa and the church of S Salvatore that were consecrated in 1685 by the future Pope Benedict XIII. Norman Douglas was very interested in her and accused her of putting undue pressure on girls to give up their fiancés and become celibate nuns - and during her lifetime there were other criticisms leveled at her. She emerged victorious from her accusers, and was able to found seven further Carmelite convents on the mainland. She died in 1699. Agitation from Capri for her beatification before the two hundredth anniversary of her death was heated until Pope Gregory, (according to Douglas) said he wanted 'to hear no more' of Serafina.

No matter whether Serafina should have been beatified or not, the gracious church of S Michele is a fine monument to her, and the story is fascinating. In 1683 the Turks invaded Austria and laid siege to Vienna. Mother Serafina was so concerned that she fired a battery of prayers at St Michael for the preservation of Vienna against the infidels, swearing that if St Michael saved Vienna, she would found at Anacapri a church and convent to 'the glory of the Lord in your honour'. On 2 September 1683 the Austrian army defeated the Turks. Serafina felt her prayers had been answered and persuaded a Sardinian, Antonio Migliacci, to give large funds for a new church. The church was built between 1698 and 1719 with the help of the Bishop of Capri, Michele Gallo, who is buried in the church behind the high altar. We must be grateful to Serafina because St Michele is a lovely church, which fits beautifully into the Capri background. Its most striking feature is the majolica floor representing the Garden of Eden, which was laid in 1761 and is the work of Leonardo Chaiaese, one of the best majolica craftsmen from the Abruzzi. In the centre is an angel, his flaming sword driving Adam and Eve from the Garden of Eden, while on high is the devil in the form of a serpent. There are exotic animals - elephant, jaguar, lion, and crocodile and in the foreground domestic animals quietly graze amid a lovely landscape disregarding the dramatic events. The floor looks its best from the organ loft. Serafina's convent still exists with an enclosed order of nuns, but it is no good trying for admission. Unless you are a relative of one of the nuns you will not be allowed in. Still if you mention Serafina to any priests or nuns on Capri, they will be delighted to tell you all about her.

A little way to the east of the piazza of Capri is the Certosa or Carthusian monastery of St James. It reaches almost to the cliff edge. This is the most visited site of Capri. It was founded in 1371 but many misfortunes overtook it. In 1553 and again in 1563 it was sacked and laid waste by the

Saracens. Fortunately for the monastery it was rich with property in and around Naples, and after 1563 it was enlarged and restored. Joachim Murat suppressed it with many other monasteries after he took possession of Capri in 1808. It became a barracks for the army as well as a prison. An important medieval survival it lies attractively above the sea surrounded by lush vegetation. Both the inner and outer cloister stand comparison with the Certosa of S Martino in Naples and the Certosa of Padula on the mainland in their elegance and dignity, but St James has a more oriental feel. The big cloister is a sixteenth century addition clearly modelled on S Martino. In recent years St James has been restored to its former splendour. The cellars and residence of the prior are interesting and are on the edge of a precipice with marvellous views. Gathorne Hardy writes that having seen the Certosa of Padula a few days before he was still 'enraptured' by the cloisters of Capri. The attractive baroque bell tower dominates the monastery. In the refectory are noteworthy works by the German painter Karl Diefenbach, who lived on Capri until he died there in 1915. They do not appeal to most modern tastes.

Marina Piccola is the most popular bathing place on Capri. The beach is narrow and pebbly and the best bathing is in the well maintained pools or by hiring a boat for a swim in deep water. The place has character. It can be reached by the main road or by the narrow Via Krupp, which winds down to it and was built at the whim of the German industrialist millionaire of the same name. The restaurant and bathing establishment Canzone del Mare (Song of the Sea) used to be a celebrated meeting place for cinema stars. It is a good spot from which to start a sea trip around the island or to some of the grottoes. The boatmen are very cooperative and friendly but it is better to fix the price in advance and make it clear exactly where you are going.

A delightful boat trip is to the three enormous limestone pinnacles of the Faraglioni rocks set in deep water just off the coast. Here are the famous blue lizards that, chameleon-like, have adapted to the deep blue of the Capri sea and sun - there are some also on the main island. You pass the port of Tragara, a good place for a deep water swim from the rocks amid Roman remains. Nearby are the Tragara Terrace and a tall rock Pizzolongo. If you follow the track above the sea you come to a stairway, that leads you to the inland cave of Matermania (always open). The Romans worshipped the fertility goddess Cybele (great mother) in this cave. It is a spooky spot. There are traces of wall decoration left by the Romans in this cave. Below is the extraordinary modern villa of the author Curzio Malaparte on a cliff. To my mind it is a mistake - although fabulous.

From here steps take us up to a little terrace with a welcome bar and down to the Arco Naturale, a spectacular archway formed in the limestone rock by slow erosion, and much admired by the Victorian British.

Another way of reaching Porto di Tragara is by walking past the Hotel Belvedere di Tragara from Capri. General Eisenhower used the hotel as a holiday resort when he visited Capri during the Italian campaign of World War Two. If you walk around Porto di Tragara you should see tortoises, woodcock, quail, falcons or even the blue lizard.

Visitors should be aware that hotel prices are higher on Capri than on the mainland and accommodation is apt to be booked well in advance. There are plenty of good restaurants at all prices although the menu varies little between the best and the cheapest. The emphasis is always on seafood and the local vegetables and fruit, while the local wine, both white and red, is excellent and good value. Capri is much loved by Italians for honeymoons. Chess is played in many of the hotels, and once I was embarrassed by playing too lengthy games of chess with a honeymooning husband and being reproved by his newlywed wife for keeping him out of bed.

British visitors are said to be tiring of the inland charm of Tuscany according to some travel writers, and Capri is becoming more popular. Certainly Capri is unspoiled and little changed. Perhaps the endless generous hospitality of the Capriots will again make it the premier Italian holiday resort for the British - certainly its charm is unending, as is its enthusiasm for the British.

Ischia

The island of Ischia (20 miles from Naples, two from Procida) is lovely, surpassing even Capri in beauty. It would be a dream for British visitors were it not taken completely over by the Germans. It was popular with the British until the late 1950s but now they are wary of going because it is described as a little Frankfurt or Berlin. Signs, café and restaurant menus are written in German and not Italian.

This is a shame because Ischia is a dream island. Pines, vines, olives, oranges, and lemons, with pink and purple bougainvillea cover every corner and garden. It is green and mountainous with delicate attractive hills along the coast so that from the curving roads you get one delicious view after another of the sea. Unlike Capri it has large unblemished bathing beaches, although the sand is dark coloured. High up in the middle of the island is an extinct volcano, Monte Epomeo; it has not erupted since 1301. The lower slopes are covered with vineyards that produce an excellent white wine of that name.

It is believed that Ischia was the first Magna Graecia colony in South Italy. It was a Greek settlement as far back as the eighth century BC; the original Greeks came from Euboea, and Ischia was called Pithekoussai. Earthquakes and lava flowing from Monte Epomeo drove many of the early Greek settlers over to Cuma on the mainland that soon far exceeded Pithekoussai in importance. Nevertheless Greeks remained and today the Ischians show many Greek characteristics and pride themselves on being different and superior to the Neapolitans. Certainly they are better looking and speak a more understandable Italian. In 1824 Lady Blessington noted how good looking the Ischians were. She is correct.

Hieron the tyrant of Syracuse, defeated the Etruscans of Cuma in 474 BC and took over the island. It seems that volcanic outbursts drove him away, and at some unknown period the Romans took control. Pliny wrote that the name Aenavia was given to the island denoting that Aeneas had anchored there. It was sacked by the Saracens in 813 and 847 AD, and in 1282 Ischia joined Sicily in the revolt against the Angevin Charles I. In 1299 his grandson Charles II recovered it and punished the inhabitants by sending 400 soldiers to cut down the vines.

Surprisingly Bishop Berkeley the English philosopher, spent the summer of 1717 on Ischia and declared that it was the happiest summer of his life, writing: 'The air is in the hottest season constantly refreshed by cool breezes from the sea; the vales produce excellent wheat and Indian corn, but are mostly covered with vineyards interspersed with fruit trees. Besides the common kinds such as cherries, apricots, peaches, etc. they produce oranges, limes, almonds, pomegranates, figs, watermelons and many other fruits unknown to our climates, which lie everywhere open to the passerby. The hills are to the greater part covered to the top with vines, some with chestnut groves and others with thickets of myrtle and lactius'. He also expounded on the beauties of the orchids and other wildflowers. Today you will find even more wildflowers because the boom in tourism has made the Ischians abandon their farming - apart from grapes for wine and some fruit farming - in favour of work in the hotels, restaurants and thermal establishments.

No other spot in Europe contains such a number of hot mineral springs. This is why the Germans flock to the island; they love hot spa water, especially when it can be combined with bathing from lovely beaches. Still if you like the Germans for company, Ischia is ideal for a spa and seawater holiday amidst beautiful flowers and scenery. Strabo and Pliny knew of some of the springs now in use, and several bas reliefs recording them have been found on the island. In 1588 a description of Ischia waters and their medicinal powers was published by Giulino Jasolino; he described 40 springs including all the principal ones now in use. Dr. Cox, a British physician practising in Naples in 1841, compiled a detailed account of all the waters, which was much read by Victorian travellers.

Steamers and hydrofoils run to Ischia from Naples, Mergellina, and Pozzuoli - mostly stopping at Procida. The harbour at Porto Ischia is a delightful circular crater lake made into an artificial harbour. The south bank of the harbour is lined with many excellent shops and restaurants; the atmosphere is relaxed and peaceful - a great contrast to Naples. The modern town of Ischia has a fine sandy beach, that runs for a mile to the south, with numerous excellent hotels that nearly all have their own thermal pools in addition to private beaches standing before nice pinewoods. An old lava flow separates this beach from another - Spiaggia dei Pescatori at Ischia Ponte, which is an older town. This unlike Ischia Porto, that is entirely dependent on tourists, has fishermen and less wealthy people. The Castello d'Ischia (Castello Aragonese) at Ponte was severely damaged by English bombardments in 1806 and 1809 It is associated with its most distinguished resident, the celebrated poetess Vittoria Colonna. She was married to the hero of Pavia, Charles V's General Ferranti D'Avalos, in the fourteenth century church of Assunta, of which only the arched ruins remain. It was completely destroyed in 1809 by the English fleet fighting the French. Vittoria retired to Ischia after her husband's death in 1455 and wrote her best poetry there.

Ariosto and Michelangelo admired her *rime spirituali*; Michelangelo composed sonnets to her. The narrow streets and 500 year old houses of Ponte are romantic, and the views from the walls superb. There are popular beaches with plenty of space at Ischia Ponte.

A good road zigzags along the coast from Ischia Porto all around the island. There are plenty of buses, and a cheap form of transport is a three wheeled taxi. Travelling west from Porto d'Ischia you pass a good (and free) little beach, Spiaglia degli Inglesi - given its name from of the British eighteenth century occupation. You come to Casamicciola Terme, which contains Henrik Ibsen's villa, with a rose garden and trellis overlooking the sea where Henrick Ibsen wrote most of *Peer Gynt* in 1851. Otherwise Casamicciola is merely a collection of hotels and thermal establishments.

The coast road leads to Lacco Ameno where there is the biggest concentration of hot water springs and the most expensive hotels. Excavations begun in 1952 disclosed Greek tombs from the seventh century. The Sanctuary of S Restituita is on the site of a paleo-Christian basilica. Here there is a recently opened crypt, which dates back to the fourth century and contains some antiquities discovered on the spot. S Restituita is the patron saint of the island and it is claimed that her body was recovered from the sea and buried here.

Nearby to the west a road leads down to the attractive Lido di S Montano - an excellent black sandy beach between two wooded hills in a very pretty situation next to the hill of Monte Vico. Here are hot springs rising out of the sand - hot enough for the locals to cook mussels in the spring water. This beach is an important archaeological site. With the adjoining and now developed seafront at modern Lacco Ameno, was the port of entry for the original eighth century BC Greek settlers from Euboea. One can imagine their boats drawn up on the sand there after their long haul from the Aegean. There is controversy over whether the early Greek settlers on Ischia used it only as a trading post or whether it became a full-scale colony. Large-scale excavations of the cemetery at the Valley of San Montano begun in 1952 continue and still show that the cemetery was in constant use from the fifth century BC until the third century AD. There are several famous finds, which cannot be seen on Ischia, as they are housed in the Museo Archaeologico Nazionale in Naples. The most important was the Nestor Kotyle (drinking cup) with several lines of Homeric verse ending with: 'Nestor had a fine cup but anyone who also drinks from this cup will soon be struck with a desire for fair crowned Aphrodite'. According to archaeologists this is probably the first piece of Greek poetry that has survived with Homeric epics written down after a long tradition of oral poetry. It is strange that these cheerful verses were found in the sad tomb of a small boy.

Another famous find was a locally made drinking pot with a painted narrative scene of a shipwreck and is the oldest figure painting found on Italian soil. It shows a capsized ship with the sailors swimming for their lives; the head of one is locked in the grasp of an enormous fish (a shark - they were common in that part of the Mediterranean); there is also a plump fish standing on its tail. The Greeks thought those who died at sea were denied all the hope of being reunited with their fellows that proper burial conferred. In the *Iliad* you can read the terrible consequences of death at sea, and the scene on this pot evokes it graphically.

Yet another fascinating find at San Montano is a pot showing a sacred tree flanked by a pair of rampant goats. Much material from San Montano is in the museum next to San Restituita the Museo Archaeologico di Pitnea. However there are excellent pictures of the three main finds in David Ridgway's book *The First Western Greeks*.

Ridgeway believes the remarkable finds at San Montano prove the sophisticated nature of the early Greek settlement on Ischia. The excavations suggest that a substantial Greek colony flourished near San Montano, even after the settlers had founded Cuma on the mainland, and that they never altogether abandoned Ischia. This is reinforced by an inscription (found over 150 years ago) on the east side of nearby Monte Vico on a large block of lava. It records the construction of a fortified wall, built by Syracusan colonists, and gives the names of Syracusan soldiers who constructed it. In 474 BC the Syracusans under King Hieron came to the aid of their compatriots and won a great naval victory over the Etruscans who were attacking Cuma. An Etruscan bronze helmet captured by the Syracusans records this victory with a Greek inscription; it was found at Olympia in 1817 and was presented to the British Museum in 1823 by King George IV. It seems probable that the Syracusans in 474 BC found a Greek colony at Valle di Montano, since they thought it worthwhile to construct a wall to defend it. Probably they added to it. The adjoining Monte Vico was the Acropolis of the settlement and has yielded much Greek pottery to archeologists, as has the neighbouring site of Mazzola. Monte Vico also shows that the Euboeans smelted iron ore that came from Sardinia or Elba and gold. Ischia has neither iron nor gold. It would not be surprising if the Greeks, despite the devastating lava flow from Monte Epomeo and intermittent earthquakes, had a permanent colony on Ischia - given its fertile soil, gentle climate and attractive living conditions. Certainly the Ischians today in appearance and manners vividly recall their Greek ancestors.

The town of Forio lies to the south two miles from Lacco Ameno. It is a picturesque little port. Here you feel you are at the edge of Europe looking out to Africa to the south. It is the centre of Epomeo winemaking. Its attractive colour washed houses and churches distinguish it from the rest of Ischia and it has an African feel. The church of S Maria di Loreto was originally fourteenth century but has been baroqued; its twin towers are covered with majolica tiles. Nearby is the Torrioni, built in 1480 by King Ferrante to repel the Corsairs. Another interesting small church is the whitewashed S Soccorso, with eighteenth century majolica tiles and crude devotional messages from sailors, and well-carved model ships on pillars. Soccorso has a Gothic bell tower, a Renaissance portal and a baroque pedestal. Sir William Walton, the late British composer, lived not far away. He and his wife created a magnificent garden and she, Lady Susanne Walton, has opened it to the public.

Forio although replete with new hotels and restaurants retains its strange old world charm. It was much loved by Harold Acton in the 1950s before extensive German tourism took over and banished the mules and white oxen from its fields and terraces that all now lie uncultivated.

Forio boasts Poseidon, the most luxurious thermal gardens in Europe. A mile to the south of the town on the seashore they are unique. There is every conceivable type of swimming pool, from an Olympic sized one with relatively cool water, to others of every shape and temperature. Dozens of terraces climbing up the hillside covered with flowers and olive trees are host to sun beds for the 95 percent German clientele. I used to particularly like the two Poseidon *knipe* pools side by side - one the cold, and the other as hot as you can bear. Jumping from the hot to the cold is wildly stimulating, and used to make me feel 40 years younger.

There are up to date facilities for sauna baths (in caves on the rocks), and pavilions for massage with mud facials and all the paraphernalia of expensive spas in luxurious surroundings - while two self-service restaurants provide enormous helpings of excellent pasta and cream cakes to cater to German appetites and tastes. Today English and Americans are scarce at Poseidon amid the flock of Germans. Still it is the Mecca of all spas and although expensive, I thoroughly recommend it. It also has a tiptop beach for sea bathing.

Two miles to the south of Forio is S Angelo - my favourite place on the island. It is too steep for buses or cars to descend to the little port, and to carry your luggage to one of the numerous hotels you need to hire a porter or preferably a mule or donkey. Cars and motorcycles are mercifully banned from the narrow alleys of S Michele. The views are lovely from many of the hotels - from several you can see the sea and bays both to the north and south.

The port is now full of luxury shops - only two small grocers and a newsagent remain. The cafés are already expensive but when a steamer approaches carrying Germans on an 'around the island tour', their price lists are turned around and the normal list substituted by one with doubled prices.

There is a tiny beach at S Angelo, with no facilities. However motorboats can provide a shuttle taxi service to the famous Maronti beach to the east, which is one of the best in Italy - equipped with hotels, cafés and all that swimmers desire. To return from Maronti to S Angelo you just wave and the motorboat pulls into the shore.

Nearly all the hotels at S Angelo have their own hot water pools and there are two very good thermal establishments with plenty of pools in their gardens, but they cannot compare in elegance with Poseidon. However for a peaceful bathing holiday in both mineral and sea water far away from motor traffic S Angelo with its smell of mules is hard to beat.

Procida

The island of Procida is only five miles across the sea from the point of Misenum, and easily reached by steamer or hydrofoil from Pozzuoli, Mergellina, or Bererello, the main harbour of Naples. It is a lovely tiny island quite unspoiled at the time of writing with a slow pace of life. The large prison in the castle has recently been closed, which adds to the peace of the island. There is talk of turning the castle into a grand hotel much to the annoyance of the islanders who want to preserve their unique atmosphere.

The contrast with the glamour and hectic life of Naples is vivid. On the island life proceeds as it has for centuries, except that three-wheeled motorcycle taxis have replaced horse carriages plying for hire. It seems idyllic. Most of the islanders still make their living from fishing or from market gardens, while many are sailors and others carve fine models of antique ships. The whole island is scented with lemons, which are said to be the best in Italy with a marked tangy taste from the volcanic soil. The orange and lemon groves and vineyards are interspersed with flat roofed houses in various bright colours, and the whole island is enchanting, with a charm all of its own.

There are only three small hotels; in the spring and summer these are all booked up by Neapolitans seeking a break, and only in winter can a foreigner obtain a room. So for nearly everyone a visit to Procida is a day trip. It is no good taking a car. The roads are too narrow and you will soon get the car scraped on the walls. Cars are prohibited from Naples except for self-hire - that keeps the roads quiet.

The fish on the island are the best in the Mediterranean. There are several internationally famous fish restaurants and Procidans take much pride in their cooking.

Procida looks delightful from the sea. As the Gulf of Naples and the Point of Cape Misenum recede, you see the charming streets of yellow, white and pink houses along the seafront. All ferries arrive at Marina Grande, which is closely linked to Marina de San Cattolico or Sanlio. Here are bars the tourist office and three fine restaurants. The island is only 4 kms long and 2 kms at its widest part.

The Romans used Procida and there are Roman remains. The Benedictines built an abbey in the eleventh century but marauding Saracens, under the infamous Barbarossa, destroyed the abbey in the sixteenth century. During the thirteenth century the island was the property of Giovanni di Procida, a Ghibelline nobleman of Salerno, who loved it so much that he named it. But Charles I of Anjou confiscated the island when he conquered Naples with his Guelphs. In 1265 John of Procida then took his revenge by helping to incite the Sicilian Vespers in Palermo where probably 8,000 Frenchmen perished. The British occupied Procida in 1799 when the French held Naples.

There is an attractive church S Maria Della Pietà, dating to 1760 at Marina Grande, that gives a foretaste of Procida's architecture, from which a nice walk leads up to Terra Murata. The houses are Arab looking with wide arches and steep staircases cascading down, while the pink, blue and yellow of the flat roofed houses is very picturesque. Together with the white and blue fishing boats that are hauled up to the doorways, it has been likened to liquorice allsorts.

The main square, about a 20-minute walk from the ferry is the Piazza dei Martiri, named after 12 inhabitants who were brutally executed by the Bourbons for having helped the French in 1799. Terra Murata site of the castle and former prison, is the highest spot on the island with wonderful views over the sea to Ischia. The castle dates back to 1521.The Via Madonna delle Grazie takes you down past the castle and disused prison through the Porta Mezz'Olmo to the pretty area of Corricella that adjoins the good bathing beach of Chiaia. Before you get there turn left up a steep narrow street to the best church on the island, S Michele Arcangelo that has three domes. It has a Saracenic appearance, and must have been rebuilt several times after the Saracen raids. Inside it is fine baroque. The parish priest has written notices - 'Children keep quiet', and 'The church is not a museum'. But it is rather like a museum stuffed with statues, paintings and glass cases filled with votive offerings. There are two important paintings. On the ceiling is Luca Giordano's *Glory of San Michele* (1699) with the archangel fighting Lucifer. The second is Nicola Rossi's San Michele defending the island with the help of delightful little angels showing Procida surrounded by numerous Turkish ships. All the ceiling frescoes are seventeenth century. Chiaiolella is a little fishing port at the southern tip of the island. It has a good black sand beach (the whole island is volcanic) - none of the beaches on the island is long, being interspersed with rocks. It is the site of the bus terminal and from here are two fine walks. One is to the promontory of S Maria Vecchia where there are the ruins of the abbey church and monastery, abandoned by the Benedictines in 1586. From here is a lovely view back to Procida.

Another walk is over a little footbridge to the island of Vivara that is a nature preserve with no inhabitants. The whole of Procida was a favourite shooting area for the Bourbons and Vivara their most favoured part. Ruins of the royal hunting lodge can be seen there. Cats are the enemy of pheasants and partridges because they take the hen bird off the nest. Consequently the Bourbons forbade the inhabitants of Procida from keeping cats, and inflicted severe penalties for any transgression far exceeding the apparent gravity of the crime. As at Capri in the early part of the 19th century, Neapolitan warships protected the coast of Procida while the King was shooting there for fear of a Saracen raid. Today there are neither pheasants nor partridges on Procida or Vivara despite their abundance 140 years ago - only a few passing quail and woodcock on Vivara that no one is allowed to shoot.

A kilometre to the east of Chiaiolella is another excellent black sand beach - Ciraciello Lido that almost links with another small beach to the north, Spiaggia Ciraccio. Punta Solchiaro to the southeast of Chiaiolella, so called because it receives the rays of the morning sun before the rest of the island, is a good place for walking - but the best walk in my opinion is to head north from Chiaiolella for four kilometres to the other tip of the island. You wander through narrow streets flanked by typical Procida houses with fields full of olives, lemons, and oranges together with grapes. Procida is densely populated but there is no grating modern development. You pass a quarter known as Olmo with the seventeenth century church of St Anthony of Padua that has a pretty cupola. Branch to the left and you find Punta Seara with the little beach of Pozzo Vecchio - captured on celluloid in Il Postino. Inland again and you find the Annunziata quarter with the church of that name full of votive offerings to its miraculous Madonna. From here the Via del Faro leads to the northernmost tip, Punta Pioppeto that has a lighthouse and a good view of the mainland.

Evenings on Procida must perforce be quiet, but if you can secure a room in one of the few pleasant hotels you will find your hosts most welcoming. Procida is the ideal place in which to relax and enjoy the sunshine away from the bustle of Naples. Long may it remain in its present pristine state; it gives one a last glimpse of the island life of southern Italy little changed from the nineteenth century.

12
Sorrento and Amalfi Coast to Salerno

S orrento is a mecca for British tourists. It is the number one choice for an Italian holiday in all the big package tour brochures. Fifty years ago Sorrento was a walled town with narrow streets and few buildings outside the walls. It was set in orange and lemon trees, masses of olive groves and walnuts stretching peacefully up the mountainside, and a few old fashioned hotels catering to the British. Protected by high hills, Sorrento has an exceptionally mild winter climate with no frosts - and there is luxuriant vegetation with palm trees and tropical shrubs.

The British who came in pre 1939 days were mostly invalids and the elderly seeking an escape from the harsh British winter, and Sorrento was a very popular winter resort. However the hotels closed down in summer because it was too hot.

Sorrento was untouched by the ravages of the Second World War. In 1943 all the hotels were taken over by the British Army as convalescent and leave centres. The orange and lemon groves of Sorrento were a welcome contrast to the battered warfronts of Italy. After the war many survivors returned for holidays in Sorrento with nostalgia for their wartime stay - thus setting up a British demand for holidays there, which has continuously increased in pace. Even in 1998 I met veterans who had come back because they had enjoyed it so much more than 50 years earlier.

Today a rash of new hotels almost as many as at Bournemouth, and other developing resorts have covered a great deal of the attractive orange and lemon groves with a sea of concrete and brick. All the same Sorrento has not lost its charm. Most of the hotels are very comfortable and they cater especially to the British, although German package tours are also common. The people of Sorrento pride themselves on their connection with Britain; their manners are very good and they are friendly. English is spoken to a large extent. It is a strange feeling in Sorrento to sit in a typical Italian café or restaurant and be surrounded by British people. The majority of British tourists going to Sorrento never visit the centre of Naples. They are content with a trip to the island of Capri, Amalfi, Ravello, Pompeii and Herculaneum. Certainly this is plenty for one week, but it is a shame that the art treasures of Naples are overlooked. Naples is easily reached in one hour on the local railway (Circum Vesuviana). I could not find a single holidaymaker in Sorrento who proposed going into Naples - they all claimed to be put off by tales of pickpockets.

The old walled town remains a joy and the narrow alleys and streets within the walls are full of shops and stalls for visitors. Here you can buy excellent inlaid wood marquetry and can see the workmen making this in the shops. Cameos are also very popular as are lace and coral necklaces a specialty of Sorrento, as well as handmade children's clothes. Prices are reasonable but prices in the smart Corso Italia shops are double those in the alleys. The old city is full of cafés and restaurants catering to tourists, and they provide good food without overcharging. The people of Sorrento are different from those of Naples, being descendants of Greeks without interbreeding and they radiate charm.

The majority of English visitors to Sorrento are middle aged. The beaches are extremely narrow so that almost all the bathing is done from jetties covered with parasols and long chairs, while waiters scuttle backwards and forwards from the cafés bringing drinks and coffee. From the platforms it is easy to swim out into the deep clear water of the gulf.

When choosing a hotel look for one in or near the old town as distances in Sorrento are great and although there are plenty of buses, they are not always easy to find. Taxis here are a racket - they are double the price of Naples taxis and many drivers refuse to use the meter.

There are not many nightclubs in Sorrento - its main charm is for the middle-aged clientele. Try to choose a hotel with a swimming pool, most hotels have one, although many are small. If you are coming in the summer, a hotel with air conditioning is essential. It is definitely not a place to bring small children for a holiday on the beach. Despite this, Sorrento is a deservedly popular magnet for British package tourists and it is likely to remain so for many years to come.

The most interesting hotel is the Imperial Tramontano, the birthplace of Tasso in 1544, and was converted into a hotel at the beginning of the nineteenth century. Milton, Goethe, Byron, Scott, Keats, Shelley, Lamartine, De Musset and Leopardi all spent holidays here - as did Longfellow and James Fenimore Cooper who wrote his 'Water Bird' here, while Harriet Beecher Stowe wrote 'Agnes of Sorrento' in its rooms. Ibsen also spent a month here writing his 'Ghosts'. Although modernized, the hotel retains its faded charm of a Victorian home away from home at rather high prices.

Close to the Hotel Tramontano is the fascinating little church of S Francesco; on no account miss the Moorish style cloisters. Classical music is performed here on certain dates in July, and no more delightful venue could be found.

The Sorrento Cathedral was rebuilt in the fifteenth century and has a twentieth century facade, although one marble doorway with an Aragonese crest dates back to 1479. The base of the adjoining bell tower (campanile) has four ancient classical columns to remind us of the antiquity of Sorrento.

I was pleased to see that the Bishop of Sorrento allows an Anglican service for British and American visitors in a side chapel on Sunday evenings at 5pm from April to October, except for August – a reminder of Victorian times when the British had their own church and resident chaplain.

Agenzio Viaggi Internationali (AVI) Corso Italia 159 (Tel 081 878 1984) will with great courtesy arrange excursions. They provide day bus tours to Pompeii, Herculaneum, Amalfi, Ravello and Paestum. There is also an escorted one-day tour to the centre of Naples. This is poorly subscribed as is the trip to Pozzuoli and Solfatara. A memorable day out by bus takes you to both the Abbey of Monte Cassino and the Royal Palace of Caserta.

Very popular are AVI's boat trips to Capri and Amalfi. The boat excursion to Amalfi has a stop at Positano and makes several stops for bathers if the weather is good. You can also take relaxing day excursions to the lovely islands of Ischia and Procida; I recommend a cruise around the whole of the Ischia coast. The boat trip around the cape to Positano or Amalfi is a joy. You get magnificent views of the headlands so elegantly described by Norman Douglas and Robert Gathorne Hardy. For the more adventurous AVI even provide, from 1 April until 31 October, a submarine to explore the lovely clear water. It will descend to 225 feet below sea level.

A very popular restaurant and café is the Foreigners Club run by an Italian with an English wife who are most welcoming. It has a large terrace over the sea where they can feed more than 200 people. It was built in the 1960s as a club with a casino above for ex-patriates - but it never had enough members. Good food can be had at the Antica Trattoria in Via Guillano. In the same street is the excellent café Mona Lisa, that sells splendid pizzas, and there are several shops nearby for cameos and corals. I especially like Bimonte, Via Guillano 62 that has a good selection of cameos, corals and jewellery. Here you can see the cameo maker working in the window and behind him, his father stringing corals.

Above Sorrento is the Don Alfonso, reputed to be one of the best restaurants in Southern Italy, where the owners produce their own olive oil and delicious organic vegetables. The Kursaal in Via Fuori Muri has tiptop antipasta, and in the smart Corso Italia, the Favorita O'Parocchiati has typical local Campania cooking in a large conservatory - situated in a pretty tropical garden. It was much appreciated by convalescent British officers during the Second World War.

The well known Coreale Museum, an attractive old palace belonging still to the Coreale family (one of the oldest in Sorrento), has a big garden, part of a large estate given to them by the Queen of Anjou in 1428. Here there is one of the best collections of interesting inlaid ivory and old Neapolitan furniture, showing the connections between Naples and the Far East. But the real prize is on the second floor where there are many pictures from the school of Posillipo. The family was friends of Declerc and Pitloo, and there are numerous attractive pictures of them together with a whole room of pictures by Giganti - with typical evocative views of Pompeii, the Sorrento countryside and scenes of Neapolitan life.

I spent a convalescent week in the Tramontano Hotel in 1943, and the concierge told me that in the 1930s the number of British declined because it had been discovered that Egypt had a better winter climate. Then the concierge still had his blackboards on which to write at what time British families required their carriages with how many horses, for their excursions to local beauty spots.

There is a delightful walk towards the tip of the Sorrento peninsula - Punta del Capo, passing the villa of Maxim Gorky. Here a charming path through olive groves leads down to the seashore where you find the ruins of the Roman Ville da Pollio Felix or Bagni Regina Giovanna. By the shore near the old Roman bath is a splendid place to relax and watch the evening sun go down behind the Isle of Ischia.

Sorrento can be recommended as ideal for non-Italian speaking British holidaymakers who want an Italian holiday; the best time to go is March, April or October. Prices are reasonable, the hotels comfortable, trips to Pompeii, Herculaneum, and Capri are easy, and the atmosphere amid the lush vegetation is completely relaxed.

Amalfi and Positano

There are two delightful mountain roads from Sorrento to Positano and the Amalfi coast. Be warned that if you take the direct road from Naples to Amalfi, the hideous sprawl of buildings continues until you are well up in the mountains, although once you are in the wooded hills it is a delightful drive especially as you near Ravello. Pompeii and Herculaneum are engulfed in horrid new development. On the scenic Strada di Capodimonte, leading from Sorrento to Positano, after 10 kilometres you come to Santa Agata dei Due Golfe and find superb views of both the Gulf of Sorrento and Amalfi. The church Santa Maria delle Grazie is interesting, as is an odd thriving café, Bar Oriando, where the owner may give you a gift of his book about his long defunct smoking cat, and make you an excellent cup of coffee. A few minutes uphill and there is Il Deserto, a former Carmelite monastery (near the O Sole Mio hotel) with a brilliant view of Capri and the two bays. Look at the bell tower for the warning inscription - Tempus Breve

Est (Time is short). Opportune perhaps for anyone too carried away by the beauty of one of the best sea views in Europe. Then it is eight kilometres to Positano.

Positano is popular with the very rich and has become a mainland Capri. Moorish style pink and white houses tumble from terrace to terrace, with bougainvilleas, orange and lemon groves to the sea; only Capri equals it for beauty and it has an Arabian feel. Exquisite hotels abound, many of them very expensive but well run and comfortable. It is the chosen resort of the ultra rich. Fortunately the authorities have carefully controlled the type of development and although it is tremendously built up, there is nothing that jars. It is a gem of a coastal town. Unfortunately the bathing beach is limited and the sand is black, but most of the hotels have private beaches and some have lifts down to these.

There are no monuments of interest apart from the attractive Church of Santa Maria Assunta, just above the sea. The outline of the majolica dome against the sea is particularly beautiful - it also has a dignified campanile. However the Palazzo Murat is a fine seventeenth century palace where Joachim and Caroline escaped from the heat of Naples to enjoy sea bathing in the dog days. It is now a four star hotel with first empire furniture to remind us of Murat. It has a splendid terrace and large shady garden only a few feet above the beach. It is the only hotel that attracts me to stay in Positano.

Despite its opulence the streets of Positano have charm. They are mostly pedestrian streets and lined with shops displaying famous international names. There is an attractive well-known restaurant near the beach, Buca di Bacco. The hotels mostly close in the winter, which seems a pity, as there is a delightful winter climate and at that time the roads around are fairly empty - while in season they are packed with large coaches carrying German and British package tourists and innumerable cars.

There is another beach at Positano - the Fornillo, to the west of the town and is reached by steps. Even this is insufficient for the numbers of bathers and both beaches are horribly crowded in the summer. Still there are plenty of bars and restaurants, many air-conditioned.

Splendid boat trips leave from Positano and many boats ply for hire. The three rocky little islands of the Sirens or Li Galli, a mile offshore and four miles to the west - much admired by Norman Douglas are popular. The largest Il Gallo Lungo, is inhabited, and the late Rudolf Nureyev had a house for the summer there. The smallest La Castellucia, has the remains of a tower. In 1827 Ramage scrambled up to the top of Il Gallo Lungo although there was no landing place, and found a marble floor and other Roman remains. He was sure it was the site of an ancient villa. Ramage also visited the tower on La Castellucia, finding an unfinished road and stairs. He thought the smallest island La Rotonda was the most suitable for habitation, but the heat was unbearable. He could find no trace of any old building there. Virgil's description (Aeneid V 864) of the Siren Islands was according to Ramage's translation :

'And o'er the dangerous deep secure the navy flies Glides by the Sirens' cliffs, a shelfy coast long infamous for ships and sailors lost and white with bones. The impetuous ocean roars and rocks re-bellow from the sounding shores.'

Although there are landing stages there is no point in trying to land on these romantic isles that are privately owned and not welcoming. So continue two miles west, passing the rock Scoglia d'Ischia where the Neapolitan actor Eduardo di Fillipo had a house, now belonging to his son, to the sheltered cove of Nerano - with very difficult access by land. Here are two good fish restaurants on stilts above the sea where you can sample the day's catch, either with spaghetti or on its own. One, the Conca del Sogno, has a pickup boat service. It is a romantic spot, ideal for honeymooners. If you are lucky enough to return to Positano while the sun is setting, the view of the town with the glimmer of lights is striking, and has been appropriately compared by one travel writer to the tiers of boxes in an opera house.

Boats also arrive at Nerano from Sorrento - a rather longer trip around the gorgeous Punta Camponella with intriguing views of Capri. It is best to anchor off and let the sons of the restaurant owners row you to the one of your choice.

Going east from Positano you soon come to the attractive Praiano. Again you find a fine church with both campanile and dome, plus numerous well-designed hotels superbly situated with lovely views. As well some have lifts leading to private beaches, which, unfortunately are black sand and far too small. After Praiano a tiny road to the right leads down to the minute fishing village of Marina di Praiano. It is a gem. Here the owner of a delightful restaurant in a cave, called Trattoria di Armando, will give you a warm greeting and you can taste his homemade pasta made with freshly caught shrimps from the bay. Unfortunately his home brewed wine is far too strong. Surprisingly in this hamlet there is a well-known diving school La Boa, and you can hire rowing or motorboats to capture delightful views of the hills from the sea.

A few miles further on you come to the Grotto dello Smeraldo discovered by chance by a fisherman in 1932, and scathingly dismissed by Gathorne Hardy in his book, 'Amalfi'. However it is well worth seeing and open all year round. A lift or steep steps take you from the car park to sea level, and inside the grotto obliging guides take you in a boat. There is no entry from the sea - the green emerald light is beautiful and eerie, and under the water a stone crib has been made. I found it more attractive than the Blue Grotto of Capri. In season boats come from Amalfi and Positano in addition to the coaches and there are such crowds that long queues form, but out of season it is quite a delight.

Go east past crumbling towers built in the sixteenth century to repel Saracen pirates and you soon come to Conca dei Maroni. Take the hill road to the left and you are quickly rewarded by the charming silhouette of a parish church façade outlined against the background of the sea. Explore this fascinating village that is completely unspoiled and encased with gardens of oranges, lemons, olives and vines, and you come to a most interesting monastery recently made into a rather strange hotel.

Drop down again to the coastal road and a few kilometres to the east you will find a turning to Agerola and Furore.[12] On the hilltops you see ruined towers, decaying monasteries and a few villas, while every spit of leveled land is terraced and covered with the typical delightful orange and lemon groves. The lemon blossom gives off an exquisite scent in hot weather, and after Naples where the countryside is ruined by indiscriminate development, it is a delight to be in an area where unauthorized development is strictly banned and little has changed in the last hundred years. On the road to Agerola you soon come to S. Elea. Walk into the little piazza and enquire of the parish priest or custodian if you can get into the church. You will find a quite important picture for such a small place (reproduced in Gathorne Hardy's book) by Antonelli da Capua of the Virgin and Child between Elijah and St Bartolomew. It is dated 1482, and is a tribute to the importance of the Amalfi area in the Middle Ages. Centuries old steps lead down to the sea from S Elea and up to Furore. Better to go by car to Furore and enjoy the magnificent views both to the east and west, and sip some of the excellent local wine at the village café of Baco.

From Furore it is a short distance to the delightful town of Amalfi that is surprisingly small. Amalfi was a favourite wintering place with the British until 1914, but now it is empty in the winter. It's a pity because it is like Positano, an ideal escape from the cold of Britain. The Hotel Cappucini

---

[12] The name is due to the fierce noise made by the sea on the rocks many feet below.

is the first to greet you. It is an old Capucin monastery with a beautiful twelfth century cloister, with the arcade resting on more than a hundred classical columns and a chapel. My brother who was a Monseigneur/Monsignor in Rome, loved this hotel and used to say mass in the chapel. The Sitwells and Aldous Huxley came in the 1930s and wrote about it, which made its pre war reputation in England. There is no road to the main part of the hotel and you have to take two lifts. Once you are up there the surroundings and view are out of this world. On the east side of the town is another disused monastery, converted into a luxury hotel - the Hotel Luna with an equally charming sixteenth century cloister. Both hotels are ideal bases for holidays and much booked up by British and German package tours. In view of the overcrowded roads the most pleasant way to arrive in Amalfi is by sea from Naples. There is a good boat service in the summer but package tours do not use this route. You need to fly to Naples independently and make your own hotel booking - not difficult because they speak English in the hotels.

Much of the way after Sorrento, the boat travels only two hundred yards from shore, and if the engines are not too loud (as on a hovercraft), one can hear crickets singing on land. Ridges of mountain 1,000 feet high, drop to the sea in under a mile and the limestone cliffs are fantastic with pillars, obelisks and arches together with ruined castles, churches and watchtowers.

Around Positano the cliffs rise to 2,000 feet, and eastwards you see all the habitable slopes covered by picturesque hamlets having many churches that feature campaniles and often domes. Once you are in Amalfi do take a trip by boat to Capri or Sorrento and back. It is a wonderful experience when the sun shines and the sea is calm, as it usually is even in winter. The landscape is dazzlingly lovely without the distraction and roar of constant motor traffic. Bernard Berenson has written, 'The landscape between Salerno and Sorrento, the Amalfiano especially, one would not believe in a picture. Indeed it recalls Mantegna to such an extent one can almost believe that he had studied it in some of his pictures ... you have to see it to believe it'.

Amalfi, formerly an independent maritime republic, is redolent with history. Her story begins in 339 AD when some noble Romans sailing to Constantinople were blown ashore by bad weather. There were no roads, but they liked the area so much that they made a settlement. Alas it was insecure against Barbarian raids, so they moved it up the mountain to nearby Scala and cultivated the rich soil, starting the terraces of orange and lemon groves

NAPLES, What most tourists never see

that you see today.

Increasing in numbers and strength, after some years they moved back to Amalfi. There is an analogy with Venice where the first Christian church was consecrated in 432 AD. At any rate, pirate invaders never ravaged Amalfi, which is almost unique in history apart from that of Venice.

Rome was tottering when Amalfi came into its classical heyday, but Amalfi practised Roman law. While Huns, Vandals and Goths devastated Italy, Amalfi, protected by mountains with no roads, remained immune. As Rome declined Amalfi became a self-governing state owing only nominal allegiance to Byzantine Constantinople. Amalfi territory stretched west to Sorrento and east to Salerno and north to Gragnano, Lettere and Cava.

When in the 800 AD Charlemagne imposed himself on Italy inaugurating the Holy Roman Empire, Amalfi remained independent, still loyal to Byzantine and building up a fleet that rivaled Pisa, Genoa and Venice.

When Lombard princes took over Naples in the ninth century and the Saracens began their conquest of Sicily, Amalfi was still fiercely independent. In 838 Sicardo, Prince of Benevento, temporarily occupied Amalfi but was thrown out the next year, and then ensued the great years of Amalfi until 1101 when the Normans extinguished their independence. Although Amalfi remained a republic in the tenth century the Doges became dictators with only a tacit commitment to Constantinople. They even made their own coinage.

In 1101 Amalfi fell to Robert Guiscard the Norman King, and from then on it was a Norman possession. After the Norman conquest the cultural and trading ties with Constantinople were lost, and Amalfi was made into a dukedom ruled by the Angevin kings. When the Spaniards seized Naples in 1502 the duchy of Amalfi did not even have a king, as Spanish viceroys from Naples ruled them and there was no king until the coming of the first Bourbon in 1738.

However in the fourteenth century the Amalfi citizen Flavio Gioia invented the ship's compass, and the only copy of Justinian's Digest of Laws came to Amalfi from Constantinople and were then sent on to Pisa. This is all part of Amalfi's fascinating history as are the laws of navigation drawn up in Amalfi in the tenth century, the Tarole Amalfitane, a code followed in the Mediterranean until as late as the sixteenth century.

Traces of Amalfi's proud history can be seen in the Duomo and Museum. Amalfi Cathedral dominates the short attractive seafront. Up innumerable steps its striking facade is probably the most photographed monument in South Italy. However it is not genuine. The original collapsed in the 1861 earthquake and its replacement is not to everyone's taste.

The Cathedral is dedicated to S Andrea, and his body (minus his head that has been taken to the Vatican), lies in the crypt. His bones according to the locals, are alleged to produce an oily substance that has miraculous powers of healing.

The Cathedral was first built in the ninth century, reconstructed in 1203, and finally baroqued in 1704. Its carved bronze doors inlaid with silver, were made in Constantinople before 1066 by Simeon of Syria and closely resemble similar doors at Lucera and Trani. The skeleton of the Cathedral is Romanesque, with fine proportions. The eastern end, transept, and northern chapel together with the crypt, are thirteenth century Gothic. Little else is left of Gothic or Renaissance work except that at the far end of the southern aisle is the monument of an Archbishop - and above it are a Madonna and child in Florentine style. The Roman pillars that support the church, are still covered over in baroque fashion. In one apse are remains of early fourteenth century mosaics and frescoes.

Those who are short of breath can reach the cathedral by car, passing through the Piazza del Municipio to the pleasant Albergo del Sole where there is a medieval stone passage leading south to the ticket office for the Museum and Cloister of Paradise. The Cloister of Paradise is a jewel just north of the portico of the Cathedral. It is thirteenth century Saracenic style architecture with striking pointed arches, and twin slender Roman pillars supporting the lunettes. From there is an imposing view of the sensational early campanile finished in 1276 and topped with nice arches in yellow and green tiles.

To the right of the Cloister of Paradise is the interesting chapel of the Crucifixion, now a well laid out museum. The numerous Roman pillars here are not encased as in the cathedral, and there are some impressive early frescoes (as in the cloister) in the style of Giotto. Originally the cathedral had five aisles but in the eighteenth century restoration, fortunately this chapel was hived off. It shows the Gothic features of the original cathedral and proves how dramatic the whole must have been when almost completely frescoed.

In the Crocefisso Museum are two fine Roman sarcophagi. Of particular interest is the Silver Paliotto (altarpiece) dated 1713, showing S Andrea's tomb in the crypt, and a twelfth century mosaic taken from two early pulpits when the church was baroqued. Do not miss a captivating ivory Madonna and Child of the fourteenth century.

At the foot of the cathedral steps on the left is a pleasant restaurant with probably the best food in town, the Taverna degli Apostoli.

Amalfi is bewitching. There are arched doorways, the remains of early merchants palaces and warehouses, recalling how Amalfi traders were so important in the Byzantine Empire. A few yards north from the bottom of the cathedral steps lead you into the main Piazza. It has turned its back to the sea and might be Venice. A road leads north to the Via dei Mulini that used to contain many water driven mills for the making of macaroni and fine paper. One paper mill remains and Amalfi is still renowned for selling high quality artists paper. A great storm and earthquake in 1343 described by Petrach, engulfed the beach between Amalfi and Atrani. In it disappeared the ancient quays and warehouses of which today there is no trace.

There are several cheaper hotels in Amalfi much booked-up during the season. We stayed economically and comfortably at the Bussola right on the sea. From my bed I could hear the sea gently lapping the shore. There is nice bathing at Amalfi, also attractive boat trips to the east and west along the coast. Lady Blessington forced by rough sea to land at Amalfi, loved the place but found the only means of transport to Castellamare was by chair, carried by four men with four reserves. Nevertheless she thoroughly enjoyed the journey.

Ravello lies six kilometres up a steep road from Amalfi. It is a dream town and everyone who visits Amalfi should go there. You can go up by centuries old steps but even in my younger days I only took the down steps. They pass myriad sweet smells - olive trees, oranges, lemons and pergolas of vine with delicious views. I found the tiny peaceful medieval town of Ravello planted everywhere with flowers, almost the loveliest place in Campania. André Gide wrote of it: 'closer to the sky than the seashore'. During the great days of the Amalfi republic it was very prosperous and reputed to have 36,000 inhabitants and its own bishop. Now little more than a village, it still has a cathedral although some of its former 12 churches, four monasteries and delightful old palaces are in ruins or converted into houses.

The American author Gore Vidal lived in Ravello for many years, and there are three captivating luxury hotels housed in beautiful old palaces. To the right of the Piazza del Duomo is the Villa Rufolo, dating book to the thirteenth century and now a well-run art centre and public gardens with open-air concerts in summer. Coaches take a long time to arrive. It has a cloister of Saracenic arches in two storeys and paths lined with palms and cypress lead to a wide terrace with a wonderful view of the coast. The little

Moorish court is particularly lovely. In the middle of the last century an Englishman Francis Neville Reid bought it and owned it until the end of the century. Here, Wagner wrote the music of the magic garden in Parsifal.

The Hotel Palumbo is in another splendid palace. It is a mixture of Sicilian and Saracen with pointed and rounded arches, and even the bedrooms are gems. It was very popular with British officers as a leave and convalescent home in 1943-1945.

Lord Grimthorpe bought the Villa Cimbrone at the beginning of the century. It was then a house, orchard and pasture field belonging to a monastery. Now it is a splendid pastiche. He reconstructed the villa using old stonework, and laid out magnificent gardens. There is a pleasant small courtyard, and the gardens and the view are truly breathtaking. Acres of lush garden with paths lined with roses, camellias, begonias, and hydrangea slope down to a wooded area with pines and chestnuts where a small folly, the Temple of Bacchus, has been built. It is now a small hotel but other visitors are allowed in until 6:30 pm. The Villa is a highlight of the Amalfi coast and should not be missed.

The former cathedral of Ravello, now a parish church, is small and peaceful but very attractive. At first you may like me feel you are drunk because most unusually the floor slopes sharply. It is the Cathedral of San Pantaleone, and overshadows the town's main square. The Byzantine bronze doors, with wonderful delicate workmanship, are famous and were brought from Trani in Apulia in 1179. Fifty-four panels depict the lives of the saints and Christ's passion. Note the two Roman sarcophagi and the traces of very old frescoes on the right nave that must have made the church brilliant before it was baroqued in the 1786. The baroque was mostly removed in the late 1970s. There are two Byzantine pulpits. The large pulpit in the central nave is the church's most important feature. Dated 1272 it is supported by six twisted columns encrusted with bands of mosaic resting on the backs of six attractive small lions. (It is very much like the pulpit at Sessa Arunca). The opposite pulpit (twelfth century) is adorned with strange mosaic representations of Jonah entering and being vomited out of the whale. In the sacristy there are three interesting pictures - two by Andrea da Salerno of S Sebastian, and the third in Byzantine style of a Madonna and child. The doors and pulpits are glorious and a striking example of Byzantine contribution to art in Southern Italy. There is a very interesting museum in the crypt.

Just opposite the Hotel Caruso (in an old palace) is the Church of S Giovanni del Toro (Bull). It is dated 1066 and used to be the church of the nobility of Ravello whose palaces were grouped in the Piazza. Its chief glory is another pulpit (twelfth century) with four columns resting on small lions that climb over the bases like mice, encrusted with similar mosaics to the Cathedral. Again a reminder of Byzantine times! On the west side of the pulpit are two bulls, and on the entrance a whale in mosaic with Jonah emerging from it. There are light blue Islamic saucers on the staircase of the pulpit. S Giovanni, like the Cathedrals, is built with massive Roman columns. In the crypt are fourteenth century frescoes, and an early S Catherine in stucco. S Giovanni has three unusually high semi circular apses, and domes decorated with interesting arches and an attractive low campanile.

Uphill from the cathedral you come to the Gothic church of S Francesco, again with Roman columns. It was rebuilt in the eighteenth century, although inside the cathedral the transept and apse retain their original appearance. Next to the church is the monastery with a small Romanesque cloister - now a mixture of baroque and gothic. There are other interesting churches in Ravello mostly with Roman columns indicating the town's classical history. The little church of S Maria di Gradillo has three apses and a very oriental cupola.

A pleasant uphill walk a mile northwest of Ravello leads to the ancient town of Scala. Exquisitely perched on the side of the mountain, this too has a medieval cathedral whose mass dominates the town. It was built in the second half of the twelfth century on the site of an earlier church and dedicated to S Lorenzo. Scala was once the rival of Ravello, and Gathorne Hardy records that 'not so very long ago' a girl from Scala could not cross the bridge to meet her fiancé without an escort of friends.

On the facade of San Lorenzo is a Gothic relief of the Virgin between two saints. A strange feature of this cathedral is the vaulted alleyway running from side to side beneath it.

The interior with a nave and two aisles is like the hall of a great palace with its striking baroque work. To the north is a staircase leading down to the fourteenth century vaulted Gothic crypt, with baroque decoration and Roman columns. Above the altar is a superb wooden crucifix to which the locals attribute miraculous powers, circa 1250. In the crypt there is also the interesting large Gothic tomb of Marina Rufolo with many figures carved in stucco and some original colours.

So steep is the hill that the crypt is above ground and you can see traces of an earlier church probably eighth or ninth century, of which part was probably the alleyway under the present S Lorenzo.

There are two great treasures in Scala Cathedral. The first is a chalice of 1337 with paten, and on the foot are beautiful enamel figures. It must come from either Limoges or Siena. The second is a mitre of the thirteenth century, worthy of display in the Vatican Museum, and elaborately embroidered with pearls and precious stones. It must be from Constantinople being Byzantine in style. The tradition is that in 1270 on the feast of S Lawrence, Charles of Anjou was fighting a naval battle with the Saracens off Tunis. The Saracens were the larger force and Charles swore that if his fleet escaped he would make a rich offering to the saint. On his return he redeemed his promise by the gift of the mitre to S Lorenzo of Scala. These two objects are *not* on display. You must ask to see them - they are well worth the view.

Scala has an entrancing "out of this world feel". For the active I strongly recommend taking a walk into the hills above, covered with cork, alder, chestnut and beech trees, especially in spring and autumn. Gathorne Hardy waxes enthusiastic about the villages high above Scala. In the 1950s and 1960s he had to walk up steep steps or mule paths, but now there are roads for cars to Campedoglio, Minuto, St. Eustachio and Pontone. Delightful walks can be enjoyed to these villages, using mainly steps.

He further devotes a whole chapter to the flowers, which flourish there in winter and spring. He describes the sweet alyssum as always in blossom, especially in December and January when 'the honey scent floats in the air'. Rosemary too flowers continually. Orchids begin in March, and there are many varieties with brilliant blooms. Different species of cyclamen are in profusion in March and April. Flowers fade in the fiery heat of July and August, but in November large daffodils sprout all over the place. For flower lovers the hills around Scala are enchanted ground.

You find all cultivatable ground has been made into terraces as you climb above Scala. Tiny Campidoglio can be reached by a steep flight of steps, and has not only a church but a sweet little medieval tower in the usual local fashion, two square storeys surmounted by a round turret. There are pointed openings and it is clearly thirteenth century.

Pontone has traces of former splendour and her three churches are worth visiting. S Fillipo Neri goes back to the twelfth century although much altered in the eighteenth. Classical columns show it to be Romanesque. In the little piazza is the church of S John the Baptist with an exceptionally beautiful campanile and a carved tombstone, dated 1346. In Pontone, arches on the walls show the relics of old palaces.

Minuto is even higher than Pontone, with breathtaking and views that will make you dizzy. It has a fascinating church. In the crypt are around 1,100 well-preserved frescoes on the walls and stone vaulting. Originally all the crypt must have been frescoed brilliantly – a reminder of the glory of Gothic churches. These frescoes may not be Giotto masterpieces but they are magical and well done and well repay a visit to Minuto.

The mountains around Minuto and Pontone were once well fortified with many castles. Ask for the Torre del Zirro. It is a round castle with a ring of decaying stone battlements, and must have been one of the most important defense sites of the coast. It probably is thirteenth century, although most of the other round towers like the one at Praiano date to the time of the Amalfi Republic. Near the tower to the west is a cave where the rock is plastered over with remains of frescoes, which appear to be fourteenth century. Obviously it was the choir of the castle chapel.

If you wander around Minuto and Pontone either by car or on foot, you are surrounded by wonderful natural beauty and in the heart of the old independent mountainous Amalfi Republic. You see how the original settlers terraced their precipitous slopes to scrape a living. What is more, you are in the old Italy that is entirely unspoiled by tourism and modern development. The people are very friendly, but the older folk only speak in dialect and are difficult to understand. Across the valley you see the towers and domes of Ravello. Below can be seen Atrani with its lovely bell tower, while traces of ruins, and at the right times of the year, masses of lovely wild flowers cover the mountains. Augustus Hare described the scenery here as 'magnificent' and you will not be disappointed.

The coast road to the east from Amalfi towards Salerno is still glorious - although not as spectacular as that from Sorrento to Amalfi. Atrani lies close to Amalfi right on the sea. The fine church of S Salvatore has interesting bronze doors – Byzantine work of the eleventh century as in Amalfi and Ravello, and an unusual marble of two peacocks. There are hotels - but the bathing is limited. It is a picturesque town with an intricate network of lanes some covered, and a stairway with white houses and colourful gardens.

Other charming and relaxing little towns are on the sea. The next is Minori with old fortifications and an especially picturesque tower upon the headland. The main church contains a fine Byzantine style pulpit. At Minori there are the most important classical remains on the whole of the Amalfi coast. This is the Villa Romano, dating from the first century BC that evidently belonged to someone very important. The part close to the beach survives - there is a pool surrounded on three sides by a portico and some interesting rooms, one of which contains the bath facilities.

Further on at the mouth of a valley is Maiori – very eastern looking with its old walls and towers more or less intact. Above are the interesting ruins of the castella di S Nicolo, and a Camaldoline monastery of the fifteenth century where you can see remains of some curious frescoes. Neither Minori nor Maiori can be recommended for bathing holidays, although both are trying to attract tourists with (ugly) modern hotels and blocks of flats. At Maiori the chief church is S Maria a Mare. At the time of the sacking of Constantinople, a ship with Venetians and Frenchmen laden with loot was about to sink in a storm off Maiori. To lighten the endangered ship the crew threw overboard a wooden image of the Madonna, whereupon the ship was able to make the harbour. The name of the church was changed from S Michael to S Maria, and in the church is a beautiful image of the Madonna in cedar wood reputed to be Byzantine. Surprisingly this church has a lovely alabaster made in England, of scenes from the life of Mary around 1400. It is a complete altarpiece in its original wood frame with Gothic lettering (reproduced in Gathorne Hardy). It was probably sold abroad clandestinely after the Reformation when the English iconoclasts were destroying statues and images wholesale.

East of Maiori the road runs uphill to the high promontory of Capo D'Orso (Bear) - the name is derived from the waves here that in rough weather make a noise like a bear. The watchtower has been converted into a restaurant with a fine view. On a clear day with binoculars, you can see the temples of Paestum.

Just below Capo D'Orso to the west is a strange building, established in the tenth century by two hermits. Steep steps lead to a pitch-dark cave that is the crypt of the miniature chapel of S Maria di Olearia above. Here surprisingly there are eleventh century paintings resembling those at S Annunziata at Minuto (also skulls). The paintings are strong and well worth seeing, especially after you have been to Minuto. Ask at the restaurant how to get in - it is a national monument and access can be obtained with persistence.

Above Maiori is the district of Tramonti bounded by high mountains but easily accessible by car through a succession of little steep hills - the lower slopes planted with lemons, the upper with vines from which much good wine is made. These green pastoral hills are especially romantic. At Polvica the centre of Tramonti there is a church whose slender tower with a nice domed turret is visible from most parts of the valley. At Figlino in the church is a fifteenth century bas-relief of the nativity, and close by is a half derelict old palace showing the former grandeur of these mountain villages. After Ceseranno with a baroque church containing a slab in the floor dated 1534, you come to Pietre where there is a welcoming restaurant. In the woods south east of Pietre, Gathorne Hardy found a profusion of wildflowers. At Polara the most southerly village of the Tramonti, there are paintings in the church that have been ascribed optimistically to Luca Giordano. The road up through Tramonti ends in a narrow pass at the tower of Chiunzi (1453). From here you can see to the south into the sweet green hills of Tramonti and also northwest to Vesuvius and the wide sweep of the badly disfigured plain and the bay of Naples. You can see the tower of Chiunzi from the motorway to Salerno. There is another café restaurant at Chiunzi.

The high mountains around are ferocious and menacing. In contrast, the gentle cultivated hills around the villages of the Tramonti have an idyllic pastoral feel. The name obviously comes from the north wind of Italy, known as the Tramontana, and this is the least protected of all the Amalfi valleys from the north. If you have a car and free time, I earnestly recommend a trip into the Tramonti. In the Tramonti you are near the tourist coast but far away in another world of the forgotten Italy, and the inhabitants greet you with old world manners and charm.

Driving east towards Salerno from Maiori the scenery is wild and impressive and you soon come to Cetara, still a small fishing village, where the road dips down to the sea in a steep valley. By some miracle this beautifully situated village is unspoiled by tourism.

In medieval times it was the port of the abbey of Cava, and was known at one time as 'a nest of Saracens'. They occupied it in 879 and it became a thorn in the flesh of Amalfi because the Saracens kept their ships in the neighbouring Bay of Fuenti and made raids up and down the coast. In 1551 the Turks occupied Cetara carrying away 300 as slaves and killing those who resisted. After that the place declined.

Here you can buy salted tunny in small vases, and excellent fresh anchovies – the large ones are super with hard-boiled eggs and fresh bread.

The approach to Vietri gives fine views of the sea and the plain towards Paestum, with the blue mountains of Picenti and Alburni behind. Above the road are the picturesque white houses of Raito where the Albergo Raito has a splendid view, and the bathing beaches of Vietri with hundreds of parasols come into view. The bathing facilities here are the best on the Amalfi coast. Vietri is grouped around the pleasant majolica domed church of S Giovanni Battista 1732), and is the capital of ceramics for south Italy.

211

The streets are lined with shops and kiosks selling the very attractive Vietri pottery.

You will get the best value by going to one of the ceramic factories where they sell cheaply at wholesale prices, even if you only want a few items. Interestingly there is an art school for designers of ceramics. The Ceramche Solimene, at Via Madonna Degli Angeli 7 (tel 089 210 243) is a striking large newish modernist factory designed in the 1950s by Solieri, the Italian American architect highly thought of in the USA. He is best known for the experimental city of Arosanto. Here they not only make ceramics, but sell willingly to tourists. It is a family run business and the daughter of the owner who knew the Italian translations of my books on Italian history, even asked me to sign one plate and most courteously greeted me, It is an elegant building, with many potters at work - a very friendly atmosphere, with much choice at low prices.

Vietri is crowded but a Mecca for shoppers wanting ceramics. Taking the one-way street seven kilometers to the north, a good road quickly takes one to the attractive town of Cava de Tirreni. As you climb note the historical old towers on the hillside. They were used until recently for netting pigeons. Finely meshed nets were strung across the narrow parts of the valleys and when the beaters threw white stones into the nests from above, the pigeons flew into the nets. Some towers were still used in this way until recently. In the 1855 John Murray handbook it is noted they were in constant use.

Cava is a delightful hill town - much cooler in the summer than the coast. It has extensive arcades like Bologna and Padua, which are cool in summer, and in winter give protection against the rain and cold winds. The hills around Cava with their hamlets, churches and villas embosomed in trees or vineyards and cornfields are lovely pastoral scenery and had a strong influence on Claude Lorraine, the French painter of exquisite landscapes, as can be seen from comparing his pictures with this landscape.

During the nineteenth century Cava was much frequented by the British. John Murray's 1855 *Handbook to Southern Italy* states that furnished apartments could be found 'at moderate expense'. Sir William Gell, British Ambassador in Naples from 1822-1825, and who later lived in Naples, in his letters makes several references to British families residing in Cava. In 1832 with Sir Henry Lushington, the British Consul in Naples, he stayed with the Misses Whytes at Cava in January and 'found the climate is quite heavenly'. He also refers to Sir Walter Scott staying with them for three nights the next month in the winter of 1832 on his way to Paestum.

Interestingly Augustus Hare in his book published in 1883, describes 'the most excellent and remarkable' Albergo di Londra as the ideal place to stay for an excursion to Paestum because the landlord made all arrangements to meet the train at Battapaglia[13] with horse carriages, so that Paestum can be 'seen in the day with great comfort, returning in time for dinner'. Augustus Hare writes of many delightful walks and rides, which make Cava 'a charming summer retreat'.

Today, the arcades are lined with fashionable shops. Rich Italians find the heat of the confined area between the coast hotels and the beach and the sea on the Amalfi coast claustrophobic and much enjoy driving up to the cool of Cava to shop in the evening. I found probably the best restaurant in Southern Italy in the arcades while sheltering from a downpour. It is the Taverna Scaccia Venti (Tel. 089 443173). Here there is no menu. The friendly owner asks you if you want a meal with its principal ingredient either vegetable, fish or meat, and then brings you delicious dish after dish until your hunger is sated, together with well-chosen wine. Masses of magnificent vegetables, sides of wild boar and fruit adorn his captivating restaurant - and prices are reasonable. Today few British set foot in Cava. This is a pity because the scenery with its mountains, woods and farms is as captivating as it was in Claude Lorraine's day. It is an ideal centre for hiking, driving or sketching in pristine countryside.

However the main attraction of Cava is the nearby great Benedictine convent of La Santissima Trinita - the biggest and most celebrated convent apart from Cassino in Italy. A richly wooded valley two miles from the town narrows into a gorge described by Valery as 'Swiss valley with the sky and vegetation of south Italy'. A few steps before the abbey you reach the tiny village of Campo di Cava. Here Augustus Hare recommended the Albergodi Michele Scapolatiello as 'occupying an exquisite position at the foot of high mountains'. The hotel is still run by the same family and is a comfortable four-star hotel with a swimming pool and air conditioning (tel & fax 089 443 611) - where you will find peace, a warm welcome and no other British.

S Alferius, son of a nobleman from Salerno, founded the monastery between 1011 and 1015. While on a diplomatic mission for the Emperor of Germany as a young man, he had fallen dangerously ill and was nursed back to health by a Cluny monk, St. Odillon. On his return to Salerno he retired to a cave and became remarkable for his piety - so many disciples gathered

[13]I could find no trace of the Albeit di Londra.
The railway from Naples to Salerno and the south was designed by the Bourbons and is one of the early railways of Italy.

around him that the monastery acquired much property and adopted the rule of S Benedict, who had founded the nearby Benedictine monastery of Cassino in 817. Pope Urbano II consecrated the abbey Church of Cava in 1095.

The portico of the abbey (1761) is out of keeping with the much older monastery that runs behind for a considerable distance up the gorge. The magnificent large abbey church is impressive Neapolitan baroque. It contains a fine large twelfth century pulpit from the earlier church with curved columns and flamboyantly coloured marble mosaics, together with lions beside, and not underneath the pillars. The organ is reputedly the best in southern Italy. Fine frescoes in the church are nineteenth century. Apart from the pulpit the other early part of the abbey church is the chapel of the SS Patri - attractive Renaissance baroque. To the left of the high altar is the tomb of S Alferio enclosed in part of the cave where he lived as a hermit, with a heavenly baroqued altar standing out against the rock. His remains are in an urn.

To the left of the abbey church is the entrance to the monastery; courteous guides will show visitors around during the morning. The chapter house was restored in 1632 with striking bright frescoes and elaborate inlaid wooden stalls dating from 1540. The spectacular majolica floor (eighteenth century) was brought from Naples from a bombed out church after the Second World War.

The thirteenth century cloister is fascinating. Pairs of short Greek or Roman columns in different colours support rounded arches and give a Byzantine effect. The central court is partially sheltered by overhanging rock so that even in downpours there is a dry area. Behind the cloister are Roman remains including part of an aqueduct, proof that the site was important in classical times. The head of a faun was found and is displayed indicating that a pagan cult had been in existence in the cave.

Two chapels remain of the original church. Here are two sculptures by the famous Tino di Camaino, who came to Cava in the fourteenth century to create the works. The two groups of pious women with Roman soldiers are brilliant, most moving and are considered to be one of Tino's masterpieces. There is also an evoking Paliotto (altar front) of the eleventh century from the high altar of the basilica consecrated by Urbano II. Fine Roman sarcophagi of the second century AD are stored here as well.

Ask to be shown the museum. This fine room had been bricked up and was only rediscovered after the Second World War. It was part of the guesthouse of the monastery and has Roman columns, some fluted, some plain and contains works of art belonging to the monastery.

Down a steep staircase is the sombre crypt of the original church containing the Lombard Cemetery. The roof is supported by a great number of Greek or Roman pillars and was brilliantly frescoed in the fourteenth century. It was used as the burial place for both the monks and distinguished outsiders. Now all the bones have been removed to an ossuary. The frescoes now lit by electricity, are a memorable record of the early days of the monastery. A ghostly staircase leads from the crypt to the old monks' dormitory.

When the monastery was rebuilt in 1765, its famous library was rehoused in sumptuous rooms with sandalwood drawers and shelves and beautifully painted ceilings. Today it has all the modern apparatus of a great library - television screens and computers. There are always researchers studying in the delightful eighteenth century rooms. It is high up but there is a modern lift. The monastery was suppressed in 1866 after the unification of Italy and its possessions sequestrated. However the State allowed the monks to continue, and now the government pays all the costs of maintenance as it is a State monument. The monastery was also suppressed in the Murat period, but he allowed a few monks to remain.

The monastery library contains one of the most important collections of over 100,000 manuscripts in southern Italy. There is a good catalogue but it is not yet computerized. I was shown inter alia a wedding contract of 792 - the earliest manuscript I have ever handled - also a gift of land to the monastery by the Prince of Salerno dated 1025, together with the 1832 signature of Walter Scott in the visitors' book. This historic library is unique in its authentic eighteenth century setting.

The abbot Dom Benedetto Chianetta graciously received me in his palatial guest chamber with brilliantly painted ceiling and doors and contemporary furniture - the equal of any great Neapolitan palace. He is the head of a community of 15 Benedictines who run a large and successful secondary day school. We had a pleasant talk about Pius XII whose conduct when the Germans committed atrocities in Rome during the 1943-1944 occupation I had criticized in my book *War in Italy*. He does not consider that the beatification will proceed. In its heyday in the eleventh and twelfth centuries 3,000 Benedictines depended on Cava, and 100 monks went to found the abbey of Monreale in Palmero, Sicily in 1176. In the middle of the nineteenth century they sent monks to found the Benedictine order in Australia.

The Neapolitan painter Salvatore Rosa (1615-1673) lived and

215

studied in the monastery and his renowned wild landscapes, like those of Claude Lorraine (1600-1682), owe much to the spectacular surrounding scenery. Turning down from the monastery door there is a beautiful walk, impossible for cars, known as the ravine and grotto of Salvator Rosa - nearby the ruined and picturesquely sited monastery of Bucato in Gobbo can be seen. In spring wildflowers cover the slopes in profusion.

The British watercolour painter Samuel Palmer, when newly married in August 1838, stayed at La Coma. He painted a well-known picture of the Benedictine monastery that recently sold for £20,000 at Sotheby's. Palmer described it 'as fine a subject as Poussin ever chose', and the two months he spent at La Cava as 'possibly the happiest of their lives'. They lived for two shillings and four pence a day, and loved the mountain air. Cava was as far south as Palmer traveled.

Salerno

Seven kilometres downhill from La Cava brings you to Salerno. Do not be put off by the enormous, hideous and already decaying post-war town that sprawls along the coast and up the hills. Hidden within it is a delightful medieval part still intact, almost untouched by bombs and shelling during the Second World War, and now a quiet, almost car free area.

The waterfront was badly damaged by naval gunfire during the 1943 landings by the Allies, but has been rebuilt in good taste. There are hotels but it is not my idea of the best choice of a town from which to explore the Amalfi coast or to visit Paestum and the Cartosa di Padula. However, the Naples *autostrada* quickly takes one to Herculaneum and Pompeii. As does Augustus Hare, I recommend Cava as a preferable base for going to Paestum and the south.

Many regard the Cathedral of Salerno as the best example of Norman architecture in Southern Italy. It has no piazza, but an excellent restaurant stands over the road a few feet from the main entrance. The baroque portico (1733) with two sweet Byzantine lions at each side of the door belies what is inside. A feature of the cathedral is the atrium or entrance. It is two storeys and supported by 28 Greek pillars taken from Paestum many centuries ago, and is a sheer pleasure (much like the atrium at Capua). At the centre of the atrium there is an interesting large Greek vase taken from Paestum and from the atrium you should look at the imposing Romanesque campanile (1137) that shows a pleasant Moorish influence. A recent earthquake revealed Roman columns under the baroque decoration within the cathedral. From the atrium you enter the cathedral through a tall bronze door with 54 panels, imported from Constantinople in 1099.

At the centre of the atrium there is an interesting large Greek vase, taken from Paestum; from the atrium you should look at the imposing Romanesque campanile (1137), which shows a pleasant Moorish influence. A recent earthquake unearthed Roman columns under the baroque decoration within the cathedral.

The interior of the church still has much of its original decoration, which luckily survived the baroquisation of the eighteenth century. On the east wall of the transept there are important mosaics in the Byzantine style of 1258-1266, restored at the request of Pope Pius IX in the nineteenth century. Look especially at the thirteenth century mosaic of S Matthew. The most renowned features are the two pulpits of the thirteenth century and an exceptionally tall candelabrum for a paschal candle also thirteenth century, (compare these with the ones at Amalfi and Ravello). In the central apse the throne of Gregory VII, used for the consecration of the church in 1084, is exceptionally interesting. He died in Salerno in 1085.

At the end of the left aisle is the fine fifteenth century tomb of Queen Margherita, wife of Charles III who died in Sorrento in 1412. It is by Antonio Bobaccio, whose carving can also be seen in S Chiara in Naples.

The baroque crypt has sensational wall and ceiling decoration - the vaulted ceiling frescoes are by Corenzo, and the walls and pillars richly decorated in polychromatic marble are by Domenico Fontana. The crypt should not be missed - it is seventeenth century Neapolitan baroque at its best.

The museum of the duomo has some outstanding exhibits - (open 9 am - noon), especially the 54 scenes from the Old and New Testaments carved in ivory in the twelfth century altar fronts. Look too for a painting by Ribera, and others by Giordano and Vaccaro.

The Museo Archaelogico Provinciale in the quiet Via S Benedetta nearby occupies almost the whole site of the former large Benedictine Convent and incorporates the remains of the royal Norman palace (some arches are now open to the public over the road). Here are rich archeological remains from a wide area around Salerno displayed in strict chronological sequence. Particularly attractive is a head of Apollo (a bronze of the first century BC) discovered under the sea in 1930. One sector houses an exhibition of remains from the nearby Etruscan town of Fratte, with much fascinating material from the Necropolis there - almost as interesting as the Etruscan museum in Rome.

The museum and the remains of the Norman palace evoke the

history of Salerno. The necropolis at Fratte dates from the sixth century BC. In 194 BC, Salerno became a Roman colony, and particularly after Paestum declined after being ravaged by the Saracens, was a thriving commercial centre. The Byzantines had gained the upper hand when, in 646 AD, it was wrenched from Constantinople by the Lombards from Benevento. It became the capital of their most southern province, although they could not penetrate into Amalfi. Salerno remained Lombard until 1076 when the Norman, Robert Guiscard, drove the Lombards out and made it his capital and a principality. The Lombards appear to have integrated with the culture of the local population, protecting Salerno from the Saracens, and allowing Christianity to flourish. Robert Guiscard brought Pope Gregory to die in Salerno. Why he did this is uncertain. A famous medical school had flourished under the Lombards - Thomas Aquinas praised it highly and it even had women professors.

When the Norman King Frederick II founded Naples University, Salerno medical school declined and was finally suppressed by Murat during the Napoleonic occupation. Now it is only a memory, although early medical diplomas are displayed in the Museo del Duomo.

The Castle of the Arechi on a hill beyond the *autostrada,* is impressive and is open to the public. It is being converted into a museum – to date there is little of interest there. It was originally Roman and rebuilt by both the Lombards and the Normans.

The medieval town of Salerno is most attractive, with some good restaurants. It is deserted in the afternoon, but in the evening the *passegiata* starts - the evening stroll or amble with everyone arm in arm. It has a more peaceful and much safer atmosphere than Naples.

It is worth looking at the romantic medieval Via Dogana Vecchia and Via dei Mercanti, that brings us under the vaulted Arco de Arechi to the remains of an eighth century Lombard palace. These old streets contain a splendid mix of bits and pieces in the walls from the remains of palaces, houses, shops and workshops.

If open it is worth looking inside the fine baroque church of S Giorgio, which has frescoes by Solimena, Andrea di Salemo and S. Pietre. Fortunately some complete eleventh century brilliantly coloured frescoes have survived. Try to go in the morning.

It is pleasant to dine in the medieval quarter of Salerno. Brace, Lungomare Trieste 11 (tel. 089 225159) and Del Golfo, Via Porto 57 (tel. 089 231581) have air conditioning and both specialize in the delicious Salerno fresh caught fish and the characteristic local cuisine. Right in the middle of Via Merostanti (73) is an excellent café - Pasticerria Pantaleone, with the interior exactly as it was in 1868. Although I have not sampled the food Trattoria da Sasà (Via Daza 42, no phone) has been highly recommended to me. The restaurant a few feet from the duomo, Al Cernaculo is good but 'touristy' - the others cater to the locals, not the travellers and have more character.

On your way out of the old town, in several places you pass the remains of a medieval aqueduct, with waterways at different levels. It is most graceful and a unique tribute to the talents of engineers of hundreds of years ago.

On 9 September 1943, a joint American and British force landed on the sandy beaches south of Salerno and Paestum. German divisions were waiting, and bitter fighting took place. At one moment it seemed that the Allies would be thrown back to the beaches. The American Commander General Mark Clark, even considered evacuation until the overall Commander Field Marshal Alexander, arrived on board his ship and restored morale. General Montgomery had landed with his 8th Army six days before, over the Straits of Messina, and met little opposition. According to the Americans he moved with reprehensible slowness to relieve the hard-pressed Salerno invasion force, and has been seriously and deservedly criticized for this. Allied warships and infantry reinforcements were rushed to Salerno and US parachute drops were made. When Montgomery's army eventually joined Clark's, the Germans withdrew on 20th September. There is a large British war cemetery at Bellizi, south of Salerno with 2,000 graves and there are American cemeteries near Paestum. They are still much visited by relatives of those killed.

13
South of Campania and Paestum

L eave Salerno and go southeast on the A3 *autostrada*. You bypass the uninteresting town of Eboli (well known for the book and movie *Christ stopped at Eboli*), and after 80 kilometres, branch north for Pertosa three kilometres away. Here are some of the most exciting caves in Europe. There are long caves, with an exceptional number of stalagmites and stalactites. You start by boat on a man-made canal, pass caverns lit by electricity and then continue on foot. It is believed that the caves were inhabited during the bronze and iron ages, but today the only inhabitants are bats. They fly out at 9:00 pm and return at 4:00 am.

The guides take a great pride in the large stalagmites and stalactites. They will point out for you an array of characteristic ones to which they have given names such as the Sphinx, the Madonna of Lourdes, the Throne Room, the Castle and the Waterfall. Remember it is always cold in these caves. The caves are closed down for a long lunch break, but are certainly well worth visiting by anyone who likes this sort of thing. Those addicted should also visit the Castel Civita caves. Ask to go to the nearby village of Controne - but I have not been there. Some say the Pertosa caves join up with Castel Civita.

Continue southeast another 20 kilometres on the A3 *autostrada* past Sala Consiliano (which has classical remains rather smothered by unattractive development), until you come to the signposts to Padula only 5 kilometres from the motorway. Here is one of the most magnificent monuments in Europe - the Certosa de Padula. The Carthusian monks left in the nineteenth century. It was a prisoner of war camp in both the First and Second World Wars, and thus has unhappy memories for some former British servicemen.

It was founded by Tommaso Sanseverino in 1306 and is enormous, and like S Martino in Naples, it confirms the grandeur of the Carthusian order in the fourteenth century. The vast complex of buildings is on a gridiron pattern as is the Escorial near Madrid, which repeats the gridiron on which St Lawrence was burned to death. There are hourly tours and the guides expect a tip. In the late seventeenth century it was baroqued magnificently, a transformation greatly admired in the 1950s by Aldous Huxley, Sacheverell and Osbert Sitwell. It has been restored to house a museum of local antiques and is also used as a cultural centre for conferences. As a result the State keeps the monument in first class condition - and the baroque interiors are outstanding. Surrounded by modern houses and not far from the main road, the huge monastery appears incongruous nowadays. However the damage done when it was a POW camp has been completely repaired.

Tommaso had set out to create the most beautiful and powerful monastery in Southern Italy and it must be one of the biggest monastic complexes in the world. The small cloister (1561) is paved in a pretty herringbone pattern and has a central fountain. The church on the right side has a gothic doorway, with bas-relief scenes from the life of S Lorenzo. These are the only pre-baroque items, except for the lay brothers' choir stalls that have wooden inlay scenes - the work of Giovanni Gallo in the early sixteenth century. The monks' choir stalls are even more elaborate, with 36 scenes from the New Testament on the backs of the seats. However the high altar is magnificent baroque, light coloured and encrusted with mother-of-pearl, lapis lazuli and coloured marble.

The kitchen nearby is very large with an exceptionally big stove and chimney. The wall skirtings have nice scallop-shaped tiles in bright green and yellow, and on the far wall there is a fresco of the Deposition (only recently uncovered). In 1535 Charles V brought part of his army to the Certosa di Padula on his return from conquering Tunis, and asked the monks to feed them, whereupon an omelette with 1,000 eggs was cooked in the enormous kitchen, which has very long worktables. The idea of the 1,000 egg omelette excites visiting schoolchildren.

The library is the most beautiful room in the monastery. You reach it by a steep spiral staircase from the Great Cloister. The excellent floor is a soft blue and cream majolica tile, while the painting on the curved ceiling by Giovanni Olivieri has recently been fully restored. The library was very important for the Carthusians because they were an intellectual order that made a particular study of classical Greek and Latin, as well as specializing in translating manuscripts and studying medicine and science.

Just beyond the library is the Great Cloister completed in 1690. It is a quadrangle with 84 pilasters supporting the arcade. The whole is a supremely important example of monastic architecture.

Each monk had his own quarters and there were guest rooms but no dormitories. The monks' accommodation consisted of a bedroom, study, and sitting room together with a small garden. These can be seen today as they always were.

The town of Padula is unrewarding but there is a hotel and some small restaurants and cafés for refreshments.

From Padula it is only 15 kilometres to the attractive medieval town of Teggiano to the west. The drive there begins with hideous shops, workshops, garages and horrible modern houses. But once you get off the main road you are in the peace of the Cilento – an unspoiled farming area. Along the valley stretch fruit trees, tobacco plants, every type of vegetable as well as olives, oranges, lemons, grapes, and much livestock - goats, sheep, pigs and cattle. Occasionally you see a horse-drawn cart, a mule or donkey still engaged in agriculture. Until recently numerous white oxen were used for ploughing, but today small tractors have replaced them. It is a world of its own and in the Cilento you find almost the last remains of the traditional way of life of old southern Italy.

Teggiano is wonderfully preserved, and the view from it is tremendous. Six hundred feet below it is the valley of Diano - farm after farm in green and brown fields, interspersed with old ochre farmhouses and buildings. In Roman times the town was called Tegia, and in the fourth century Diano, from the name of the valley it overlooks. It has now reverted to a derivation of the original. The Visigoths destroyed the town when they descended from Rome in 410. In the fourteenth century it fell under the influence of the rich Certosa di Padula and it prospered under the Angevins and Aragons. In the thirteenth century the Sanseverino family built the castle that still dominates the town. With its arches and crenellations it's a reminder of feudal times.

The Cathedral Church of Santa Maria Maggiore is rich with the town's history. The carved portal dates from 1279, but an earthquake heavily damaged the church in 1857. Look at the elaborate paschal candlestick with a lion at its base, the marble pulpit (1721) and the Sanseverino tomb (1336) in the style of Tino di Camaiano. The Gothic church of S Andrea is built upon the remains of a Roman temple dedicated to Juno - it has two good fourteenth century triptychs. Close by is San Pietro also built on a classical temple. This is now a civic museum, that has interesting Roman remains and other exhibits from medieval times evoking Teggiano's fascinating history. Another Gothic church is the Pietà that has a small fifteenth century cloister, while S Agostino has a pretty sixteenth century cloister. There is a Roman mosaic in the church of S Marco and also a Roman bridge with reliefs and inscriptions to remind you of Roman times.

It is a joy to walk along Teggiano's narrow winding streets and look at the old palaces, crammed side by side with other houses. Outside staircases are packed with flowers, and long lengths of red poppies descend from stone balconies. The town recalls the Middle Ages and the Renaissance as much as Sessa Aurunca.

One snag about Teggiano is that although there are several nice cafés and bars, there is no restaurant, trattoria or pizzeria in the town. However there is one attractive hotel the Eldorado, above the castle that is family run and supplies good inexpensive meals. It has splendid views from most bedrooms of the valley and the castle below.

Paestum is only 37 kilometres south of Salerno and easily reached by bus, train, or car. Whereas the other Greek cities like Cuma, Sybaris, Metaponto and Velia have disappeared almost into rubbish dumps, Paestum retains the glory of her three ancient Greek temples. They stand out from the excavations of the streets and forum of the later Roman town. Only by visiting Paestum can you envisage what Cuma and Naples looked like in Greek times. It is less ancient than Cuma, and was not founded by settlers direct from Greece. Instead it was a colony thrown out by Sybaris further south, which itself was famous for its good living. Virgil wrote of twice-flowering roses in Paestum, and that the gardens where they bloomed were the loveliest he knew. You will not see many roses today - but there is nothing to stop the archeologists from recreating fine rose beds. Ariosto compared the roses of Paestum to the bloom on a lady's cheek. In the air above Paestum there is the constant twittering of small birds, while green and brown lizards glide in and out among the shadows of the columns. Try whistling to them and see if they look around at you. New excavations are in progress under the guidance of an American professor and there will soon be more exhibits in the museum.

In 510 BC Sybaris was destroyed and many Sybarites came to Paestum, that was called Poseidonia in honour of Poseidon, the god of the sea. Their gravitation to Poseidonia was natural, as Sybarites had founded a colony there at the end of the previous century and were sufficiently developed to have completed the Temple of Neptune (dedicated to Hera), c 450 BC. The town now flourished and two more magnificent temples were built, that survive today - the Basilica c 550 BC, and the Temple of Ceres c 500 BC. The Basilica and the earlier Temple of Neptune are lovely buildings with perfect Doric temple architecture. The Temple of Ceres (in fact dedicated to Athena) was built chronologically midway between the other two. It is notable for its use of two different orders, Doric externally and Ionic capitals adorning the columns of the vestibule. At the time this was quite an innovation. They are yellow and the stone looks like painted wood from a distance.

Probably sometime in the fifth century BC Paestum fell to the Lucans, and according to the somewhat unreliable historian Aristoxenos, the inhabitants were not allowed to speak Greek. As a result they used to meet outside the walls once a year to talk in Greek about their lost freedom. After

Pyrrhus left Italy Paestum became a Roman town in 273 BC, and the amphitheatre, forum and gymnasium were built. Excavations in recent years have brought much to light about the Roman town, that at one time was very large and prosperous.

There is some mystery about Paestum's decline. It was probably due to a combination of malaria, Saracen raids, the deforestation of the hills that changed the course of the rivers - and the opening of the roads to Taranto and Brindisi. This diverted the military and commercial traffic so that Paestum was no longer on a main trading route. Gradually it became a small village and was completely abandoned in the eighth century AD. This was fortunate in a way because being remote there was then no demand for building stone from the three Greek temples - allowing them to survive, unlike the temples at Cuma and Naples.

Under the Bourbons in 1752 a new state road to the south was built, crossing Paestum, and the forgotten temples began to attract much attention. In 1787 Goethe and the artist Kneip visited Paestum and wrote that his first impression was one of complete amazement. 'I found myself in a completely alien world because the eyes of our times are attracted to slender delicate architectural forms and here great masses of stones and imposing columns have a terrible daunting effect. I thank my good genii for having brought me to such a place to see with my own eyes those wonderfully preserved remains, this sense of the fullness of life which the architect sought and so admirably created'.

The temples are among the most magnificent Greek monuments, which have come down to us. Twenty five centuries ago they were embellished with statues, bas-reliefs, and splendid terracottas and finished with painted stuccoes. That must have been a riot of colour set against the nearly always blue sky. In the museum you can see many pieces of the temples' original friezes. In ancient times the sun only penetrated the temples at mid-day, and inside was an air of mystery in which priests continually tended the cella, or holy of holies. They were roofed in. Today all is in full sunlight.

The Forum slightly north of the Temple of Neptune is one of the most interesting Roman rectangular forums and is larger than the forum of Pompeii. The Romans broke into the sacred area of the Greeks to make the Forum at some time in the third century BC when Paestum was becoming very prosperous. The Forum was surrounded on all sides by an arcade of Doric columns - on the southern side, the foundations of some 60 can still be counted, and there are others under the road built by the Bourbons. The town walls date back to the Lucanian period and were mainly constructed in the early fourth century BC. They are well preserved with a circumference of nearly three miles, have four main gates and numerous posterns (small gates).

Situated between the Temple of Neptune and the Forum is the Roman theatre that was only discovered in 1907. It is an exceptional example of a theatre building erected during the Augustinian period (first half of the first century BC). There is a second theatre known as the *ekklesiasterion* or open-air theatre to the north of the Forum. Unfortunately the Roman Temple of Peace was built in 273 AD across its southwest corner. The Greek temples faced east - this Roman temple has its façade to the south.

To the east of these structures is the amphitheatre built about the time of Christ. This has been partly excavated but sadly is dissected by the road.

To the west of the amphitheatre lies the gymnasium. Here there are the easily identifiable remains of a fine large swimming pool, which excites the hordes of Italian school children that visit Paestum. There is evidence that it was used for swimming and diving competitions with wooden stands for the competitors.

If you are at Paestum a visit to the excellent museum is a must (Museo Nazionale). Its treasures range from prehistoric to Roman times and are exceptionally well displayed, with a magnificent collection of Greek vases, remains of friezes and a good collection of terracotta statues of Juno dating back to the seventh century BC. There are many exhibits from the Heraion situated 12 kilometres to the north of Paestum and only discovered in 1934. There is nothing to be seen at this site, only foundations, but numerous metopes of temple friezes dating from the sixth century BC, were unearthed during the excavations. In the museum the friezes have been placed in chronological order showing the myth of Hercules. Anyone who knows about the life and legend of Hercules can reconstruct the story from the stones, and would find it most fascinating.

However the most attractive exhibit in the museum is the Tomb of the Diver (*Tomba del Tuffatore*). This was discovered in 1968 and is one of the most extraordinary archeological finds of the century. The tomb consists of either Greek or Etruscan tomb paintings of around 470 BC, when such frescoed tombs were rare. It is a normal box shaped tomb formed of five slabs, and what is unique is that the four inside walls and the covering slab are completely frescoed. A banquet is painted on the first long side, with two persons making homosexual love, and three others playing a Greek game known as *Kottabos.*[14] The third person is overtly looking around to watch the love play between the older man and the good-looking ephebe. On the second side there is a funeral banquet, and on the third a naked ephebe pouring wine from a vase. On the second short side a dancing ephebe is preceded by a girl in white playing the flute (the only feminine figure in these frescoes). On the covering slab is the picture after which the tomb is named. In an open space bounded by two elegant small trees, a naked man dives into a pool of blue water from a diving board. Experts believe this fascinating fresco represents the soul leaving this life for the hereafter - symbolized by the exhilarating plunge into cool water. It is the best-known fresco of its period.

Quite disconcerting for visitors to the Museum is the terracotta bust of a woman shorn of her hair with three unmistakable Nazi swastika insignia in black. In fact the swastika was an ancient symbol often used as an ornamental motif with a religious significance, and found frequently in both Byzantine and Buddhist inscriptions and as far a field as America.

Other Lucanian tomb paintings in the Museum tell much of the life of the Lucanians, about which otherwise little would be known. There are vigorous scenes of funeral games, hunting expeditions, chariot races etc. *The Horseman in Black* with a sad face and tired gesture of his right hand, alone and absorbed in thought, clearly represents the passing from this life into the next. An amphora of Nikozenos, found in 178 fragments in 1952, is splendidly decorated with two scenes. In one scene four Amazons prepare for battle, with one grasping an axe with her bow and arrows attached to her belt. The other scene is dominated by the goddess Athena who, with the help of Hermes, confronts Cerberus on the threshold of Hades.

Before you leave Paestum, be sure and look at the early Christian basilica tucked away near the northern side of the Museum in a small square. This has recently been excavated and is one of Paestum's treasures. The overall appearance of the small church is of restoration work carried out in the fifteenth and sixteenth century, but recent digging has disclosed a much more ancient floor, belonging to an early Christian basilica that was recorded in the days of Pope Gregory the Great (sixth century). This shows that the early Christians did not always use the ancient Greek and Roman temples for their rites. It is surprising that this early Christian basilica has survived the Saracen raids and overall decay of the town.

---

[14] Kottabos was a Greek game of aiming the last drop of wine left in a cup at a moving target such as a small vase floating in a big container of water.

Until the 1960s, a visit to Paestum had to be a day trip. There was only one small restaurant and no hotels. Today there are some hotels near the ruins and two good restaurants. Five kilometres to the south of the ancient site a bathing resort has sprung up at Laura beach. Here are plenty of hotels and excellent bathing facilities on sandy beaches. Thus it is possible to enjoy the antiquities of Paestum at the same time as taking a bathing holiday. But remember that in July and August all the hotels are filled with Italian holidaymakers.

South of Paestum

From Paestum to the south there are two roads. The coast road leads to Agropoli with long sandy beaches, and inland to the delightful fertile Cilento covered with olive groves. Around Agropoli you come to scrubby green hills. The fishing villages along this coast area are now hosts to camps for Italians in the summer months. They love the beach and taking boats to explore the coast. These villages are not for British tourists.

However Agropoli, founded in the fifth century by the Byzantines has a wonderful old quarter. A Byzantine castle much enlarged by the Aragons, dominates the town. The other part of Agropoli is unattractive - although the hotels are said to be good value.

Twenty kilometres south of Agropoli is S Maria di Castellabate via an enjoyable drive through low hills with the blue Tyrrhenian Sea on the right. Castellabate is a pleasant seaside place with two good sandy beaches, and can be recommended for a seaside holiday. The town is on top of a hill with gorgeous views and there are several good hotels in beautiful locales. Four kilometres to the south is Punta Licosa, a small attractive port with good deep-sea swimming from the rocks. The tiny island of Licosa has a lighthouse and the remains of ancient walls. You can take a small boat to it but it is uninhabited. The name comes from Leucosia, the siren who is alleged to have thrown herself into the sea here when she failed to lure Ulysses on to the rocks.

Continuing down the coast road (N 267) brings you to Acciaroli and Pioppi that are both pleasant seaside resorts. Pioppi on a small inlet protected by hills, has a Saracen tower and a seventeenth century castle. The church of S Maria was built in 994 but is disguised by a modern facade. From here there is a fine view to the south as the road climbs, flanked by olives and figs. The harbour at Acciaroli is packed with colourful fishing boats, and there is a twelfth century church of the Annunziata at the Marina.

Soon after Acciaroli you rejoin the N 447. A short distance inland lies the ancient Greek town of Velia (Elea) near Ascea. There are no spectacular ruins, but much stone has been carted off piecemeal from here over the centuries. It was not large but famous for its beautiful setting, and its school of philosophy. It produced brilliant minds such as Parmenides (circa 475 BC) who participated in a Platonic dialogue. When Persians attacked various Greek cities in Asia Minor around 540 BC, some Phophaeans fled and founded the city of Hyele or Elea. It was the last south Italian colony to be founded, and was probably situated where trading with Greece was already established. It was also famous also for medicine and rivalled the Pythagorean school (of medicine), which flourished at Croton Originally it was much nearer the sea.

One of Parmenides' tenets was that there should be no change. Much respected by Plato, he gave the town a code of laws. There is considerable dispute over his philosophy but no one disputes his great influence. Even Hegel drew inspiration from him. His disciple Zeno, whom Aristotle called the inventor of dialectic because he argued theories in which he did not believe, followed him.

What can be seen at Elea is disappointing in view of the importance of the town in history. We know that in the fourth century BC it warred with the Lucanians who threatened her from the mountainous country inland. It was one of the last strongholds of Greek culture in Italy.

Around 272 BC Elea allied with Rome and provided ships for the Roman fleet during the Punic war. Cicero often stayed in a villa, and had a dramatic talk with Brutus here. The soil of the area was of poor quality and the inhabitants had difficulty in scratching out a living. Stabo wrote that they had to establish fish salting factories and other such industries in order to survive. When the harbour became silted up the site was doomed. Virgil refers to several harbours.

The south sea gate is now well away from the sea, but the remains of a town were found in one of the harbours. The sea gate itself has a square tower and is part of a stretch of town wall dating back to the fifth century BC. Near the gate are inscriptions relating to the medical school of Elea. There are also the remains of a bath building. Further along is Porta Rosa a rounded arch supporting a road or pathway - and is the only existing rounded Grecian arch in Magna Grecia. A track leads to the acropolis under which the modern railway passes, and here is a medieval tower. Between the acropolis and Porta Rosa excavations have revealed a sacred area with small temples. The marketplace that originally had fountains has been found here also. Excavations continue at Elea, and archaeologists hope to find the town's theatre and other public buildings.

Crawford Ramage was a well-known traveller who arrived at Elea in 1818 by way of the beach in the cool of an evening. He found it completely deserted and noted that in Roman times the balminess of the air made it the residence of invalids. Horace seems to have visited it in this vein due to the weakness of his eyes. Ramage found the ruined medieval castle (the Castello della Brucca) and traced the circumference of the walls for about two miles. He described the walls as 'Cyclopean Architecture' with 'large polygonal masses of stone fitted to each other without cement by their own superincumbent weight', but he could find no trace of temples. He found several Greek inscriptions especially on tombs, and noted the '*Hic jacet*' of the Roman period. ('Here lies'.)

He had an unfortunate experience while trying to climb the ruined staircase of the castle, and found himself attacked by 'a host of stinging insects' that turned out to be 'nothing else than fleas'. He found himself in a 'state of the utmost torture' and the only relief was for him to strip down and dash into the sea, only a few hundred yards away. He discovered that the tower had been used to house flea infested pigs.

On Ramage's second trip to Elea, an Ascean landowner directed Ramage to the remains of the Temple of Proserpius. Ramage considered it to be a medieval building, and he also found many more inscriptions. Ramage was hospitably entertained at Ascea by the landowner who had shown him the ruins. He noted the prolific fruit, which can still be found at Ascea, especially the pears, apples and apricots. Ramage called Ascea 'miserable' - today, it is a cheerful, pretty little town perched high above the sea, with a fine view. On the seashore 2 kilometres away are plenty of bathing paraphernalia in quite pleasant surroundings. The large house of Ramage's landowner can still be identified in Ascea.

Pisciotto where Ramage found the natives unwelcoming is larger than Ascea. The hills come down to the sea here and Pisciotto dominates the hilltop. It is said to produce more olives per acre than any other town in the region. It has a good beach on one side of the harbour and is popular with yachtsmen and campers.

Palinuro is 20 kilometres further south and it is named after the pilot who died at the helm in Virgil's Aeneid, and who is buried here, according to Book V:............'But Aeneas sensed that the pilot was gone and the ship was drifting, and himself steered her through the waves of night; sighing and numbed at what had befallen his friend; trusting too much to clear skies and calm seas. The end is, 'Palinures, you will lie naked upon an unfamiliar shore.'

The ruins of Palinures's tomb are at the entrance to the harbour by the beach. They may well be genuine.

The demands of tourism have forced the town to develop unattractively, but the coast has remained rugged and wild. There are nice caves and sandy inlets both north and south of Palinuro. They can only be reached by boat, but there are plenty of boats for hire. The Grotto Azurra is not quite as beautiful as that at Capri, but it has good stalactites and the water is a shimmering blue. The most famous cave is the Grotto delle Ossa (Cave of Bones), full of bone fragments now encased in stalactites and stalagmites. It was once believed that these were the bones of seafarers shipwrecked in Roman times, but later research has revealed that they are the remains of bears and horses that were possibly consumed by prehistoric man.

Above Palinuro are the ruins of Molfa, believed to have been an outpost of Elea. Ramage had found Palinuro 'a village of fishermen' but believed that the ruins of Molfa were medieval and not Greek or Roman. Today there is no way of telling, but the ruined watchtower is definitely medieval - although there is evidence from classical literature of a Roman town in the area. It is worth making the half hour walk to the site just to see the views from this isolated region.

Once around the headland of Palinuro to the south there are excellent beaches and splendid views of the Gulf of Policastro, which is as large as the Gulf of Naples but without the presence of a single factory. The first venue is the unattractive Camerota Marina, with six campsites and innumerable hotels and restaurants. However 300 metres above is the attractive old town of Camerota, renowned for 1,000 years for its ceramics and especially for the long terracotta amphora used for holy wine.

Camerota Marina and the succeeding towns of Policastro, Villamare and Sapri are barely worth a visit - although the blue sea of the Gulf of Policastro is always fascinating. Inland however lies the delightful and fertile country of the Cilento, with its very friendly inhabitants. This was much appreciated by the soldiers of Field Marshal Montgomery's 5th Army when they landed on the toe of Italy in September 1943, and advanced unopposed to relieve the hard-pressed American Army at Salerno. According to the war correspondent Christopher Buckley, the Cilento was a welcome contrast to bleak winters and scorching summers in the arid North Africa. Buckley wrote: 'There are more unpleasant ways of passing ten days in early September than driving along a country road with the Mediterranean at hand on one's left and a daily increasing abundance of autumnal fruits waiting to be picked. Usually we did not need to pick them - the villagers thrust them upon us!'

To Montgomery's shame, Buckley's party of war correspondents actually arrived at 5th US Army's HQ at Paestum in advance of the British combat troops. This occasion embarrassed Monty in failing to spur on his troops to link up with the Americans who so badly needed help.

The road to Maratea (which is just outside Campania in Calabria) from Sapri reaches a site of intense beauty where the hills come down to the sea again, soon after leaving Sapri. Maratea can also be reached from Teggiano. From Teggiano, drive south on the *autostrada* to Lago Negro, and branch off again to the south to drive through wild country with sheep and shepherds and the scent of thyme and oregano. Just as you see the Gulf of Policastro, the road dives down in a series of serpentine bends to reach the sea just east of Sapri.

The drive from Sapri to Maratea is unforgettable. The road is edged into the side of the mountain and the views are as spectacular as from the Amalfi peninsula. This route is advantageous in that instead of encountering another vehicle every 15 seconds, they come at intervals of about 15 minutes.

Ten kilometres before Maratea is Aqua Fredda, where there are hotels with lifts down to the sea. Maratea is a fascinating old town well above the sea with a marina and port below. The coast here is unrivalled. Development is strictly controlled. No new houses are to be built except to replace existing ones. What a contrast to the suburbs of Naples! Here is all the beauty of Sorrento and the Amalfi coast, without the crowds. At Maratea Marina and Maratea Port there are boats for hire to explore the 20 miles of crystal clear blue water that lies between Campa and Calabria.

In old Maratea we are tracing Ramage's footsteps. It comprises a huddle of medieval houses built out of view of the sea to shield them from the Saracen raids. Ramage thought it superior to anything he had encountered on the way from Naples. He found comfortable lodgings with the Barone San Biagio to whom he had been given a letter of introduction. Ramage notes that Maratea was surrounded by hills and situated in a narrow valley, so that from November until the end of January the rays of the sun did not reach it. The town was famous for its cheese, and in Naples most of the cheese and pork sellers had come from Maratea - where excellent cheese may still be bought.

Ramage was shocked that the monks of San Biagio monastery sold 'manna' that they claimed came from the perspiration emanating from a statue of Our Saviour and 'was a cure for all sorts of diseases.' The monastery of San Biagio is beautifully set above the town, but the monks who offended Ramage with their 'manna' have long since all departed. Instead of seeking 'manna', you can admire the unrivalled view of Calabria.

There is a nice drive south to Praia a Mare (10 kilometres away) in Calabria along a rocky corniche. At Praia the mountains begin to recede from the sea and you come to the Madonna della Grotta. It is a natural cave, 50 yards long and 60 feet high. It originally had a large baptistery in the cave and a small chapel where the famous Statue of the Madonna is kept. It is still a place of pilgrimage, but has nothing like the importance it had in Ramage's day. A tale was told to Ramage that Our Lady is so fond of Madonna della Grotta that when her statue was removed to a church in nearby Ajeta (up a steep hill), it physically removed itself back to Madonna della Grotta. Like the statue at Maratea, the one at Madonna della Grotta was said to exude 'manna' that would cure diseases. Ramage actually had a long talk with the judge officially charged with investigating this mystery. Despite the judge's insistence that miracles occurred Ramage was doubtful.

Another interesting excursion from Maratea is to the medieval town of Vibonati (54 kilometres). To reach Vibonati take a winding hilly road 2 kilometres west of Sapri for 3 kilometres. Like Maratea, Vibonati was built away from the sea to evade the ravages of the Saracens. Time has stood still here and the old houses cluster around the church and bell tower along with plenty of trees. A walk along the narrow streets and up and down the steps evokes the past and you see many well cared for porticoes, dating back to the sixteenth and seventeenth centuries. The imposing church of St Anthony Abbate, with three asymmetrical naves, was built upon the ruins of a fourteenth century castle. Like Teggiano at the other end of the Cilento, it is an unspoiled farming town, with very friendly inhabitants.

A modern 60-foot statue of Christ, modelled on Rio de Janeiro's Redeemer with outstretched arms stands on a commanding summit but does nothing to spoil Maratea.

Maratea itself has an attractive luxury hotel in a former convent in the old town (Le Donne Monache). This is a splendid place to stay and enjoy the peace and romance of the medieval town. On the coast and in the low hills there are a number of good hotels. I recommend this area as the ideal spot for a seaside holiday, far away from the brashness that has engulfed so much of southern Italy's delightful coast.

For generations tour operators and travel agencies have spurned the coast of Italy south of Salerno as having little to offer. As the popular resorts to the north become more and more exploited, this southern region is bound to become more popular with Italians and foreigners. One hopes that it may long be protected against brash development as has occurred on the coast of Maratea.

The Appendices

Naples is rich in architecture, but the Angevin Gothic architects mostly came from outside Naples, as did the Renaissance and baroque ones.

The Spanish kings encouraged Renaissance architecture. However, the first great Renaissance monument, the tomb of Cardinal Rinaldo Brancaccio in S Angelo a Nilo, is dated 1428, sculpted by Michelozzo and Donatello and sent complete by ship from Pisa. The style was novel, but it was not imitated in subsequent years.

One of the first acts of the Aragonese King Alfonso I was to rebuild the Gothic Castel Nuovo built by Charles I around 1280. Alfonso added the celebrated triumphal arch in 1451 to honour his victory over the French. This now forms the entrance to the castle and has a wealth of carved sculpture created by Neapolitan artists of the time.

Alfonso also built the Porta Capuana completed in 1490 by Neapolitan, Luca Fancelli in Florentine style. Neither site should be missed.

During Alfonso's reign and patronage wealthy nobles constructed many palaces and churches. Palazzo Carafa di Montono (121 Via S Biagio) bears the date 1466 and is worth viewing because of its mixture of Gothic and Renaissance - as is Palazzo Penne. Notice their fine marble balconies and ornate doors.

There is little church architecture remaining from the Renaissance (1460-1550) in Naples. Still there are two attractive chapels in the church of Monte Oliveto (also called S Anna dei Lombardi) - both by Florentine sculptors that recall the Renaissance. There are also two remarkable Renaissance chapels in the large church of S Domenico Maggiore (1283) - Cappella di S Martino and the Cappella del Presepe. A third is The Lady of Assumption Chapel in the Duomo.

Until the end of the fifteenth century the main Neapolitan architects were distinguished foreigners. This changed in the sixteenth century with Tommaso Malvita and his son Giovanni Malvita. They were responsible for the crypt in the duomo with its lavish and delicate decoration and the wonderful chapel Caracciolo di Vico created in S Giovanni a Carbonara (1516) commissioned by Galeazzo Caracciolo (....).

A Neapolitan architect De Palma Mormanno, designed SS Severono e Sossio and the church of Donna Romita (1535).

An important church of the Neapolitan Renaissance is S Giacomo degli Spagnoli (1546) that has an altar painting by Titian. Other Renaissance features of Naples are the Campanile (bell towers) of which the most impressive are at S Chiara and S Lorenzo Maggiore.

Little remains of the furnishings of fifteenth and sixteenth century Neapolitan churches because most of them were redecorated during the baroque period. Fine wood carving can still be found at the old church of Donna Regina, the ceiling at S Maria do Constantinopoli, the door at S Angelo a Nilo and on the sacristy of S Martino.

After 1570 Neapolitan architecture during the transition to the baroque became increasingly independent. Then Giovanni Dosio and Domenico Fontana came to Naples. Dosio designed the magnificent church of the Gerolomini,[15] the Cappello Brancaccio in the duomo and the great cloister of S Martino.

Domenico Fontana arrived in Naples in 1596, having been invited by the Spanish Viceroy, and died there. He designed the Palazzo Reale and the Museo Nazionale. The latter was much changed in the eighteenth and nineteenth centuries, but one fine room remains - the Gran Salone del Atlanta with a magnificent ceiling.

A Jesuit architect Giuseppe Valeriano came to Naples in 1582. He was mostly responsible for the brilliant and ornate Gesu Nuovo that is highly original with an exceptionally spacious interior - too flamboyant for some tastes.

Towards the end of the sixteenth century a distinct local school of architecture evolved in Naples. Fabrizio Grimaldi, a priest of the Theatine order, designed four important churches in Naples - S Paulo Maggiore, S Maria degli Angeli, S Maria della Sapienza and SS Apostoli. He also provided the plan for the Capella del Tesoro in the duomo. Later he began the church of S Maria degli Angeli at Pizzzofalcone.

A pupil of Grimaldi, Giovanni Cavagna, also a Theatine, built the new church of Donna Regina in 1620 - a magnificent baroque church with a broad and spacious nave without aisles. Cavagna also built Monte di Pietà in Via S Biago in 1599. This was a charitable bank and has a grand façade to the palace and a delicate and feminine one to the chapel.

Domenico Vaccaro (1678-1745) trained under Solimena. He designed three chapels in S Martino church - S Rosario, S Joseph (in gilded stucco) and S Gennaro, with white marble, much carving and statues. These should not be missed. One of his most important churches is at Sessa Aurunca, S Annunziata (...). Another is S Michele at Anacapri (...) and another at the Convent of S Giovanni at Capua (...). Vaccaro specialized in designs for the exterior of churches and especially in altars. He gives

---

[15] Blunt disputes this.

enormous character to many Neapolitan churches - rails with elaborate white period columns, and full-length cherubs swinging on the scrolls as if on the branches of a tree. His finest memorial is the formal garden in the cloister of S Chiara with its unique majolica.

Vaccaro was imitated by Giuseppe Sanmartino (1720-1793) whose celebrated work can be found in the Cappella Sansevero in the form of the extraordinary Veiled Christ sculpture (1753). He and Vaccaro are the founders of the Neapolitan Rococo.

Ferdinando Sanfelice (1675-1748) was a contemporary of Vaccaro. Sanfelice specialized in domestic architecture especially in open staircases for Neapolitan palaces that he accomplished brilliantly, giving them a place of honour. Alas almost all of his palaces are now broken up and let out to small poor tenants; the interiors are now battered and the exteriors in squalor. His most impressive church is the Annunziata at Pizzofalcone, with a single vaulted barrel nave and a fine tomb by him is that of Caetano Argento in S Giovanni a Carbonara. His staircases can be seen at Palazzo Cassano and in Salerno at Palazzo Genovesi. His staircase in Palazzo Cassano is spectacular, as is his staircase to S Giovanni a Carbonara. His own palace (Palazzo Sanfelice) should be seen - especially for the entrance doors.

The most remarkable surviving rococo is the porcelain room at Capodimonte designed in 1717 by the German Johann Fischer who came from Meissen. There were several fine Rococo villas at Portici and along the coast. Little survives, and what remains is hidden by hideous modern and unplanned development.

Cosimo Fanzago

Cosimo Fanzago was born in Naples in 1591 and died there in 1678. He was a wonderful sculptor and decorator and to a lesser extent an architect. A bad tempered and violent man, his artistic career was damaged by quarrels and lawsuits, including a long running legal dispute involving the monastery of S Martino. He frequently robbed one church of material for another.

He designed the churches of S Maria degli Angeli alle Croci and S Maria Egiziaca at Pizzofalcone and others. Blunt describes his architecture as 'uninventive', although 'highly original', with his façades. Take a special look at the façade of S Maria degli Angeli.

He achieved his greatest distinction as a decorative sculptor. Naples and the surrounding area are full of his brilliant work. He was a master of the art of marble inlay and is unequalled in Italy for this. His best work is in the Certosa S Martino particularly in the layout and configuration of the big cloister, with white marble, grey marble and fluted panels. He also designed the interior of the S Martino Abbey church that Blunt emphasizes, is one of the few cases in which a Gothic church has been given a satisfactory baroque covering. This magnificent monastery is a splendid monument to Fanzago, and it helps one to appreciate his many lesser works, which appear so often in Naples

His famous palace of 1642 is Don Anna on the seashore at Posillipo that recalls the palaces in Claude Lorraine's paintings. His style of decorative sculpture dominated Naples until the mid eighteenth century when more classically inspired designers reacted against him. You will encounter numerous chapels in Neapolitan churches designed by Fanzago. They include the church of S Ignazio in the Gesù Nuovo and those of S Antonio and Cacale in S Lorenzo.

Franco Solimena (1657-1747) the renowned Neapolitan painter was also an architect. His important architectural works are the façade of S Nicola della Carità, and the high altars of S Martino and the Capella del Tesoro in the duomo. Blunt believes that he relied heavily on his pupils for his architectural designs and it is as a painter, not an architect, that he should be famous.

The Last Generation

Guiseppe Astarita, a Neapolitan who died at the early age of 55 in 1755, set a new style in the church of S Anna a Porta Capuana. It was a combination of baroque and classical. Mario Gioffreddo (1718-1785), who built the Palazzo Calascienda and Palazzo Cavalcanti on the Via Mezzocanone between 1758 and 1762, continued this style although these are more classical in essence.

In 1751 Charles II invited two already well-known architects to come from Rome to Naples - they were Ferdinando Fuga born 1699 and Luigi Vanvitelli (1700-1773). Fuga designed the enormous but monotonous Albergo dei Poveri with a classical façade front 1,000 feet long. He also designed the façade of the Girolomini.

Luigi Vanvitelli was a Neapolitan by birth but worked in Rome until 1754 when he was called to Naples to design the giant palace at Caserta for Charles II. It was intended to rival Versailles and was supremely successful in the classical style (...). Vanvitelli also designed the magnificent Caserta gardens, and rebuilt the church of S Annunciata, that had been destroyed by fire.

With this new generation Neapolitan architecture caught up with the

239

rest of Europe and entered the neoclassical period. Much of what had been created in the baroque period was swept aside in the rebuilding of the late eighteenth and nineteenth centuries. A vast amount has survived providing the most impressive baroque to be found in any European city.

Food and Wine

Neapolitan food is considered by many to be the best in Italy, and Cucina Napolitana prevails all over Campania. Full of flavour from the use of only the best olive oil plus fine tomatoes, garlic, many herbs like parsley, basil, oregano (marjoram), together with anchovies and good cheeses, it is unique. Tradition claims that the Neapolitan method of using herbs and spices has come down from Roman times, and judging by what has been found at Pompeii and Herculaneum, this is probably true.

A customary Neapolitan meal consists of antipasti (hors d'oeuvres), soup, or pasta, followed by fish (often in a risotto), vegetables as a separate course, cheese, or dolce (sweet dish). Beef (manzo) is not very good, and veal varies in quality. On the other hand, the fish, including shellfish and oysters, are exceptional - while the fruit and vegetables from the lush countryside are always excellent.

In the more expensive hotels food tends to be good international cuisine, so that the best local food is found in the restaurants and trattoria where the Italians themselves eat. In some hotels popular with British package tourists, the food can be frankly bad or monotonous. Choose an eating-place well patronized by Italians and you will not be disappointed. The southern Italians are so keen on their food that any restaurant producing bad food would last only a few weeks.

Antipasti can be vegetable, fish or meat - soup will be either vegetable (minestrone) or brodo (broth). Both are usually excellent and a great contrast to English cooking. Zuppa di Pesce (fish soup) is a specialty, and varies from restaurant to restaurant and from town to town. It is a meal in itself, but it is best to order it somewhere where there is a big turnover. Zuppa di Vongole (clams), or Zuppe di Cozze (mussels) are excellent. If you are on Capri ask for Zuppa di Pesce Caprese, served with bits of bread fried in olive oil and containing a considerable variety of vegetables and fish together with lemon. Also try their Ravioli Caprese.

Of course Naples is famous for pasta. Spaghetti or Maccheroni alla Neapolitana with special plum shaped tomatoes and Parmesan cheese are very reliable. The pasta is cooked quickly so that it stays firm on the teeth (*al dente*). Probably the best pasta is Spaghetti alle Vongole (clams) or Spaghetti alle Cozze (mussels) cooked in a variety of ways and always delicious. Do not add Parmesan to these dishes. Neapolitans consume enormous quantities of pasta, so if you are also facing a second course, ask for a '*mezza porzione*' (half course).

I am no fan of pizzas but my grandson, when he was my companion, definitely was. I must say pizza tastes better in Naples than elsewhere. Neapolitan pizza makers are hired to cook pizzas in far off Italian summer resorts. It requires skill to flatten out the leavened dough of the circular pizza, usually with pats of the hand. When really flat and decorated with a selection of tomatoes, ham, anchovies, capers, garlic, herbs, mushrooms and mozzarella cheese it is slipped on a long handled spoon into an igloo-like oven heated by wood. In a few minutes it comes out crisp, with an appetizing aroma. The Neapolitans are adamant that pizzas must be cooked on a wood stove and not by electricity. They say electricity ruins the flavour. I can well believe it, but am not sufficiently expert to judge.

Having seen the colourful variety of fish displayed in the markets and street stalls you must sample them in the restaurants. Red mullet (*triglia*) has the fresh tang of the sea and is a lovely pink gold in colour. Sea bass (*spigola*) is excellent, as is dentice (that has no English equivalent). They can all be eaten roasted, grilled or boiled. Do not pass on the cheaper sardines (*alici*) and anchovies (*acciughi*). If fresh and fried they are splendid. Not to everyone's taste is the popular fritto misto of fish - octopus, squid and cuttlefish (ink fish). They are very popular with Italians, but too hard in the mouth for the British palate. Lobsters (aragosta) are expensive but delicious. Oysters and scampi are cheaper and excellent. Swordfish (*spada*) and tuna (*tonna*) are mouth watering when grilled.

Mozzarella cheese is one of the region's specialties and tastes far better in its own country than in the packaged varieties sold in England. It cannot be exported properly because its true flavour is only retained if it is soaked in a mixture of milk and water. You can buy it at stalls along the main roads where it is always fresh and at its best. It is made from the milk of buffalo in the plains south and north of Naples. Insalata Caprese often appears on menus and is an appetizing dish with slices of mozzarella and fresh tomato with basil, olive oil and salt. It originated in Capri, but popular everywhere.

For anyone with a sweet tooth I thoroughly recommend sfogliatelle, crisp shell shaped puff pastry filled with ricotta cheese and fruit, often with candied cherries. The café Scaturchio in Piazza Domenico has been

241

renowned for this pastry for over 100 years. Sfroccolati are delicious - skewered sticks of dried figs stuffed with fennel seeds.

Peaches, cherries, figs and apricots are among the best in Italy as are the oranges and lemons (especially from Procida and Sorrento). Tomatoes, especially the small ones, have a special southern and exquisite flavour. The fig season lasts a long time, beginning with the picking from trees at sea level and continuing until the last figs are picked from trees high up on the mountain slopes of Vesuvius and Mount Epomio.

The Neapolitans eat late in restaurants. Lunch goes on until 3:30 and dinner until after midnight. On Saturday evenings the restaurants become very crowded and it is best to reserve a table.

Cafés are always welcoming even when busy. Neapolitans insist on good coffee made from freshly ground beans, and generally Neapolitan coffee is the best in Italy. Peter Gunn declares it 'the best in the world'.

Cappucinos are popular and better than one may obtain in London. A café lungo is a generous portion of espresso - a café latte is apt to have too much milk.

Restaurants are known as Ristorante, Trattoria, or Osteria. Despite the different names they are all much the same inside. Prices vary according to the décor and the menu varies little. Some specialize in innumerable hors d'oeuvres (antipasta) and will not mind if you make your whole meal out of warm seafood delicacies, different forms of salami, good vegetables, olives, pâté, etc., all served with wonderful sauces. The least expensive restaurants are known as Vino e Cucina, where the food will be simple, but if you find one well patronized by locals, it's likely to be good.

At any of the many grocers (*alimenti*) scrumptious picnics can be bought. They do not go in for pâté as do the French, but there is always a selection of salami, hams, mortadella (galantine), sardines, anchovies and eggs in mayonnaise etc. Most will also make sandwiches for you and mozzarella with ham is ideal picnic food.

The best local wine is Gragnano (11%) and is deep red, dry and full-bodied. Falerno wine much praised in antiquity comes from the Phlegraean Fields. Although frequently consumed it is inferior to Lacrima Christi, which comes from around Vesuvius and can be white, red or rosé. Some is very dry and excellent. There is also a slightly bubbly (frizzante) version that is most refreshing at the start of a meal. Vesuvio (10-12%) also comes from Vesuvius and is most drinkable. Asprino (8-10%) is an excellent mild white wine from nearby Avellino. Both Ischia and Capri are famous for their wines. Capri wines have deteriorated, but Ischia wines are still excellent.

The best is Epomeo (11-12%) either white or red. At Ravello the Caruso vineyard produces a famous Rosé (12%) and white wine that are much prized. At Minori on the Amalfi coast there are good white wines, but as you proceed south from Naples the quality of the wine deteriorates. Most restaurants stock good wines from Tuscany and with the richly flavoured Campanian cuisine nothing is better than good Chianti.

Neapolitans like to finish the evening meal with a digestive liqueur. Yellow Strega made locally at Benevento is the favourite, and mighty good it is although currently unknown in Britain. Limoncello made at Sorrento from lemons is also popular, but appeals more to Italians than to the British.

Index

Printed in the United Kingdom
by Lightning Source UK Ltd.
107955UKS00001B/18